YOUR 40-DAY TRANSFORMATION

GET YOUR HEALTH BACK, NATURALLY

JANELLA PURCELL

HAY
HOUSE

Copyright © Janella Purcell, 2019

Published in Australia by: Hay House Australia Pty. Ltd.: www.hayhouse.com.au
Published in the United States by: Hay House, Inc.: www.hayhouse.com
Published in the United Kingdom by: Hay House UK, Ltd.: www.hayhouse.co.uk
Published in India by: Hay House Publishers India: www.hayhouse.co.in

Design by Rhett Nacson
Typeset by Bookhouse, Sydney
Edited by Margie Tubbs
Author Photo by Mark Lane, lanewayphoto.com

ISBN: 9781401959708
Digital ISBN: 9781401959715

22 21 20 19   4 3 2 1
1ˢᵗ Australian edition, 2019

Printed in Australia by McPherson's Printing Group

CONTENTS

PART THREE TURNING THINGS AROUND

PART FOUR 40-DAY RESET PROGRAM AND RECIPES

introduction

WHERE THIS JOURNEY BEGAN...

Sometimes life throws you a curve ball, and I was on the receiving end of mine in September 2013. I was working way too hard for too long, then had a miscarriage in my mid-forties. Although it was traumatic, what I didn't know then was that I was soon about to crash even harder. It used to be called burnout or 'having a breakdown' and more recently adrenal fatigue or adrenal collapse. Here I was, and perimenopausal. A lethal mix.

Sometimes when we're not listening hard enough, something happens to make us stop and listen. It often comes as a health issue—or ten—and Western medicine has let us down.

On top of the physical repercussions, I was trying to deal with the grief of knowing that I would probably never have a child of my own. The miscarriage was my 'trigger' but what became apparent was the underlying Adrenal Fatigue (AF) and chronic Small Intestine Bacterial Overgrowth (SIBO) that also desperately needed to be addressed. That was when my health seriously started to decline, and rapidly. That's often what happens when you ignore what your body is trying to tell you: its voice gets louder and harsher.

Here I am five years later looking back, and I couldn't be in a more different place—a happy and well place. My recovery wasn't easy, or anything close to that. On the contrary, it was probably the most difficult period of my life. But what I've learnt during this time about myself, the human body, body/mind connection, media hype, Western medicine, Big Pharma, genetic engineering, and the food and health industries is enormous, and somewhat frightening.

During this period, in an attempt to heal myself, I was at one point or another diagnosed with everything from adrenal collapse to SIBO to hypothyroidism, and tested positive for a MTHFR* gene defect and pyrolluria—all the while gaining weight, becoming irritable as all hell, losing lots of hair, ageing prematurely, losing my memory (and mind) and having trouble even getting out of bed. Plus I was single, watching myself quickly age, becoming frumpy, with chronic lower back pain and an ever-decreasing bank balance. No wonder I was depressed! Still, I wasn't listening …

When I was diagnosed with a homozygous A1298C MTHFR gene mutation I was relieved. This was it! This was why I had suffered with food intolerances from a young age, why I'd been estrogen dominant, gained weight easily, had broken capillaries and Stage 4 endometriosis. This is why I was highly emotional and a bit of a perfectionist. At last, I'd found it—the missing link!

But had I? I followed strict protocols for three months, but my symptoms continued to worsen. I started to wonder why, if I'd had this gene my entire life, I had never been so sick before? It was my guess that the miscarriage and subsequent adrenal fatigue I'd been living with for decades had caused this gene to 'express' or 'turn itself on'. So why couldn't it be turned off? Medical doctors told me it wasn't possible. Hmpf!

So I went on a five-year journey. When you've been unwell for some time, it's not uncommon to feel a little obsessed about finding a cure. Just a diagnosis would do, really. This causes some of us to

---

* Methylenetetrahydrofolate reductase (MTHFR) helps to make a certain enzyme we need for proper methylation. Methylation is a major pathway essential to the health of a wide range of important bodily functions, such as detoxification, immune function, circulation, mood, fertility and more.

get **really** forensic, and maybe just a little 'obsessive-compulsive' about our health issues. It's increasingly common in the 21st century **not** to find the one diagnosis we desperately crave (because there often isn't just **one**). So on we go, seeking out countless health practitioners and feeling increasingly hopeless, alone, broke and despairing.

I continued my research. Looking back, I didn't know how to stop. My head was stuffed with so much new info, it literally felt like my brain was going to explode. And I still couldn't hear what my body (the unconscious mind) was trying to tell me. I know now that it was to slow down, go within, practise stillness and take off my masks, so I could live an authentic life. Like myself as **me**. Acknowledge that I was enough. But how very far from that I was.

Orthorexia nervosa means having an 'unhealthy obsession' with healthy eating; it literally means 'fixation of righteous eating'. Um, tick. Maybe this fixation keeps some of us from going within and consciously listening to what our body **really** needs. Maybe being stuck on our diet prevents us from looking at all the other aspects of our lives that need attention. Your diet is relatively easy to change, especially when compared with dealing with childhood trauma that's been lodged in your physical body for decades or generations, as becomes apparent when you really start to listen to your body/mind.

Good health is not just about diet, and that's for sure. Our weight is not only about the antiquated belief of eating less and moving more. There is no doubt these things need to be considered and addressed, but as many of us who already have a good diet, exercise routine, healthy relationships, sound sleep and a spiritual practice know, it usually goes much, much deeper.

Deep healing isn't as easy as taking a pill. It takes time, patience, dedication, forgiveness and self-awareness, and can only occur once we address the underlying cause of the symptoms. And they're not always easy to track down, let alone find the time, will or resilience to do what's needed next.

Belief is going to play a big part in the state of our health, and our view of the world around us. So I have a suggestion. Let's start believing in ourselves, once and for all. It's time.

It's worth remembering that you can eat a fully organic, plant-based diet and still not enjoy good health. We read about people living to be 100 years old and more, having a drink every day, eating fatty bacon on white bread with butter, and perhaps still smoking. What's **their** secret? Is it where they live, a trauma-free childhood, the pleasure they gain from tending their own organic veggie patch, the alkaline water they drink, their genes, a great marriage, or how much surfing or yoga they've done and still do? Do these individuals practise mindfulness or other forms of meditation? Are they mentally tough enough to have the ability to effectively compartmentalise their thoughts and emotions? Or perhaps it's about how well they love, and whether they allow themselves to be loved in return? Is their default emotion set to love, rather than to fear? Some would argue this is key to a long, rewarding and healthy life; others swear it's by eating chlorella and hemp. Where we are right now, it's looking like a balance of all of these factors. After seeing many clients in my practices over the past two decades, I am inclined to agree.

Wellbeing (health plus happiness) is not about eating an organic diet because you're scared you'll get cancer if you don't. It's about eating an organic diet because it **empowers** you to do so, knowing you're giving your health and that of the planet the best chance of living a long, healthy, balanced and happy life, without leaving a heavy footprint.

Your 40-Day Transformation, and the accompanying Program came out of this journey. It's an easier way to live and eat. It is not a diet, nor a short-term detox, nor a punishment. It is basically how our great grandparents lived, before we industrialised and globalised our food. Before we were told low-fat foods, margarine, refined carbs and diet sodas were healthy, and coconut, cheese, avocado, chocolate and nuts weren't. Our ancestors ate mostly plant food, not too much, with the occasional animal product included for celebrations—using the entire beast, after killing it respectfully. They ate fermented foods (mostly by accident, due to fridges being scarce); they used less or no toxic chemicals to grow their food; they had access to clean water; they had more relaxation and less screen time. More often, they had a supportive community and extended family, went to bed earlier, had periods of fasting and exercise, and lived closer to nature.

The future of medicine, I see as a continuation of our investigation into the gut and our individual genes, how they're 'expressing', and what's causing it. Why can I drink coffee without getting jittery, while someone else is jumpy all day? And why do bright lights, loud noises and artificial fragrances bother some but not others? We now have access to this kind of exciting information, but genetic testing is still in its early stages. But remember, your diet, lifestyle and beliefs dictate around 95% of your health; your genes dictate the rest.

There are eight factors that can add to or subtract from our wellbeing: of course our diet is one, the different types of stressors (emotional, physical and chemical) another, the quality of the air we breathe, our sense of connection and belonging, and how much we laugh, exercise, meditate and sleep. During your 40-Day Reset Program, you'll learn how to achieve a healthy body/mind by addressing all of these factors. And in the process, you'll find an even happier you. You'll also finally learn how to put an end to chronic digestive discomforts, such as embarrassing and painful gas and bloating, aching joints and your entire body, thyroid and immune issues, drab skin, crushing exhaustion, terrible sleep, a crap mood, no sex drive, weight gain, infertility and so much more.

I will show you how I did it. How I helped my body return to good health by balancing my hormones and gut bacteria through diet, supplements and lifestyle, the way I spoke to myself, meditation, as well as by changing long-held beliefs about myself, the world I live in, and my part in it. This may sound overwhelming, but it's simpler and cheaper than you might think, and a hell of a lot more empowering.

WHY 40 DAYS?

Our ancestors knew the power of 40 days: the number for waiting, preparing, testing. The time it takes to transform, renew, repair and regenerate. The start of a new chapter. Rebirth. This is a universal understanding. Most of us just didn't get that memo.

This period is honoured by many cultures around the world from India, South America, Islam and Greece to mothers in Ethiopia. Likewise in the Sikh tradition and in China, where mother and child do not leave home for the first 40 days after birth. To this day, a newborn is protected and supported in a safe and sacred environment for 40 days after birth, with only mother and intimate family present.

Muslims devote themselves to God for 40 days, to 'see the springs of wisdom break forth from their hearts and flow from their tongues'. Yep, sign me up. There is also the long-held spiritual belief that it takes 20 days to break old habits and 20 days to form new ones. Our skin cells take 40 days on average to renew. Sperm count can be increased in 40 days, and red blood cells start breaking down from 40 days onwards.

In Kundalini yoga, it's said that practising for 40 consecutive days gives you the opportunity to make or break habits, deepen your intuition, and unleash the unlimited creative potential that exits within all of us in the quantum field. Yep, I'm up for that also. And if you've picked up this book, I'm pretty sure you are too. The period of 40 days holds both a mystical and practical significance for transformation in many areas of our lives.

In keeping with the rhythm of the cosmos of which we are a part, I'd like to guide you through your own 40 days to transformation—to becoming the real 'you'. Your authentic self, free of dis-ease, living the life you're capable of and yearn for. And it's not that hard. It just takes determination, will (thought transformed into energy), focus, and a desire to want to be your best self.

part one

WHERE ARE YOU AT?

chapter one
TIME TO TAKE A STEP BACK

Before we begin our transforming journey, we need to pause and consider the many ways in which diet, medications, thought patterns, upbringing, relationships and lifestyles can affect our health. Some diseases are different and more complex than they were in grandma's day. There's a lot going on in our body/mind at any given time.

------- ------- ------- -------

It's not a 'one size fits all' diagnosis anymore. Most
of the time it's a number of different things all going
on at the same time, in a body called you.

------- ------- ------- -------

Twenty years ago, most people came to see me about losing weight, or for bloating, constipation, period pain, premenstrual syndrome (PMS), sleeplessness, arthritis, reflux and maybe a bit of fatigue. Today, there isn't even a name for most sets of symptoms my patients present with. There are so many 21st century conditions—and even more symptoms—that most doctors are at a loss to know how to handle each person's body/mind imbalance. This can leave us feeling resigned, angry, frustrated and not heard.

21st century dis-eases are unique to each person; there's no 'one size fits all' diagnosis anymore. Even with the same diagnosis, one person's symptoms can be so different to the next person that it's often hard to imagine it's the same condition. And most of the time it's not; it's a few different things all going on at the same time, in a body called **you**. So considering this, it's not difficult to see why one or many of the different drugs that have been prescribed to you just aren't going to fix the problem (just as removing an organ that we apparently don't need won't). Not only is modern medicine not honouring the 'first, do no harm' ethos; worse still, it's leaving behind serious side effects and physical and emotional scars that are worsening our health. Not to mention the cost to the tax payer (us) and to our environment.

Finding the root cause of the suffering, then the right treatment, is a skill for sure. Natural medicine doesn't usually provide you with a quick fix; the body needs time and the right circumstances to heal, deeply and from within. If only we could get out of its way and let the body do its job, healing will occur naturally most of the time. In these pages I provide you with the tools you need.

Health is a big topic these days, and that's probably because we're a sick lot. We've also become curious about our own bodies and what foods and emotions they do and don't like; and which ones affect our wellbeing by not properly detoxifying them. Health care has become 'sick care'. We also have access to the internet, so we can easily get more info now. So no longer do we need to take what an advertisement or the doctor says as gospel. We're beginning to realise that something's not right—that perhaps modern medicine and the food industry may not be the 'best things since sliced bread' after all.

So many more of us want to know the truth about what's going into the food we eating, how and what it's been grown with, and how our health might be affected. We're also far more likely to choose natural cosmetics and cleaning products that haven't been produced using toxic chemicals left over from World War II. On the bright side, at least we now are easily able to access information around the industrialisation of our food, if we choose to. So if you'd like to see change, plus make a difference to the world our future generations will be living in, vote with your wallet. Every time you buy something, you're voting for the kind of world we're living in, and will leave behind for our children.

Prior to this decade, only hippies or greenies seemed to care about the environment. And man were we mocked for this, even though Rachel Carson's bestseller *Silent Spring* told the world for the first time about the detrimental effects caused by the indiscriminate use of pesticides. This groundbreaking book was published in 1962 and sold millions of copies worldwide. Even so, wanting to live a natural, healthy, worthwhile and long life seemed immature, ignorant and ridiculous, compared to making your fortune at any cost. And cost us it has!

Most people still believe that a particular food, whatever it is, will have the same effect on all of us. But current research is proving what many of us already know—this is just not the case! A recent study found that blood glucose levels could vary by up to 20% in the same individual, and up to 25% across individuals, after eating exactly the same meal. Researchers have found that eating identical foods can lead to very different effects in each of us. So what causes this to happen?

Metabolomics is a fairly new field of study that identifies the molecules that vary between us, our unique footprint. Now it's being applied to nutrigenomics (the study of the interaction of nutrition and genes). It's all pretty exciting stuff. Basically, some of us can and do gain weight from eating (say) carbs, while others don't. It's the same situation for other food groups. No wonder so many of us are confused about what to eat, and when. I know I'm not the only one who has had a gutful of all of the conflicting and often misleading information out there.

So where does the truth about how to live as a well being really lie? All medicine is evolving, and I see this as something really positive. Perhaps what we're currently discovering about the gut and genes will bring modern and ancient medicine together by using a wholistic focus, so once again we can practise 'patient-centred medicine' rather than 'disease-centred medicine'. Health care instead of 'sick care'.

The soul always knows what to do to heal itself.
The challenge is to silence the mind.

CAROLYN MYSS PHD

chapter two
THE LAW OF ATTRACTION

Anyone living with chronic illness knows the feeling of panic, the terror of possibly never ever feeling good again. At some point the fear kicks in. And then we have a vicious circle.

In 2014, about a year after I first 'crashed', my desire to know why I was so unwell took me to Europe to one of the world's top health clinics. I was really desperate. It was a year after my miscarriage, the 'trigger' to my adrenal collapse and I was getting worse. I prayed for an answer. I spent a week fasting, detoxing, swimming in alkaline lakes, sleeping lots, foot baths, salt baths, infra-red saunas, massages, meditating and seeing many health practitioners, both Western and complementary. In the end, no-one knew what was causing my ill health. Yes, I lost weight there (that happens when you don't eat much at all for a week), but my gut and my state of mind worsened. Stress of any kind is not a good idea when you're already depleted.

So there I was, terribly unwell, alone again, on international flights into the unknown, fasting, surrendering myself to a tribe that weren't my own, in a retreat centre that had been a busy hospital during World War II. Many stressors were now activated, and loneliness and exhaustion were killing me.

What I now know is that prolonged physical, mental and emotional stress set me up for the crash, and the miscarriage was my trigger.

I believe that a good diet, loving tribe, optimistic nature, and healthy lifestyle kept my MTHFR gene mutation from expressing itself earlier. (Our genes need to be turned on, or 'up-regulated', in order for them to cause dis-ease.) Yeah, I was born with a sensitive gut, had weight issues and endometriosis most of my life, but there were periods when all three seemed to go into remission at the same time. That's probably because they stem from the same thing: emotional stress/estrogen dominance/adrenal fatigue. The MTHFR gene mutation now expressing itself wasn't the cause of my health issues, it was a symptom. It wasn't my new gluten—my life and my beliefs were!

What followed was the realisation that instead of listening to my body/mind, I had become a 'victim to my illness'. I was letting it define me. I was attaching myself to my illness, because I was familiar with it. I was becoming it. This made sense, as most of what I was thinking, doing and feeling was related to illness, not wellness. The Law of Attraction had never felt so real. Something clicked. Oprah would call it an 'aha moment'.

Living with the final stages of adrenal fatigue forces you to slow down. It's not a gentle plea from your body anymore; it demands you do so.

> *Imagination is everything; it's the preview*
> *to life's coming attractions.*
>
> ALBERT EINSTEIN

chapter three
THE LAW OF LEAST EFFORT

I decided to just **stop everything and start again**. Then something started to shift. I put this uncharacteristic behaviour down to burnout, forcing me to slow down and wake up. But now my 'shadow' had shown up.

Each of us has a shadow, and it tends to show up when we least expect or want it to. It's that part of ourselves that our culture, family, church or education have told us is unacceptable, so we go to great measures to hide those parts of ourselves we don't want anyone to see. My fear of being still, of being unproductive or lazy was right in my face. How could anyone love me behaving like that?

At that time, I started taking a few specific herbal medicines and natural supplements to aid hormone balance, improve digestion and nourish my nervous system and adrenal glands. The most significant thing I started doing was to meditate and practise surrendering. Okay, so I'm not saying this is a walk in the park, but it is essential if we wish to live an authentic life. It starts with being okay with vulnerability: letting your shadow out and seeing how that feels, then just sitting in that discomfort. More than likely it will be horrible at first, as we're so used to shoving those less attractive parts of ourselves down deep. But in a matter of days it becomes normal and starts to feel really good and right and freeing.

The things we believe as children sometimes need to be unlearned. For me, the past five years have been exactly about that. Almost everything I thought about myself has been questioned throughout this 'dark night of the soul'. The mask I had been wearing for 45 plus years needed to come off. What I found was that once you have the pieces of the wellbeing puzzle on the table, deep healing is possible. This includes being true to yourself, living an authentic life with the mask removed, and embracing your shadow. This is tough stuff, yet essential if you **truly** desire lasting, good health.

I literally had had a gutful of depriving myself, wishing for a different body, feeling unlovable and being unkind to myself. Clearly I wasn't hearing my body telling me that it was time for a change, time for a new way of thinking. Time to slow down and start accepting me. Time to step into the feminine place of 'being'. Just being myself, and loving me there.

My story hasn't ended, but where I am now is probably the best version of me I've known. I'm content, grateful for my life, and continue to share what I learn about health, happiness, connection, female empowerment and deep healing. It's a work in progress and something I am highly committed to.

> *Nature's intelligence functions with effortless ease ...*
> *with carefreeness, harmony, and love. And when*
> *we harness the forces of harmony, joy and love, we*
> *create success and good fortune with effortless ease.*
>
> DEEPAK CHOPRA

chapter four
YOUR SHADOW SELF

Before we move on, let's look deeper into our shadow. This is the mask we wear, hiding those parts of ourselves we don't want anyone to see, those parts of ourselves that are angry, wounded, hurt, sad, unkind, lazy, unproductive, addicted, lonely. Those parts of ourselves that we feel aren't loveable, or we've been **told** aren't loveable or acceptable, so we just shove them away to never see the light of day. Part of our healing is learning to accept these parts of ourselves, and to love them.

In our shadow, we have the opportunity to truly heal and live an authentic life. To understand ourselves better, diffuse harmful emotions, reclaim those parts of ourselves that have been shoved in the closet, and accept ourselves fully—including our past, our quirks, our weight—seeing them as gifts rather than something shameful.

Mindfulness is a way into our shadow, catching unhelpful repetitive thoughts and behaviour, as is listening to what your body is saying. The time just before your period can also help you access your shadow, as you tend to feel a little more vulnerable then, more internal. Use this time to listen to it, without judgement. Maybe it's something you've avoided or been hiding. Feelings of grief, fear or shame around the consequences of letting some anger or hurt out. Feeling these emotions, being vulnerable, takes courage.

Shining some light on your darkness—on the things you feel ashamed of—transforms them, enabling you to lighten up and accept that old grievances are nothing to be ashamed of anymore. Talking about your 'stuff' with those you can trust brings them out into the open, helping you to laugh about any embarrassing or shameful things holding you back.

We all have a shadow. Realising this helps us feel more compassion towards each other. What a bonus! If you can't hear or see it, you can't heal it.

The shadow is hidden or unconscious aspects of oneself, both good and bad, which the ego has either repressed or never recognised.

DARYL SHARP, *JUNG LEXICON*

chapter five
TURNING YOUR GENES ON AND OFF

The relatively new area of epigenetics tells us that our genes are constantly changing, in an intimate relationship with our environment. They're not our destiny, set in stone as we once thought, but quite the opposite. Epigenetics tells us that the expression of our genes are changing all the time, around every 20 minutes, in response to our environment, and signals from other cells. It's not the genes we've inherited from our parents that determine our health; it's what we do with them.

Until very recently, we were told that our genes don't change; what we inherit is there for life. This theory is still being sold to us, but has never been proven. This particular dogma says that if your mum has high blood pressure, then you probably will too; if your father has diabetes, you can look forward to that as well. It's just the hand you've been dealt. It's the luck of the draw. But that's just not true, and it never has been. This dogma sets us up for a lifetime of living as victims—as if nothing we do will make any difference to our wellbeing, and the only way to deal with dodgy genes is to take prescription medications for the rest of our lives. How wrong that is!

Belief is going to play a big part in the state of your health, and your view of the world. If you see yourself as a victim—fat, sick, broke and alone—then that's probably what you're going to attract.

Likewise, if you believe you're one of the lucky ones, then it's likely you're living a life you're grateful for.

Genetics alone makes up only about 1–8% of all disease (and we're not yet sure it's even this small a percentage). Thought patterns, lifestyle factors, environment, diet and our belief system make up the rest.

It's a fact that stress hormones down-regulate genes ('turn on' their expression) to create dis-ease. So, the answer? We need to start living a more peaceful, clean, joyful, creative and fulfilled life, connected to nature. Otherwise our bodies, minds and spirits will continue to suffer.

Epigenetics hands us back our individual power, the power over our own destiny.

I am the master of my fate; I am the captain of my soul.
WILLIAM ERNEST HENLEY, *INVICTUS*

chapter six
ARE YOU STRESSING YOURSELF OUT?

So let's take a closer look at stress, and how it may be playing out for you. When we talk about stress, we're usually referring to **emotional stress**. Things like the feelings we experience during a relationship break-up, a custody battle, losing a job, having a sick child, going bankrupt, fighting with your best friend, or too much to do in one day, and the resentment, fear, jealousy, anger and frustration that breeds from there. However emotional stress, as damaging as it is, is not the only stressor we'd be better off avoiding in the quest for wellness.

Usually, the greatest stress we will be exposed to in a single day is **physical stress**. This includes the way we hold our body while we sleep, sit, think, drive, stand or argue. How much we're pushing our bodies via the type of exercise and work we do, the hours we keep. How much we run around all day, usually not breathing deeply, but holding tension in our tummies, neck and shoulders, reproductive organs or lower back. It also involves how many chemicals we're being exposed to through our diet and life on planet Earth: how much alcohol we drink, party drugs we take, junk food we eat, medications we're on, and how efficiently we're detoxing these waste products from our bodies. Heavy metal toxicity also stresses our bodies physically, as do hormonal and gut imbalances.

And then there's the **invisible stress** we're exposed to. This includes electromagnetic waves from microwaves, ultraviolet and infra-red radiation. Your mobile, your computer, bluetooth speakers and other devices that connect to them, because they use radiofrequency (RF) waves to make and receive calls. Radiation from a cross-country flight; medical imaging tests like X-rays, CT and PET scans; stress tests for the heart (the highest levels); and iodine scans for the thyroid gland. These tests all involve radiation, and the amount varies depending on the test. (By the way, ultrasounds and MRIs don't involve radiation.) The highest radiation exposures occur among women and older adults, with 80% occurring during non-hospitalised visits. We're also exposed to UV radiation from the sun and some solariums. Ionising radiation, being constantly with us, can and does affect us as much as the more obvious stressors, like calling Telstra. (But we aren't always aware of it, unlike calling Telstra!) In many cases, these insidious and invisible forces create the environment for the physical, emotional and chemical stressors that trigger changes in our cells.

Then there's the stress that you were born with. This explains why some of us lean towards particular emotions and others don't. Trans-generational studies have shown us that trauma is inherited, three generations on, so far discovered. It's in our DNA. For example, if someone in your ancestral line was a prisoner in a concentration camp, this will have an effect on the way your own body uses food, and your reaction to stressors will be heightened.

When our **sympathetic** nervous system (SNS) is activated, our body/mind thinks we're in survival mode (fight or flight), due to the stress our body is experiencing. This is okay and actually helpful in the short term. But if we're living with these stressors 24/7, we have a wee problem. Conversely, when our **parasympathetic** nervous system (PNS) is activated, we are generally in a state of calm (rest and digest) and at peace. We need our nervous system to be moving between both to live with the greatest resilience and ease. But today we're often stuck with our SNS running the show, so our bodies are in a constant state of chronic stress and distress. The result? Chances are our body is inflamed, resulting in chronic fatigue and immune issues, constantly feeling like crap, and setting the stage for chronic illness.

GETTING BACK ON TRACK

The good news is that we can do a lot to get back on track. Nature has an intelligence far wiser than our own, and one way to access it is via our breath. Answers to our problems rarely come to us by thinking about them more, but by allowing our mind to be still. Conscious breathing is a simple way to do this, and another is by closing our eyes and focusing our attention downward and inward towards our hearts. You'll notice that when your mind is in overdrive you'll be looking up, whether you're in bed trying to sleep or trying to meditate. By bringing your attention in and down, you'll quieten your mind, allowing inspiration and higher consciousness to enter.

Getting eight hours sleep every night is vital, as are the following:

- being part of a tribe you rely upon and trust
- doing moderate, regular exercise that you enjoy
- eating a nutritious, wholefood diet
- practising deep breathing exercises right into your abdomen
- having a daily meditation
- doing and being around what you love and gives you joy, while steering away from anything that does not

All of the above help you feel healthy, nourished, safe and nurtured, and on the road to restoring your health.

chapter seven

TOO MUCH EXERCISE?

Yes, there is such a thing and many of us are guilty of it, especially the cardio (aerobic) or 'yang' type of exercise. While there are many benefits to this type of exercise, there are a few things to consider before you go ahead and book in for yet another boot camp at dawn.

Twenty minutes of aerobic/cardio exercise daily will turn on the production of BDNF (brain-derived neurotrophic factor), the brain's 'growth hormone'. This is a good thing in most cases. Fast walking, running, cycling and anything else that stimulates your heart and increases your breathing rate for 20 minutes or so falls into this category. But doesn't this also sound like anxiety? That's exactly what your body/mind thinks. Oh no, she's in danger! We better keep that fat on her belly, thighs and bum, just in case we're heading for a famine! Our bodies produce stress hormones when our heart rate increases, because they can't distinguish whether you're in a pump class or your boss is calling you in for a 'chat'. If you've already exhausted your adrenaline and cortisol from a lifetime of doing, then it's not such a good idea to push it even further.

If you choose to ignore this advice, as I did, then you'll crash like me. When I hit the first stage or two of adrenal fatigue, I started to notice a bit more of a muffin top. Of course, I freaked out and immediately upped my exercise. I found a personal trainer who I saw a few times a week (a crazy 30-minute drive away and a 6am start), and she pushed me hard. I kept up my runs to the top of the Byron Bay lighthouse and back, a few times a week, and naturally I didn't stop my daily four km jog up and down a very steep hill near home, plus swimming a kilometre once or twice a week.

Watching your weight increase and your gut issues worsen, when you think (not feel) you're doing all the right things is just devastating, isn't it? But seriously, when your back goes or something else stops you and you literally can't move anymore, you know you're in trouble. This is when the weight really piles on. If you haven't listened to your body telling you it's really tired, then not being able to move will certainly make you rest. Try not to get to this point, eh? Instead of constantly pushing yourself by doing a cardio style of exercise (usually to keep our weight down, while drinking wine or eating lollies), balance it out with more feminine movements.

Regular and moderate exercise is vital for us, but it's easy to not exercise when you're feeling rubbish. When suffering from fibromyalgia, adrenal fatigue, an autoimmune condition or just plain depression, then consider 'mindful' walking, swimming (breaststroke preferably), slow cycling, yin or hatha yoga, Pilates, qi gong and tai chi.

Research has shown that two 75-minute yoga sessions a week reduces pain, balances cortisol levels and increases mindfulness. That'll be enough, for a while anyway. Exercise regularly and sensibly, and not when you're in pain. Not too little and not too much. That's going to be different for everybody, and at different times during our journey to wellness.

Exercise is a natural anti-inflammatory, if you don't overdo it. If you do, then it becomes a source of inflammation, of physical stress.

chapter eight

YOUR FOOD HAS A HORMONAL EFFECT

As you move towards your exciting reset, it's important to become more aware of the foods you eat.

For the past sixty years we have used genetic selection, irradiation, chemical pesticides and fertilisers to increase crop yield and decrease 'pests'. A further 31 substances have been added to processed foods to preserve, colour, flavour and texture it, with potential 'fake estrogen' effects. We need natural estrogen for strong bones, blood clotting and reproduction, but these fake estrogens enter our bodies and increase our estrogen levels, resulting in **estrogen excess**.

These synthetic fakers mimic our own estrogen and mess with the delicate balance of our hormones. They're also mighty difficult to detoxify, so they recirculate through our bodies and build up, especially if the liver isn't working well. The signals our hormones are meant to give our tissues get blocked, and this is particularly bad news for hormone-sensitive organs such as the uterus, breasts, and our immune and neurological systems.

As these fake or xenoestrogens are not biodegradable, they get stored in our fat cells. An excess of estrogen is associated with many conditions, including breast, prostate and testicular cancer, obesity, ovarian cysts, migraines, severe PMS, uterine cysts, infertility, increased breast cancer, reduced testosterone in males and even behavioural changes, infertility, endometriosis, early onset puberty, miscarriage and diabetes.

SO WHAT SHOULD WE DO?

We really need to steer clear of food grown with pesticides, herbicides and fungicides. Any food not certified organic or labelled 'spray-free' can have estrogenic effects. This is everything from nuts, fruit and veggies to legumes, grains and oils, as well as all animal products.

Peel and wash all non-organic fruit and vegetables, preferably in a tub full of clean water and vinegar. (This may help to remove some of the toxic chemicals present on the outside only.) It's especially important to avoid eating conventionally produced (non-organic) meat and dairy, such as pork, chicken, beef, milk, cheese, butter and ice cream, as they are highly contaminated with antibiotics and fed genetically modified (GM) feed, exposing us to a significant amount of xenoestrogens.

And what about salmon? In Australia, the only fresh salmon available has been farmed. This means additives like synthetic astaxanthin (used as food colouring), GM crops (used in the feed) and loads of antibiotics (meaning 'anti-life') have been involved somewhere along the line. For these reasons, salmon is not something I recommend to my clients.

As we lose weight, pesticides are released from the fat tissue. This allows more estrogen to circulate, if we don't help our bodies detoxify it.

Diindolylmethane (DIM) is a phytonutrient which occurs naturally in cruciferous vegetables, such as broccoli, cauliflower, cabbage and kale that helps remove excess estrogen, so we have a better chance of maintaining a healthy hormonal balance. Calcium D-glucarate (CDG) also helps us remove toxins and excess hormones, as well as support liver function and detoxification and boost immunity, although it not as reliable as DIM. Both need to be taken as a supplement.

Other ways to detoxify are listed in *Chapter 21, Excess Estrogen.*

Someday we shall look back on this dark era
of agriculture and shake our heads.
How could we have ever believed that it was a
good idea to grow our food with poisons?

DR. JANE GOODALL, *HARVEST FOR HOPE*

chapter nine
WHAT YOU NEED TO GET ABOUT YOUR GUT

The gut is an organ in our body that weighs as much as our brain. We all have a different balance of bugs in our gut that to a large extent determine our weight, what foods we crave, our mood and overall health. As we look to rebalance, let's go to our gut or 'second brain', as it's described more commonly these days.

Controlled by a super complex nervous system made up of millions of neurons, our gut and brain communicate through signals (via the vagus nerve) by releasing gut or stress hormones. Modern science is only now catching up with this ancient wisdom and realising the importance of a healthy microbiome (the bacterial ecosystem in our gut).

Everyone's gut is full of bugs that can be good, bad, indifferent or displaced. Microbes are everywhere. They hang out all the way from our mouth through to our anus. They live on and inside us, and cover most things we come into contact with, including our personal belongings.

The microbiome is so important that these gut bacteria can be considered as an organ in their own right. Until very recently, this is a fact we have been oblivious to. Gut bacteria have been shown to influence increasingly common modern diseases such as cancer, heart disease and diabetes; other research has found links between the composition of gut bacteria in overweight and lean people. We now know that there's a whole lot more to our broadening girth than how much and what we eat and how much we are moving.

Over the past 60 years, disruption to the gut's microbiota has been linked to everything from gastrointestinal conditions such as irritable bowel syndrome (IBS), obesity, allergies, immune disturbances, fertility issues, allergies, higher rates of autism, multiple sclerosis (MS), dementia and so much more. Something has clearly gone wrong, and it's looking like the wealthier of us are the most affected.

Things like medication, stress, chemicals in our food, water, cosmetics, antibacterial wipes and hand sanitisers all negatively impact on our gut's health. Taking probiotics really helps some of us with gut issues like SIBO and leaky gut syndrome, but after we stop taking them, our gut flora tends to return to its initial balance of species.

MICROBIOTA OR MICROBIOME?

The difference between the terms 'microbiota' and 'microbiome' is this:
- microbiota refers to the microorganisms and viruses living in our gastrointestinal tract;
- microbiome refers to the genetic make-up of the whole of the microbiota—the genes from all the bacteria, fungi and viruses.

The microbiome in our gut is made up of about a thousand different species of bacteria; trillions of cells that together weigh between 0.5 and 1.5 kg may well play a key role in many diseases. For example, when we're under stress and feeling anxious about public speaking or going on a first date, it's not uncommon for us to experience diarrhoea or feel butterflies in our stomach. At such times, our mood actually changes the production of stomach acid through brain-gut nerve connections. This is your environment altering the way your genes are expressing themselves.

------- ------- ------- -------

If signals are sent to our brain from the gut as well as in the opposite direction, could it be that changes to our gut flora are actually driving anxiety, rather than the other way around? It's looking that way. Gut issues can bring on psychological distress, and vice versa. Things we do and think can change our microbiome.

------- ------- ------- -------

Only one in eight people actually feel an issue in their gut. Things like bloating and reflux tell us something's wrong with our digestion. But what about the other seven of us? Could it be that symptoms and conditions like allergies, insomnia, infertility, thyroid issues, asthma, eczema, psoriasis, autism, MS, Alzheimer's, weight gain, obesity, diabetes, autoimmune diseases, hormone imbalance and some cancers can all be traced back to poor gut health? Current cutting-edge research says 'yes'.

We have long known that our emotions can directly change the function of our gut. Now we're learning it works the other way around as well—that our gut has a huge effect on our brain. So healing the gut could also treat some chronic psychological and brain diseases. What goes on in the gut influences our digestion, immunity, metabolism, and how we think and feel. It's very exciting!

Interestingly, to some extent it has been shown that different cultural dietary preferences have a huge impact on an individual's blend of bugs, so much so that gut bacteria can even be used to identify where in the world you are from and who you live with. Incredibly, owners and pets can be matched by looking at their skin and gut microbiomes. Regular physical contact with the people you live with is a huge factor, with those in close relationships sharing the most microbes, including your pet. It doesn't matter if you're genetically related our not; if you live in the same household, you share a similar microbiome.

One of the best ways to increase exposure to good bacteria is to open your windows and let the microbes in. Welcome them into your home, your car, your office—the more, the merrier! Working or living in an air-conditioned space, without access to fresh air and all the healthy microbes it brings, is detrimental to our gut health and our health in general.

chapter ten

WHAT ABOUT GERMS?

While we're on the subject of bugs, it's helpful to know that getting our hands dirty in the garden is beneficial, as the organisms living there (bacteria and worms) make for a healthier immune system. They help reduce our chance of developing allergies and gut problems, and also act as natural vaccinators, thanks to the *Bifidobacteria* and *Lactobacillus* in the soil.

The problem is we live in a time of antiseptic overkill, with antiseptic wipes, detergents, Dettol, cleaning products and nasty hand sanitisers everywhere. It's all too much. We're obsessed with cleanliness and hygiene. If you ask most people, cleanliness comes with the smell of bleach and chemical disinfectant. We are compromising our immunity by killing off good bacteria as well as the not-so-good ones in our gut, and destroying our health and the Earth at the same time.

For cleaning, all you need is vinegar and water; if you like, add a few drops of an antibacterial or antiseptic pure essential oil like tea tree, oregano, lemon or eucalyptus to the bucket or spray bottle. Chemical-free cleaning products and hand soaps that don't contain any napalm-like antiseptics are also readily available in mainstream supermarkets. Also easily available now are cleaning cloths that require no cleaning agent at all, just the wipes.

And our food is not helping matters either, as it's mostly devoid of the natural probiotics it once contained. In part we can blame the refrigerator for this; it keeps everything cool so food doesn't have a chance to ferment and create the live bacteria we need. (Enzymes needed for proper digestion are also destroyed, if what we're eating is too cold or too hot.)

So go ahead and get dirty occasionally in uncontaminated soil, and get your kids out there with you. Pull out some weeds. Build a compost heap. Plant some flowers. Mow your lawn, roll down the hill, or do anything else that will connect you and your immune system with the trillions of beneficial microbes in the soil. Don't go washing off the dirt from the garden with an antibacterial soap; just wash your hands and body with a natural soap and clean water. The dirt is beneficial to our microbiome, as the relationship between the inside and outside of our body is very important and something we've been lacking for the past sixty years.

THE IMPORTANCE OF A HEALTHY GUT MICROBIOME

A healthy gut microbiome is necessary for our entire health. Gut bacteria do more than simply break down food for digestion. They also work on vitamins and other nutrients, and affect our immune responses. A healthy microbiome is also needed for keeping our weight stable, as it allows us to access calories we might not have been able to use before, meaning less food is needed (and eaten) and more energy is gained.

Bacteria colonies are everywhere, not just in our gut. We are covered in bacteria from our ears to our toes, our mouth to our anus and everywhere in between. From birth onwards, bacterial communities in our gut get to work, each with specific jobs to do. Some love fats, while others prefer proteins. It is only through a mix of bacterial species, each with their own preferred taste, that the gut can form nutrients, vitamins and enzymes for proper digestion. And help us decide what we feel like eating today.

Our own microbiota is decided during pregnancy, rapidly increasing in the last two months, and continuing after birth. This means that babies born prematurely or via caesarean (C-section) have their young guts exposed to an external world that they are probably not quite ready to deal with.

Bacteria are placed in our gut mostly during and just after birth—from our mother, the immediate environment and our first feed. A child develops in utero thanks to its 20,500 or so human genes, and is then hugely affected by the billions of genes expressed by its microbiome, inherited from the mother's placenta and amniotic fluid, her vagina, breast tissue and breast milk, and other places too. So the way we come into the world can make a huge difference.

Research over the past ten years has shown us that C-section births negatively affect the gut microbiome of the child. And they're on the rise. Of course, C-sections are sometimes needed to protect the life of mother or infant, but not as many as are performed these days. China's rate of C-section is now approximately 50%, while in Brazil it's 80%, along with increasing levels of Crohn's disease, diverticulitis, allergies, immune and psychological issues.

A baby needs to push through the birth canal and be covered with the mother's microbiome to give some defence against the world it's about to enter. The next contact a baby needs is with the mother's skin, mouth and nipples. This is the time the infant starts to develop its own immunity. Wiping a baby down with an antiseptic cloth; bathing it in toxic liquid soap aimed at killing any and all germs; handing the baby to a nurse wearing latex gloves; then leaving him or her to sleep in air conditioning, wrapped in GM cotton nappies and clothing are possibly the worst things we can do for an infant with developing gut flora.

The emerging practice of spreading the mother's microbiome over a baby born via C-section—in the ears, around the eyes and mouth and into the nasal cavity—in the hope that this will somewhat take the place of collecting bacteria via the journey through the birth canal is so far looking promising.

I have a personal interest in the effect of traumatic birth on a child's life, and how it affects a baby's developing flora, together with the risk of developing an autoimmune disease, obesity, anxiety and/or spectrum disorders later in life. I was one of those babies, and I am pretty sure that my gut, reproductive and weight issues and a lot of my personality traits can be contributed, at least in part, to my rocky entry into the world. My mother agrees. I am one of four siblings, the only one with a difficult birth, and also the only one with digestive and weight issues since early childhood.

The emerging field of neurogastroenterology is a very exciting one. This is the study of how the brain and the gut interact, shaping how our gut functions and what kind of condition it's in. Specifically, it looks at the stress response and how this affects our digestion and vice versa. Cool, huh?

chapter eleven

STOP DIETING AND START LOVING YOURSELF

I've always had gut issues, even before it was considered 'normal' to have gut issues. It was never really a big deal, as I just knew I couldn't eat a lot of foods without feeling sick and tired. That was my reality, and it got worse as I reached puberty. My weight ballooned and on top of digestive and weight issues, puberty brought with it endometriosis. No wonder my adrenals wore out.

So onto the merry-go-round of fad diets I went. I was always on some sort of a diet or fast, even in my teens. I was constantly restricting, denying, removing and experimenting with food. As a result, my weight has fluctuated by 20 or so kilos, more than a few times. I was always exercising so I could be thinner/more loveable, not realising that it's a great way to completely mess up your metabolism.

------- ------- ------- -------

Research has proven that remaining the same weight is far healthier than losing and gaining as little as one kilo, and can even extend your life span. Eating pretty well during the week, then bingeing on junk food over the weekend, is likely to be just as bad for your gut health as eating junk food all the time.

------- ------- ------- -------

I had self-worth issues that stemmed from my weight, which was probably a result of a traumatic birth and consequent gut issues, which led to overgiving and overdoing, in exchange for love and acceptance. I was so busy trying to gain approval by being helpful and thin, that I wasn't listening to my body's needs. No way! This little people pleaser just kept on going to the point of beyond exhaustion, but my adrenal glands (and entire being) did not. They still do not like that kind of anxious behaviour, and tolerate it even less today.

The years passed, antibiotics were taken like Tic Tacs for a recurring sore throat, with numerous abdominal laparoscopies to 'treat' chronic and severe endometriosis. (If only I knew then what I know now!) Then in my twenties, my calling to take the 'food as medicine' message to the Western world was so strong that I rarely heard what my own body was trying to tell me. It was in fact screaming at me to slow down, masked as numerous gut issues, anxiety, anger, resentment, throat issues, endometriosis, guilt, lower back pain and fatigue.

The things we believe as children sometimes need to be unlearned; for me, the past five years have been exactly about that. Almost everything I thought about myself has been questioned throughout this 'dark night of the soul' period. The mask I had been wearing for more than 45 years needed to come off. That's really scary, right? But I had to trust that I was more loveable being myself, even when not at **my** ideal weight. Otherwise, my weight would just keep yo-yoing.

I needed to catch those damaging thoughts before they became my beliefs, then my behaviour, then my disease. Those old thought patterns, that success and being thin equal love and acceptance, clearly weren't working for me.

Wanting to live an authentic life doesn't mean it will happen overnight. But regular mediation, practising mindfulness and believing that you will be different, that you will be true to yourself this time, makes wellness so much more possible.

chapter twelve

ARE YOU OXYTOCIN DEPRIVED?

As we hone in on all areas of our health that need attention, we need to look at oxytocin. This is a hormone that plays a key role in the way we relate socially, how much we trust, and in sex. It helps us feel connected and bonded to another.

Oxytocin is produced during orgasm, childbirth and breastfeeding, something not all of us automatically do anymore. So could it be that the rise in female empowerment is causing our fertility, relationships and orgasms to be compromised? Is our need for equality, at the very least, contributing to the loneliness, weight gain, hormone imbalance, memory and hair loss many women are now living with, due to oxytocin deprivation, at least in part?

A lot of the (mostly female) patients I see are frantically busy. Is it a coincidence that many haven't experienced the 'pair bonding' that happens when a woman feels she can depend on her significant person/s? These days, women feel they have to grow the bacon, cook the bacon, look sexy while they serve the bacon and make sure the bacon is free-range, grass-fed, organic, antibiotic and nitrate-free, as well as bring it home in BPA and plastic-free packaging, without breaking a sweat and in heels! Consequently, production of the bonding hormone oxytocin as well as other feel-good hormones like serotonin, dopamine and progesterone are all under threat, with our stress hormones adrenalin and cortisol in overdrive.

Seeing this made me start to think, as oxytocin has a significant effect on establishing monogamous relationships. It is released into the bloodstream as a hormone in response to orgasm, stretching of the cervix and uterus during childbirth, and from stimulation of the nipples during breastfeeding. Could it be that many of us are oxytocin deprived?

Are we **feeling** alone, rather than being alone? Of course we are. We don't live together in a matriarchal (mother-centred) community anymore, bringing up the kids together, sharing the duties of the group, as well as our worries and concerns. So how can we feel connected to and supportive of each other when we live in isolation, even within a family environment?

Oxytocin makes women want to share details and stories in a more emotional way. Women release oxytocin when they talk. Men don't. For men, it is thought that oxytocin increases their romantic attraction and attachment, to help support loyalty. (Oxytocin supplementation for men is becoming increasingly popular, and I'm not sure this is a good idea.)

LET'S GET TOGETHER

Does the new model of the alpha female, short of feel-good hormones such as oxytocin, prevent women from successfully partnering or having babies easily, and therefore feeling like they don't belong, to anyone or anything? We're not meant to be doing this alone. And it's only in the past few thousand years that we have been—five minutes ago, relative to the human timeline.

We all really need to start hanging out together more. Sharing our lives and loads. We're born this way. This is our natural environment, so it's essential that the goddesses gather together.

Oxytocin, the 'cuddle chemical', makes women want to attach and bond to each other, to 'tend and befriend'. But it can't be present when our stress hormones are always hanging around with gusto. You can't be happily breastfeeding when a sabre-toothed tiger is charging towards you and your bub. Or the modern equivalent, being 'unliked' on Facebook, or checking out the women who seem to have it all on Instagram. Have our busy, anxious, competitive, multi-tasking personalities used up all of our stress hormones like adrenaline and cortisol, thereby putting our other hormones out of balance, resulting in a life alone and sick?

Women of my generation, born in the 1960s, were among the first to be told we can have it all. And have it all we do. We do things women weren't allowed or encouraged to do before the first wave of feminism of the 1960s. We've educated ourselves, have whatever career we choose **and** have babies, have our own bank accounts, own and renovate property, vote, drive, go to bars, have sex with whomever we choose, say no, marry who we desire, divorce without (too much) shame, and we travel—a lot. We have looked within, wanting to better ourselves wherever we can (sometimes because it looks like other women are 'having it all' better than we are). So yes, we have it all; but there's a price to pay. We're lonely for other women's company, exhausted, resentful, feel isolated and unlovable, would rather be on Instagram than have sexy time, increasingly infertile and unwell. It's a big problem.

TEND AND BEFRIEND

So where to now? Unfortunately, being a capable woman with no apparent needs of her own is still glorified. However, being self-sufficient is not such a blessing, especially when men in general aren't adjusting to the relatively recent paradigm shift at the same rate as women. We need to start taking care of ourselves and each other, and all the kids. We need to seek out other women to 'tend' (all the children) and 'befriend' (other women).

According to the 'tend and befriend' theory, one of the first things women do in response to stress is to seek social contact, as opposed to the 'fight or flight' response. Support from our tribe or community is associated with increases in our oxytocin levels. This means that this bonding hormone leads to a decrease in our anxiety levels and stimulates the calming down hormones, by decreasing the stress hormones released with the fight-or-flight response. Women respond to stress in a way that makes us want to make and maintain friendships with other women, and encourages us to tend children and gather with other women. We feel safe together. Interestingly, this calming response does not occur in men, as their biological response is to produce higher levels of the fighting hormone testosterone (to provide protection and security) when they're threatened, and this in turn reduces the soothing effects of the oxytocin they may be producing. Estrogen in women, however, enhances oxytocin.

A spanner has now been thrown into research from the last half century in the area of 'fight or flight', primarily conducted on males. As it turns out, women's behaviour in response to stress is so much more than just fight or flight. We need to have baths, read, dream and mediate; to leave the washing up, ironing, gardening, dropping off, picking up, paying bills, cooking and taking on the entire mental and emotional load of the family, our workplace and our world.

If we can relearn how to be together, receive and admit we need help from our fellow sisters, maybe our stress hormones will settle down. Yes, I can hear you. If you don't do it, it won't get done. So, call Hire a Hubby or Jim's Mowing. Your oxytocin will hear you make that call and start showing up again. And guess what else will? Hello mojo! Promise.

chapter thirteen
DIGESTING EMOTIONS

Over the years in my practice and private life, I have been a keen observer of people. What I've learnt is this: it's not only food we need to digest, but information and energy as well. Some of us are really good at either one or both or neither. Like our food, information/energy shows up as feelings, intuition and emotions; like food, it needs to be broken down into easily digestible bits, so we can assimilate and use it. However, some things are just too hard to digest, either physically or emotionally, so we end up storing them away, undigested, causing such issues as SIBO, candida, skin issues, anxiety, oedema, joint pain, insomnia, heart disease and weight gain.

If we are digesting well, we take what we need and eliminate the rest. We let go of what we don't need. Unfortunately, the inability to process our emotions produces as much toxic residue as undigested food. From what I've witnessed, undigested feelings of grief, guilt, anger, sadness and resentment, as well as too much information coming our way from books, TV, movies, the internet or other people are just as harmful as physical digestive issues. It's almost impossible to have good physical digestion if you've shoved an old hurt way down deep inside, just as it's difficult to feel good if you have a few kilos of undigested food in your gut.

It's helpful here to understand the difference between feelings and emotions. Feelings are the awareness of sensations in our body. They only become an emotion if we find a memory to connect that feeling to. So if we can merely observe a sensation in our body, allowing it to give us the message it's intending, then chances are we won't get so easily caught up in past events that lead us to feeling pissed off or vengeful. Besides, only 50% of our memories are anywhere near accurate.

Ayurveda tells us that the most subtle essence of the food we eat goes on to form our mind, after digestion. So we receive information not just in our brains but through our whole body, as our mind is our whole body after all. As our skin is our largest organ and a sense organ, we are continuously receiving information literally through our pores, whether we're conscious of it or not. And it all has to be processed, or else stored as stagnant energy in our body/mind. That is when we start to feel the symptoms of not listening to our body/mind.

In Ayurveda, there is a particular type of energy called Samana Vayu—which is the integrating/digestive capacity of the human mind-body system. The energy of Samana Vayu is what enables us to digest and absorb the nutrition from the food we eat. It's also the force responsible for digesting our life experiences. In other words, the same force that enables you to extract nourishment from food, allows you to extract sustenance from life. When this force is dampened due to emotional upheaval, or just the modern stressors of daily life, it can have a direct effect on our capacity to digest food, as well as our feelings.

AYURVEDIC TEACHER DR. VASANT LAD

chapter fourteen
WHAT INFLAMMATION IS TELLING YOU

As we become more aware of our bodies, it's important we understand what inflammation is telling us.

When our body becomes sick, there's often some inflammation. This may result from a poor diet, emotional or physical stress, a toxic chemical overload, and/or an overexcited immune system. Basically, anything that deprives our cells of oxygen and other nutrients for too long causes inflammation. One of the best and easiest things we can do to correct a highly inflamed body is to alkaline our system, by detoxifying our mind, diet and lifestyle.

Inflammation is one way our body lets us know we're out of balance, that our toxic cup is full. Our yang 'always on the go' lifestyle isn't in harmony with our yin's need for rest and relaxation. The acid is outweighing the alkaline in our system. Fear has overthrown love. We're feeling bad vibes more often than good vibes. Get the picture?

Reducing stress in even one area of our life will have a ripple effect onto other areas. So if you're eating mostly processed foods, by cutting down on them you'll feel an enormous improvement in other areas of your life. Likewise, if you're under a lot of stress at work, reducing that particular stress by taking decent lunch breaks and eating healthy snacks will usually lead to some balance again.

We don't have to do a complete overhaul of all areas of our lives at the same time to be healthier, although some of us do prefer to do it that way. Start with your diet, then go from there. Use *Your 40-Day Transformation* as a guide to reaching your highest potential.

> *Laughter is a most healthful exercise; it is one of the greatest helps to digestion with which I am acquainted; and the custom prevalent among our forebearers, of exciting it at table by jesters and buffoons, was in accordance with true medical principles.*
>
> — CHRISTOPH WILHELM HUFELAND

chapter fifteen

WHERE ANTIBIOTICS ARE TAKING US

It's essential we consider where we're at with antibiotics. Many of us have recently become aware that some things are better for the microbiota in our gut than others. Antibiotics and laxatives, medications for fever, inflammation and pain, the contraceptive pill, as well as hormone replacement therapy (HRT) to reduce the symptoms of menopause, all give our gut a thrashing. They really mess up the delicate balance of our gut flora.

When prescribed responsibly, antibiotics are obviously a good thing. They have saved countless lives and eliminated many diseases. But they have caused others, and the overuse of antibiotics has got us into some serious strife.

It's kinda hard to avoid them. Even if you're a raw food vegan who's rarely sick, it's still likely you've been exposed to antibiotics. We're exposed to antibiotics every time we eat or drink, as the manure your veggies are grown with comes from animals that have been fed antibiotics (80% of antibiotics manufactured worldwide are for animal feed). Antibiotics are in our food and in our water. A small amount of antibiotic taken regularly is a whole lot worse than one big hit when you're sick, when you might actually need them.

It's encouraging to see that more environmentally conscious farmers are now using herbs and essential oils (like oregano oil) to replace the expensive and damaging antibiotics used in commercial farming. The overuse of antibiotics is destroying our gut flora and smashing our immune systems, increasing rates of anxiety and depression, and making us susceptible to whatever we're exposed to. Not to mention the damage they're doing to our animals, plants, waterways and our planet as a whole.

ANTIBIOTIC RESISTANCE

So far, Western medicine's answer has been to increase the prescription of these drugs (or rebrand them as Roundup). We have now arrived in a scary place called 'antibiotic resistance', meaning some infections are untreatable. Methicillin-resistant *Staphylococcus aureus* (MRSA) is a type of staph that has developed resistance to a family of antibiotics similar to penicillin. When we take an antibiotic, the drug kills many bacteria, but a few survive. These surviving bacteria are now resistant to that antibiotic, and then they multiply. This means that every time we take antibiotics, we're creating more drug-resistant bacteria.

And antibiotic use is increasing, which directly affects antibiotic resistance. By about twelve months of age, two-thirds of our kids have already taken a course of antibiotics, negatively affecting their microbiomes, reducing their resistance to allergens, and causing weight gain and autism—three of the biggest childhood issues in developed countries. This is bad news for the long-term health of our kids.

Bacterial infections respond well to antibiotics, as those infections will only get worse if left untreated. Such serious infections in a baby under twelve months are meningitis, whooping cough, pneumonia and blood and urinary infections. However, antibiotics won't do any good for common viral infections, such as infections of the ear, throat and chest, so treating these with antibiotics results in none of the benefits and all of the disadvantages. It's really about choosing the right situation to use antibiotics and making sure they are used for as short a time as is necessary.

To make matters worse, scientists often modify seeds using anti-biotic-resistant genes in the genetic engineering process. Some people wonder if there's a link between these GM 'Frankenfoods' and the ever-increasing rate of antibiotic-resistant bacteria. Seems likely though, doesn't it?

The thing is, nature has provided us with many effective alternatives to synthetic antibiotics, so it's upsetting that we don't use them more often. Herbal medicine and essential oils have both undergone much research and the results are exciting.

part two

CONDITIONS TO
BE AWARE OF

chapter sixteen
COULD YOU BE SUFFERING ADRENAL FATIGUE?

Adrenal fatigue (AF) is nothing new. Of course, we humans have lived through periods of chronic stress before, surviving terrible wars, famine, natural disasters and disease. The French doctor, Emile Sargent, first described AF in medical literature over 120 years ago, after an epidemic of influenza.

The adrenal glands are about the size of an almond and sit on top of our kidneys. They may be small, but they pack a serious punch. Responsible for the production of a host of hormones and neurotransmitters—cortisol, adrenaline, noradrenaline and dopamine—they have a massive impact on how we handle illness, stress, look, feel, sleep and breed, and how we function in general.

Adrenal fatigue can be the major cause of excess fat storage, irritability, brain fog and immune issues, as well as a problematic gut, achy body and extremely low energy levels. The adrenal glands also control our blood sugar, burn protein and fat, and regulate our blood pressure. AF can lead to adrenal collapse (burnout), chronic fatigue, fibromyalgia, thyroid issues, autoimmune disease, infertility, cancer, gut and immune issues and many more health problems.

Prolonged stress—physical, emotional, chemical or invisible—contributes to adrenal fatigue and to many other health issues today. When our body perceives danger, our adrenal glands release such stress hormones as adrenaline and cortisol. This release should last about 20 minutes, giving us the extra energy we need to get away from danger or just hide. Nowadays we release stress hormones 24/7, even in our sleep. High cortisol interferes with our immune system, and if this continues it can break down proteins, cause muscle wastage, then eventually lead to a condition known as hypocortisolemia (an abnormally low level of cortisol in the blood), creating chronic to severe inflammation that will eventually cause premature ageing, weight gain and fatty tissue deposits, as well as a shorter lifespan.

How did we get to this place? Do-ing is yang (action) and be-ing is yin (inaction). With AF, there's often too much **doing**, and not enough **being**—and for way too long. Too many CrossFit or 6am Bikram yoga classes, constant negative thoughts, late nights, anger or self-medicating with drugs, alcohol, food or work. Too much pain, both physical and emotional. Too much giving.

If you are suffering adrenal fatigue, it's time to give yourself a big break by doing **less**. This can be challenging. It's about feeling okay about taking daytime naps. About going to bed earlier, especially when there's still housework and study to do (after a long day at work). Saying 'no' to exciting opportunities. Not going for that run today or tomorrow or even this year. Not being there for your distressed friend. Self-care is different from 'self-ish', and AF teaches you this.

Many factors contribute to adrenal fatigue. Continued negative thinking, chronic fear, loneliness, anxiety, feeling unsafe or unworthy. A prolonged illness, surgery or injury—either your own or that of a loved one. Emotional trauma, either recent or in the past. Long-term sleep problems. Grief after the death of a loved one. Miscarriage or infertility. Stressful experiences like living with teenagers, relationship break-up, divorce, poor internet connection, bullying, work stress, compassion fatigue, financial stress. Some medications also contribute to AF, as does taking certain medications for years. Exposure to environmental toxins and pollution are also culprits.

Adrenal fatigue is often found holding hands with thyroid disease, so you're putting on weight (or losing it), especially around the abdomen, not sleeping, losing your hair, weeing a lot, your body aches, you're having trouble concentrating or remembering very much. Your breath is shallow. Your skin is sagging and dry, with new age spots, stretch marks, broken capillaries, skin tags (especially around your neck and groin) and cellulite. Gawd!

To add injury to insult, that bottle of wine is looking like your best friend at about 5pm, and you rather fancy some chocolate or chips with Netflix more than anything or anyone else in the world. After your binge, nodding off in front of a screen, you find that those swollen ankles, aching calves and feet you've had all day are now worse, so you can't sleep. In the morning, after a shocking night, you're cranky, tired, intolerant and teary, and don't want to eat (think or talk) until about 11am. Then it all starts again, along with the constant cravings for sugar and salt, plus a nap. Your mood changes frequently, from irritability and depression to anxiety and frustration. And when this is added to PMS, perimenopause, full-blown menopause or an autoimmune issue—welcome to the nightmare of a chronic health issue. Now is when you're starting to dream of an *Eat, Pray, Love* number, or a getaway for a weekend, a year or forever.

THE 3 STAGES OF ADRENAL FATIGUE

Stage 1: Excitement
The enjoyable stage when we're doing things that are exciting, and possibly nerve-racking. Bringing your new baby home for the first time. Writing a book when you're past your deadline. Starting a new relationship. Moving overseas. Stress is high, but you manage to relax in between it all. If it's short-term stress, then we seem to bounce back after the period is over. But if the stress goes on too long, our adrenal glands slow down and eventually stop producing cortisol. Recovering

from the first stage of adrenal fatigue takes about six months with the right treatment and headspace.

Stage 2: Too much excitement

This is when we start to realise something's not right. We're on high alert 24/7 and can't slow down. We start to put on weight, can't sleep, and would rather clean the pantry than have sex. When we can't manage to get the break we desperately need between all the stress, our cortisol levels start to drop and don't always come back up again. Kind of like our car's petrol tank running out of fuel after a long trip, without a chance to fill it up again. If we don't heed the warning signs and keep going with our foot firmly on the accelerator, a crash, a breakdown of you (as you know you) is inevitable. Recovery time is approximately one year, with the right treatment and attitude.

Stage 3: Burnout!

By this stage, your cortisol levels are always low, so you feel exhausted 24/7. This is when you realise the difference between being tired and completely exhausted, especially in the morning. When we're tired but in good health, we have a good sleep then feel better. But when our cortisol isn't showing up for work and you somehow manage to sleep, you don't feel any better. Other than crushing fatigue, especially in the morning, you're also going to feel completely overwhelmed, dizzy and lightheaded, especially when getting up after lying down, or getting out of the bath, as blood pressure is unstable. Recovery time is one to three years, with the right treatment and mindset.

IMPORTANT HORMONES AND NEUROTRANSMITTERS

Cortisol

Chronic stress leads to the overproduction of cortisol (then underproduction), which in turn may cause the symptoms above. It can also cause our blood sugar to increase, leading to acidic blood, which feeds into diabetes, heart disease and cancer. Cortisol also reduces collagen production, an important component of connective tissue, and is needed for a happy gut and lovely, dewy skin. It is also needed for healthy muscles, tendons and joints, and in fact for most parts of our body.

Adrenaline

This hormone is secreted by the central nervous system in response to stress, such as anger or fear. If you are continuously producing too much adrenaline, you will likely be cranky and moody, not sleeping well, be in a constant state of dread, crave sweet and salty foods, and find it hard to get up in the morning. And as adrenaline converts glycogen into glucose in your liver to use as energy, watch the number on your bathroom scales go up, and for some people down.

Noradrenaline

Both a hormone and neurotransmitter, the term 'noradrenaline' is derived from Latin, meaning 'at/alongside the kidneys'. It is inter-changeable with 'norepinephrine', the preferred term in the US. Too much noradrenaline can cause high blood pressure, nervousness, heart palpitations and headaches.

Dopamine

This neurotransmitter looks after the brain's pleasure centres and oversees the way we move and respond emotionally. It allows us to see the rewards available to us, and a way to get them. People with low dopamine may be more prone to addictions like gambling, food, video games, sex, drugs and alcohol, shopping, social media, cigarettes, love, work, supplements or exercise. Low levels can affect our ability to focus, our creativity, and can also cause insomnia, concentration issues and weight gain.

Serotonin

Serotonin is a neurotransmitter (although some consider this chemical to be a hormone), responsible for maintaining an even mood. The majority of the body's serotonin (between 80–90%) can be found in the gastrointestinal (GI) tract, where it regulates bowel function and movements. It also plays a part in reducing our appetite while eating a meal.

DIAGNOSING AND TREATING AF

Being diagnosed with adrenal fatigue can be overwhelming, not least because it doesn't fit nicely into a neat box of symptoms, or get a widely accepted diagnosis, apart from depression or PMS. It's so much more complicated than that. Every person will experience AF differently.

You can feel like you're in over your head, trying to manage on your own. You may search for a practitioner to guide you through it all and not make you feel like it's all 'in your head', before prescribing the pill, antidepressants or HRT. Ultimately, despair kicks in because you're so tired. What often results is the old 'head in the sand' number, as there usually isn't even the tiniest bit of energy left for anything. This is when you need to ask for help.

How much cortisol your adrenal glands are using is one of the most reliable indicators of what shape your adrenal glands are in, and how well your body is handling stress. A simple saliva test is all it takes, spitting into a small tube four times on a single day, to see how your cortisol fluctuates over a 24-hour period. (It's not a fun thing to do, but hey, compared with a poo test it's totally doable!) It's not essential to have this test performed, as you know you feel terrible, but it's validating to know there is a real reason for it. (Other steroid hormones, such as estrogen, progesterone, DHEAS and testosterone, can also be measured along with the cortisol in the 8am saliva sample.)

Once you've filled all four tubes, you mail them back to the lab and your health care practitioner will receive the results within two weeks. Unfortunately, many medical doctors are still unaware of adrenal fatigue and the benefits of saliva testing, so thankfully, some labs allow patients to order tests directly. Search 'saliva test' online. However,

I rarely order this test for my patients, as symptoms more than tell me that adrenal fatigue is what we are dealing with.

To treat adrenal fatigue, I truly believe that the number one thing is not to **do**, but simply to **be**. It's important to take your human **being** easy during this time. It could take up to three years to fully recover from AF, and that's only if you really, truly take care of yourself and make the necessary changes to your diet, lifestyle and thought patterns. Remember, how you've been living up until now is how you got where you are, so some changes are needed in order for you to regain your health. But you **can** heal from adrenal fatigue.

When I see patients with adrenal fatigue, they often have no idea how to slow down. The fear of what's involved is written all over their faces and in their body language. All the things they have to **do** run through their mind. *Who is going to do everything, if I slow down?* Then the anger hits, usually directed at me, as they think I have no idea what they're up against. Um … I do.

I liken it to trying to get off a roller coaster, mid-ride. It's very scary, and not so easy in the beginning. You have to wait until the ride slows down a little, before you can think about how to get off. You didn't get to this point overnight, and you won't get back to a slower place in a hurry either. But starting the process of slowing the roller coaster down is essential, otherwise the rollercoaster will crash, **forcing** you to slow down. That's what happened to me, so I want to help as many people as I can avoid this seriously challenging situation.

Nature does not hurry, yet everything is accomplished.

LAO TZU

chapter seventeen
LEAKY GUT SYNDROME

Interestingly 'Intestinal Permeability' has been discussed in the medical literature for over 100 years, yet currently many if not most western medical practitioners deny (or aren't aware of) its existence. Most doctors will prescribe antacids and/or anti-depressants, as there is little else they can do. To date no drug has been designed to specifically treat LG, plus as yet doctors haven't learnt about this condition, nor the causes, symptoms, nor the safer wholistic treatment options available. This makes it especially important that you know what the symptoms are, and how to treat them yourself, naturally.

As Hippocrates said, all disease begins in the gut, and I think we're beginning to understand just how true this might be. Fatigue, joint pain, thyroid disease, other autoimmune conditions like Type 1 Diabetes, Endometriosis, Hashimoto's and Alzheimer's Disease, and psychological symptoms such as anxiety and depression have all been strongly linked to LGS. Adrenal Fatigue, headaches, skin issues such as eczema and rashes, a foggy head, spectrum disorders like autism and ADHD. Other symptoms including whole body inflammation, candida, SIBO, weight fluctuations, bloating and excessive gas, as is overall digestive pain and abdominal cramps. Other telltale signs can be allergies and food intolerances.

This common condition could just as well be called Leaky Small Intestine, as this is the part of the gut where the leaks are located, and a lot goes on here. In fact, the majority of the nutrients from the food we eat are absorbed here. Well, that's what's supposed to happen anyway. The process of digestion takes about 6 hours from the mouth, through the stomach then into the small intestine. Before food gets to the small intestine however, our digestive process is supposed to break down relatively large food particles into individual molecules, tiny enough to squeeze through the gastro-intestinal lining in the small intestine and be assimilated into our bloodstream where it transports the nutrients to our muscle tissue and bone, then bone marrow, and finally to our reproductive tissue. Another possibility is that without this absorption, then delivery of nutrients, we may become deficient in certain vitamins and minerals including zinc, iron and vitamin B12, causing us to become malnourished, infertile, cranky, fatigued, iron deficient, slow, prematurely aged and sad, with a fluctuating weight.

'Junctions' are the net-barrier that decide what moves out of your intestines to the other side, that is, your blood stream. When your small intestine is healthy, the 'junctions' remain 'sealed' just enough, carefully keeping toxins, microbes, undigested food and waste within the digestive tract where they belong, and then eliminated; instead of spreading throughout your body.

So, what happens if instead of the tiny holes in the small intestine there are nasty, big tears in it, allowing toxic substances like gluten, casein, lectins and disease-causing bacteria, yeast and microbes, not to mention big chunks of undigested food through? Our hard-working immune system (and the female immune system is about three times stronger than men's by the way, probably due to us carrying babies) then targets these invaders, seeing some of these particles as a threat, so facilitates an immune response to attack them. There lies the connection between Leaky Gut and auto-immune diseases, and possibly why females have triple the rate of these diseases as males.

According to the *Journal of Diabetes*, there is evidence that Leaky Gut Syndrome is a major cause of autoimmune diseases, including Type 1 Diabetes.*

It is also known to work the other way around as well: once you develop an auto immune disease, you will also have increased Intestinal Permeability, (and the likelihood of developing another auto immune disease). Your immune system will then begin to think these 'leaked proteins' are something other than what they are, so you will experience symptoms that you'd unlikely relate to a food issue, since they are not felt in the gut. Instead we experience brain fog, pain, fatigue, poor sleep, anxiety, headaches, and hormonal dysfunction.

Considering how common this condition is, it's interesting to know what's causing so many of us to suffer with it. The birth control pill for one, and other commonly prescribed medications like HRT, statins and other heart meds, pain killers, steroids and antibiotics are all major contributors, as is having a diet of processed foods high in trans-fats, and conventional (not organic) cow's dairy, (casein, the A1 protein in cow's dairy is 26 times more inflammatory than even gluten, and by the way has over 20 different toxic chemicals and additives.) Limit or remove gluten found in most grains. Around 30% of us have sensitivity to it, coeliac or not. Avoid artificial sweeteners like Splenda and Nutrisweet as they cause too much damage to our gut and kill off beneficial micro biome. Sugar, as it feeds the growth of yeast, and unhelpful bacteria, leading to conditions like candida, SIBO and Fructose Malabsorption, which will further damage your gut lining.

To start healing from LG, reduce the amount of raw and cold foods you're eating, as they're harder to digest. I recommend you eat like a baby for a month whilst your gut heals. That is, cooked, easy to digest foods. The 40-Day Reset Program will be really helpful here. Other culprits are the chlorine and fluoride in tap water. GMO

---

* https://www.greenmedinfo.com/article/consumption-cow-milk-a1-beta-casein-associated-increased-risk-ischaemic-heart-

foods destroy the probiotics in your gut and cause organ inflammation. Mould can cause LG, as do xeno-estrogens in our food, cosmetics, soft furnishings and so many more places. *See Chapter 21, Excess Estrogen, Chapter 49, Prebiotics and Chapter 50, Probioitcs.*

Also include Resistant Starch. Whereas most foods we eat feeds only 10% of our cells, RS feed the other 90%. RS intake allows for increased production of butyrate by our gut microbes, and this is good because butyrate acts as an anti-inflammatory agent for the cells of the colon and functions to improve the integrity of our gut by decreasing intestinal permeability, therefore keeping toxins in the gut and out of the bloodstream. *See Chapter 41, Butyrate.*

Beef, fish or chicken bone broth cooked for less than 12 hours to produce collagen is going to be helpful here to heal the gut lining, as will be oats, if there's not a gliadin sensitivity present. Soak them overnight anyway, and buy them organic as they're usually highly contaminated with glyphosate (*Roundup). Include healthy unsaturated oils like avocado, coconut, tahini, flax, olive, hemp and those in nuts and seeds. Include Omega 3 oils from wild Alaskan salmon and mackerel, anchovies and sardines. These oils are anti-inflammatory and especially healing for the gut. Some of the microbes in your gut specialise in fermenting the soluble fibre found in konjac noodles and fruits and vegetables, and this helps nourish the cells lining your colon, helping to heal a LG.

A compound in cruciferous vegetables called indolocarbazole (ICZ) may be very helpful in the treatment of colitis and leaky gut. ICZ boosts immune function and improves the balance of your gut microbiome by binding to and activating certain receptors on your gut lining, You'd need to eat about 3.5 cups of broccoli per day to get the healing effects, or you can obtain an equivalent amount from one cup of brussels sprouts, as they contain three times the ICZ of broccoli.

Removing trigger foods and situations will help only to partially heal a leaky gut. It won't repair all the damage done to the intestinal wall. This is where glue-like foods like aloe vera, glutamine and slippery elm come in. Include aloe vera to help cool and heal the gut lining. Take it twice a day on an empty tummy. *See chapter 35, Aloe Vera.* Slippery Elm (and Aloe) has gooey properties called mucilages that will help glue the holes in the small intestine together. Zinc has been found to be quite effective at tightening up the intestinal junctions and well. Digestive enzymes before meals will help breakdown your food into smaller more useable particles. A multi-strained probiotic twice a day, will help you digest your food better, and recolonise healthy bacteria. L-Glutamine is an amino acid that will help repair intestinal permeability, reduce IBS symptoms, and improve detoxification. It is *only* recommended for short- term use and contraindicated if there are any neurological issues present. *See Chapter 65, Stocks and Broths.*

Herbal Medicine to include are those that will repair reduce the inflammation in the mucous membranes. Restorative herbs that coat and soothe the membranes in the digestive tract are Marshmallow Root, Licorice Root and Plantain. (Avoid licorice if you have high blood pressure.) Also include an immune boosting herb such as Echinacea or Astragalus, and another to restore balance to the gut microbiome. Barberry or Japanese Knotweed will be great here.

Essential Oils that benefit digestion are Ginger, Peppermint and Chamomile. And to reduce emotional stress use Lavender and Lemon Balm. Oregano will get into your gut and kill off a lot of the bacteria causing some of the problems. Use it only for 3 weeks at a time.

Lab' test for leaky gut are available from *Nutripath, Healthscope or Functional Pathology in* Australia.

It looks like many more of us than we initially thought have some degree of LG at any given time. As with all other conditions in this book, you can heal a LG, it just takes time, patience, the right diet and lifestyle, a mind focussed on healing and gratitude, and some quality natural medicine. Once your gut flora is healthy, your leaky gut should improve naturally. Heal your gut properly, then most of us should be able to digest anything, sometimes.

See also Chapter 28, SIBO, and Chapter 6, Are You Stressing Yourself Out? And the *40-Day Reset Program.*

chapter eighteen
DEALING WITH DIABETES

Approximately one million Australians have now been diagnosed with diabetes, and another two million currently live in a pre-diabetic state, putting them at high-risk of developing type 2 diabetes. The total annual cost for Australians with type 2 diabetes alone is up to $6 billion, and the sad thing is, it's easily preventable and reversible. The growth of diabetes is a major health issue, and the importance of prevention as well as the appropriate natural treatments cannot be underestimated.

The drastic and relatively sudden increase in the diagnoses of Diabetes tells us that this disease cannot and is not caused by genetics alone, and secondly, it really does indicate that something many of us are doing, or have been advised to do, is terribly wrong. Diabetes is an example of yet another emerging lifestyle disease we can safely blame on a decline in the quality of our food, lack of physical activity, overprescribed and not necessarily the right medication, and too much stress, of all kinds.

Being overweight, usually from a diet high in carbohydrates, trans-fats and sugar put us at a higher risk of developing diabetes. Those who aren't exercising regularly, or have high triglycerides and low HDL cholesterol, and/or high total cholesterol, or high blood pressure also. Other groups with a higher risk include First Australians, women with

Polycystic Ovarian Syndrome, or Metabolic Syndrome, and women who have had diabetes in pregnancy (gestational diabetes) or have given birth to a big baby (more than 4.5kgs).

Not many of us have heard about leptin yet. It's a hormone produced in our fat and other cells, and is a key player when it comes to regulating your appetite and body weight. This is the hormone that tells your brain when it's time eat, how much, and when to stop. It then lets your brain know what to do with all this available energy. Simple right? Ah, not really! If you're Insulin Resistant, you're more than likely to be Leptin Resistant (LR) as well, especially if you're overweight. When we eat foods high in sugar, insulin is released from our pancreas. This happens so it can direct the energy from the sugar into storage. A small amount is stored as a starch called glycogen, but the majority is stored as fat. Leptin is then produced in these same fat cells, so, the more fat you have, the more leptin is being produced. Now we have Leptin AND Insulin Resistance, and a viscous circle begins.

When you develop LR, your brain can no longer hear leptin's signals telling us we've had enough to eat. This is bad news as we're now constantly hungry, causing us to over-eat. Adding fuel to the fire is the newfound inability to properly burn fat, so now we're not only getting seriously chubby, and resistant to insulin, ultimately type 2 diabetes will follow. Leptin has the ability, even in low doses, to lower blood glucose in both type 1 and 2 diabetics, so its importance in the treatment and management of diabetes is very promising.

Diabetes can be split into five different categories.

1. *Pre-Diabetes*, also known as *Impaired Glucose Tolerance (IGT)*, is a term used to describe the earlier stage of Insulin Resistance. It is medically diagnosed by having a fasting blood sugar between 100 and 125 mg/dl. It's not necessary to think of Pre-diabetes as a life long disease, as it is easy to reverse.

2. *Metabolic Syndrome.* As Insulin Resistance progresses, our liver makes too much sugar and fat, and our muscles are less able to

use them for energy, or to make glycogen, which is how glucose is stored in your muscles and liver. But what happens to all that sugar and fat now? It builds up in your bloodstream that's what. This in turn, leads to high triglyceride (fat) levels and increased body fat—especially around your abdomen, and higher blood pressure. You'll be diagnosed with Metabolic Syndrome (previously known as Syndrome X) if you present with 3 or more of a group of symptoms caused by Insulin Resistance. These are 1. high triglycerides 2. low HDL 3. High blood glucose 4. High blood pressure 5. Increased belly fat.

3. *Type 1: Insulin-Dependent Diabetes.* The onset of type 1 diabetes usually develops before the age of 20, although it can occur at any age. This is an autoimmune disease where your immune system destroys the insulin-producing cells of your pancreas, resulting in an inability to produce significant amounts of this hormone. This is why type 1 is called 'insulin-dependent' diabetes, as the patient is dependent on getting insulin artificially. It is a serious condition, and there is currently no known cure for this (and other) auto immune conditions. However research from a Columbia University study claims that by turning off a particular gene, human gut cells can be converted into cells that produce insulin in response to dietary sugar.*

Type 1 is a very different condition to type 2 as it's looking like type 1 may not stem from dysregulation of insulin and leptin caused by too much dietary sugar and carbohydrate. Instead, research is pointing to two predisposing conditions, that we can control.

 – Vitamin D deficiency. The further away from the equator you live the greater your risk of being born with, or developing type 1 diabetes.

* Ryotaro Bouchi, Kylie S. Foo, Haiqing Hua, Kyoichiro Tsuchiya, Yoshiaki Ohmura, P. Rodrigo Sandoval, Lloyd E. Ratner, Dieter Egli, Rudolph L. Leibel & Domenico Accili. 'FOXO1 inhibition yields functional insulin-producing cells in human gut organoid cultures'. *Nature Communications*, vol 5, (2014) Article number: 4242

- Dysbiosis (abnormal gut flora). In 2008, animal research suggested that beneficial bacteria could protect against the development of type 1 diabetes.[*]

4. *Type 2: non-insulin-dependent diabetes.* This is an advanced stage of insulin resistance, which is typically caused by a diet that is too high in sugars. Insulin's primary role is not to lower your blood sugar, but rather to store this extra energy as fat for future needs when food may not be available. With type 2 the pancreas is (probably) producing too much insulin *and* leptin, but isn't able to recognise it in order to use it properly. This means the sugar can't get into your cells, so instead builds up in your blood. Type 2 diabetes is about a loss of insulin and leptin sensitivity, which makes this condition easily preventable and nearly 100 percent reversible without drugs.

Type 2 diabetes is not the result of insufficient insulin production, but the result of *too much* insulin being produced, typically the result of eating the modern high carbohydrate diet. Chronically elevated insulin and leptin levels deafen your receptors, making your body 'resistant' to understanding the signals sent by the 2 hormones. From this you can see why prescribing insulin is one of the worst things we can do for type 2 diabetes, as over time, yet more insulin will only worsen your insulin and leptin resistance, allowing this disease to increase, as it has, to epidemic proportions. More insulin is not needed. Proper Insulin and Leptin signalling needs to be re-established by keeping their levels low! Taking more insulin just makes you fatter, and sicker.

To add insult to injury, the insulin given to diabetics is GMO (genetically modified), that in some of us may trigger an autoimmune response to produce antibodies that destroy their insulin producing cells (pancreatic islet cells). This then produces

---

[*] Carding, Simon, Verbeke, Kristin, Vipond, Daniel T, Corfe, Bernard M, and Owen, Lauren J. 'Dysbiosis of the Gut Microbiota in Disease.' *Microbial Ecology in Health and Disease 26*, no. 1 (December 1, 2015): 1–9.

a condition in which you have both type 1 and type 2 diabetes simultaneously. Recent research published in the Journal of Clinical Endocrinology & Metabolism has confirmed that insulin treatment can provoke otherwise reversible type 2 diabetes to progress into type 1 diabetes in patients with genetic susceptibility. So now we know why giving insulin to type 2 diabetics is just a bad and worrying trend.*

A low carb, high fibre and high fat diet is needed here, and harmful habits need also be addressed, and replaced with healthy ones. Avoiding too much sugar is absolutely necessary, especially fructose, the most harmful form of sugar, as it can cause an extreme increase in blood glucose quickly. Fructose can be found in the highest concentrations in high fructose corn syrup (HFCS), and the many processed, packaged food and drinks that use it. Fructose is also high in fruit juices and dried fruit. Complex sweeteners will be ok in small amounts, occasionally. More so when you have your blood sugar somewhat under control. Your total fructose intake should be limited to 15 grams a day until your insulin/leptin resistance has resolved. After that, keep it to 25 grams or less for maintenance. And it's not just a fructose issue. Another major cause of type 2 diabetes is the excessive of amount glucose we're getting from a high carbohydrate diet. Yes, the same diet high in grains and low in fat 'health experts' have been recommending for over 50 years now. About the same time frame that we've seen diabetes drastically increase. Again a high fibre diet (not from grains) is key.

5. *Type 3: Alzheimer's Disease.* In 2005 after research was published proving the brain—not only the pancreas—produced insulin, Alzheimer's disease was coined 'type 3 diabetes'. Scientists found that brain cells depend on 'brain insulin' for survival. We were already aware of the correlation between diet and our risk of both

---

* https://academic.oup.com/jcem/search-results?page=1&q=diabetes%20insulin&fl_SiteID=5591&SearchSourceType=1&allJournals=1

Alzheimer's disease and glaucoma, (an irreversibly blinding disorder with almost 65 million sufferers worldwide, currently with no cure) via similar pathways that cause type 2 diabetes, before this mounting evidence confirmed the theory that fructose consumption needed to be drastically reduced in the prevention of Alzheimer's disease. So things were starting to get really interesting.[*]

As with other types of diabetes, eating too many sugars and grains will keep glucose levels elevated, thereby interfering with insulin's and leptin's job/sensitivity. This contributes to thinking and memory problems that will eventually cause permanent brain damage. On top of this, your liver has trouble making the cholesterol it needs for healthy brain function as it's busy processing fructose into fat. And then the cycle continues.

So if grains and low fat foods aren't recommended in the treatment and prevention of diabetes, what are we meant to be eating? At least 75% of our plate should be plant based (not grains), preferably organically produced. Include as many non-starchy/low carb veggies as you want. Eat quality protein, but not too much. Include wild-caught fish, organic eggs and dairy (preferably goat and sheep's) products, sea vegetables, legumes, hemp, seeds and nuts. If you choose to eat some animal-based protein, make a decision to buy them only organically raised, as the GMO feed and pesticides used, as well as the antibiotics routinely administered, need to be avoided.

Healthy fats are essential to include in our diet, especially omega 3's in the form of ALA, as it works with the pancreas to naturally treat diabetes. 50–80% of your daily calories should come from healthy fats. Stay on the lower side if you have fat to lose though. *See Chapter 52, Fats and Oils.*

Cinnamon is a wonderfully helpful spice that helps balance blood sugar levels and can also improve insulin sensitivity. It has outstanding

---

[*] de La Monte, Suzanne M, and Wands, Jack R. 'Alzheimer's Disease Is Type 3 Diabetes-Evidence Reviewed.' *Journal of diabetes science and technology 2*, no. 6 (November 2008): 1101–1113.

health benefits especially for the diabetic and those living with PCOS, obesity and high cholesterol. When buying cinnamon be sure to buy true or real cinnamon. This type of cinnamon is native to Sri Lanka and sourced from the plant *Cinnamomum Zeylanicum*. (Also known as *Cinnamomum verum*. 'Verum' meaning 'true'.) Unfortunately the inferior type of cinnamon - *Cinnamomom cassia* is what is widely available, and cheaper. Take one teaspoon in the morning for breakfast, and then one teaspoon for lunch or dinner. Lots of my recipes in the 40-Day Reset Program include cinnamon.

Avoid most dairy. The protein in cow's dairy called casein can trigger an immune response similar to gluten, so it needs to be avoided. *See Chapter 44, Is Dairy Good for You?*

As discussed above, avoid too many carbohydrates. This means foods that are highest in carbs like refined grains and sugar, and in more serious cases you'll also need to avoid whole grains, fruits and veggies with a higher carb content. Include some carbohydrates, but just a smaller amounts, as a side to healthy fats, fibre and protein. They shouldn't be the main feature of your plate. Aim for 35g/day or in more serious cases 20g. This protein causes our gut to inflame, which will have a negative effect on hormones like cortisol and leptin. Gluten free of not, grains have a high carb' content that quickly turn into sugar, so they'll mostly need to be avoided. Including properly prepared whole grains a few times a week on the 40-Day Reset Program will in be ok in most cases though, and preferably before 2pm. *See Chapter 53, Carbohydrates*

Avoid trans fat, as this is the absolute worst type of fat, and in fact one of the worst foods you can eat, and really needs to be avoided altogether. Processed trans fats can be found in just about all pack-aged and take away foods, and can increase your risk for diabetes by interfering with your insulin receptors. Healthy fats do not do this. *See Chapter 52, Fats and Oils*

When it comes to supplements, chromium picolinate helps our body control the amount of sugar our cells take in, thereby keeping our blood glucose in a good place, creating an even energy. You'll find an abundant amount in broccoli, but taking a supplement might be recommended in more severe cases. Magnesium has been proven to help keep blood sugar level balanced, and most of us are deficient in it, due to our soil being stripped of minerals, and our high levels of stress. In a supplement, an increase of 100 milligrams a day of magnesium was found to decrease the risk of diabetes by 15%.[*] Always choose a wholefood supplement, and regularly include pumpkin, flax and chia seeds, avocado, green leafy veggies like kale, spinach and sea veggies, almonds, cacao, tofu, and some organic beef.

Healthy Vitamin D levels are essential in treating both Type 1 and 2 Diabetes. Try to get 20 minutes of daily sun exposure to 40% of your body. In some cases supplementation (with regular monitoring) may be necessary until your levels get into a healthy range, between 50–70 ng/ml. It's important to note here that if you take a vitamin D supplement, you create an increased demand for *vitamin K2*, so it's recommended you take a supplement that has both.

Herbal medicine as always is incredibly effective in the treatment (and prevention) of diabetes. Choose anti-diabetic herbs like Gymnema and Bitter Melon. Manuka and Barberry to improve gut health, and herbs to help your body handle stress better like some of the adaptogenic herbs—Withania, Rhodiola, and Astragalus.

The three essential oils specific here are Cinnamon, Coriander and Lavender. Cinnamon because it has a positive effect on the pancreas, controlling insulin release; Coriander because your liver loves it to help balance out blood sugar levels, and Lavender to chill you out. Rub a little on the soles of your feet to help keep you calm and your blood sugar stable. For other ways to use them, *see Chapter 42, Essential Oils.*

We now know that overweight people have different, and not as much beneficial gut bacteria than leaner people. Balance your

---

[*] Rodríguez-Morán M1, Guerrero-Romero F. 'Oral magnesium supplementation improves insulin sensitivity and metabolic control in type 2 diabetic subjects: a randomized double-blind controlled trial.' *Diabetes Care, 26, no.4* (April 2003): 1147–52.

microbiome, and watch your leptin and insulin sort themselves out. *See Chapter 9, What You Need To Get About Your Gut; Chapter 19, The Thing About Candida and Chapter 51, Fermented Foods.*

Studies have shown that exercise, even without weight loss, increases insulin sensitivity, and any form will do, especially if you enjoy it and it's regular. Interval Training is proving to be really beneficial here, but not if you're already fatigued. Weight training and cardio' is good as well if you're trying to naturally reverse blood sugar imbalances. *See Chapter 7, Too Much Exercise? and Chapter 16, Could You Be Suffering With Adrenal Fatigue?*

Incorporate Intermittent Fasting. By following the 40-Day Reset Program you'll automatically be doing this, as 2 out of 7 days a week you'll be consuming far fewer calories. Mimicking our ancestors way of feast (within reason) and famine (within reason), benefits us in many ways including improving both insulin and leptin sensitivity, to help eliminate sugar cravings, and burn fat. You'll also be releasing ketones whilst burning fat, and ketones (not glucose) are what your brain prefers as fuel.

Increased and sustained stress means elevated cortisol, which in turn means increased insulin resistance. This is bad news for your blood sugar, among other things. Stress alone can bring about Diabetes, so it's mighty important to learn a way to control your responses to fear and anxiety. *See Chapter 6, Are You Stressing Yourself Out?*

We need no less than 7 and no more than 9 hours of sleep a night. A lack of sleep raises adrenalin and blood sugar, messing with our insulin and leptin sensitivity, resulting in increased hunger and weight gain. You must address the reasons why you're not getting the right amount of quality sleep. *See Chapter 25, When You Just Can't Sleep.*

chapter nineteen

THE THING ABOUT CANDIDA

Candida isn't pleasant. It happens when a naturally occurring fungus is out of control. Normally this fungus helps you absorb nutrients and supports good digestion, and it protects your gut and vagina against excess yeast. However, candida overgrowth syndrome is challenging.

Typical candida issues include digestive problems, gas and bloating, bad breath, and possibly skin and nail fungal infections. Oral and vaginal thrush are also common, as are cravings for sweets, carbs and alcohol. Or you may present with chronic sinus, eczema, psoriasis or allergy issues. Or an overactive mind with repetitive thoughts. Also, you may complain of a foggy brain or recurring urinary tract infections. A white coating on the tongue is another indicator, as is an itchy inner ear, or bottom (rectum). Commonly you're suffering chronic exhaustion, as your hormones have most likely taken a hit along with your immune system, resulting in drained adrenal glands.

Basically, candida overgrowth permeates the walls of your intestine, allowing toxins to leak into your bloodstream and tissues, causing leaky gut syndrome. So, hundreds of toxic waste products—undigested food molecules, bacterial toxins and other chemicals that should be flushed down the toilet—end up causing the nightmare we call candida.

Estrogen supports the growth of candida, and candida overgrowth creates excess estrogen in the body. This creates a vicious cycle, causing ovarian cysts, endometriosis, fibroids, infertility, heavy menstrual flow, breast swelling and tenderness. Candida can also be responsible for some forms of breast cancer, hair loss, migraines and headaches.

Some yeast toxins can even block proper communication between hormone receptors, creating PMS and endometriosis. These toxins enter the blood causing weight gain and inflammation, while hampering your immune and central nervous system. Others block thyroid function, interfering with female hormones, causing symptoms of PMS. There's some suggestion this toxic overload may worsen menopausal symptoms.

A candida overgrowth can also create fluid retention, as the body tries to dilute the toxic overload. Yeast can also decrease thyroid function and lead to lowered metabolism, causing weight gain. When it comes to food cravings, it's often not what **you** crave, it's what the yeast in your system craves. Yeast loves sugar, found in such refined carbs as breakfast cereals and bread, as well as alcohol and sweet foods. You gain weight as the carbs turn into fat, and also feel super bloated from the yeast expanding in your gut.

HOW DO WE GET CANDIDA?

If you've been on antibiotics, this can cause yeast overgrowth in your system, as can refined wheat, sugar and baker's yeast. If you're feeling overloaded, your stress hormones can go into overdrive, flooding your body and setting up the right environment for a yeast infection. Chemotherapy and radiation work to kill cancerous cells and tumours, but like antibiotics, they can also kill off the healthy bacteria needed to fight candida naturally.

Women taking the contraceptive pill are far more likely to have candida, as yeast feeds off estrogen. When on the pill, you're getting 150 times the estrogen you would otherwise make. Asthma sufferers using inhalants are more susceptible to candida—at first in the mouth, then it becomes 'systemic'. So when using a puffer, it's important to swish your mouth out after each use.

TREATING CANDIDA

When you start treatment for candida, your body has to deal with the die-off of this fungus. The severity of your symptoms will depend on how fast the fungus is dying off. Too quickly, and you'll feel really terrible. Some practitioners see symptoms of die-off as a sign the treatment is working; I see it as too harsh, which can worsen adrenal fatigue and other symptoms. Be gentle and kind to your body.

When candida is dying and trying to leave your body, it releases over 70 different toxins. So if you're facing very strong reactions, back off a little with the treatment. Otherwise, these symptoms usually disappear in about a week.

I remember one time (of many) experiencing extreme die-off. Besides feeling terrible, my finger and toenails started to flake off, and in some cases the **whole** nail. My hair went really dry and frizzy. I was nauseous and could fall asleep at any time. Plus my skin broke out with a rash and pimples. At the time I was thirty years old, managing a health food store, looking like a fungal nightmare, with the patience of a two-year-old. Needless to say, it wasn't ideal. So don't rush this process.

If this process happens too quickly, you're going to feel as if you've got the flu. Or you may feel nauseous, suffer headaches, extreme exhaustion, sweating and fever. Some people end up with skin break-outs, others sinus infections. Bloating, gas and constipation are often evident, as the gut struggles to cope. When your body is dealing with a range of symptoms, it's hard to think straight and you may feel depressed.

Get back on track by limiting (preferably completely avoiding) all sugar, including fresh and frozen fruit, dried fruit, maple syrup, honey, and all processed foods and sauces. Sugar feeds yeast, weakens the immune system and blocks hormone receptors. Avoid all wheat and refined grains; in fact, avoid most grains. However, some grains and quasi-grains like quinoa, barley, teff, sorghum, millet and amaranth can actually help to dry a 'damp' (a term used in traditional Chinese medicine to describe an overgrowth of candida in the gut), so one serving a few times a week should be okay. Avoid dairy, as it creates a damp environment that supports candida's growth. Avoid fermented foods, until you have the infection somewhat under control. No alcohol is best. Beer, champagne and sugary mixes are the highest in sugar and yeast, so be sure to give these a wide berth.

Eat an 80/20 plant/animal food diet, to feed the microbiome in your gut. Garlic is a proven antifungal and is effective against candida, inhibiting both the growth and function of *Candida albicans*. Garlic will also support your immune system. Eat one or two cloves a day and chew some fresh parsley afterwards, if you're concerned about your breath. Coconut oil can effectively fight candida, due to its antimicrobial properties. Millet has been shown to reduce an overgrowth of candida; be sure to soak it for a few hours, then drain before cooking.

In some cases, supplementing with a probiotic may effectively kill off candida. The best ones are acidophilus, saccharomyces and bifidus. Try to get products that guarantee 2–10 billion organisms per capsule. Take a high-quality omega-3 supplement to relieve inflammation, and vitamin C for your drained adrenal glands and reduced immunity.

Grapefruit seed extract is worth taking. You can get this very potent medicine from your health food store. Be mindful when taking it; if your candida is chronic (long-term), you could experience die-off symptoms. Reduce the dose if this is the case.

Oregano oil is antibacterial and antifungal. It's strong stuff. Research shows that *Candida albicans* (the strain of candida that leads to systemic candida overgrowth) is often resistant to both fluconazole and itraconazole, the antifungal drugs most often prescribed for candida.

Plants from nature's garden will help to reduce a candida overgrowth more quickly. I use antifungals like horopito, calendula, pau d'arco, calendula, usnea and barberry. You'll need liver herbs to help the excess estrogen detoxify from your body, so include dandelion root, burdock or St. Mary's thistle. Immune-boosting herbs like astragalus, echinacea, holy basil and turmeric are also healing.

Nature's oils can really help you get back on your feet, but go gently at first. Clove, lavender, oregano and myrrh oils help to kill a variety of parasites and fungi in the body, including candida. They also inhibit the growth of candida and are effective at preventing the spread of the infection. Mix a couple of drops of one of the above oils with one teaspoon of coconut oil daily during *the 40-Day Reset Program*, to help to kill off the offending candida. Essential oils should only be taken internally for three weeks or less, and are not dependant on the time of day they're taken.

For oral thrush, use two drops of clove or tea tree essential oil with one tablespoon of coconut oil. Swish in the mouth for 5–20 minutes, first thing in the morning. Tea tree oil is antifungal and antiseptic. Dilute with clean water to use on fungal skin problems like psoriasis, athlete's foot and fungus under the nails, or add one drop to a douche for vaginal thrush. You can also add a drop to coconut oil and use topically for vaginal itch.

LIFESTYLE CHANGES

- Exercise, rebound or use a Zen Chi machine, to increase lymph circulation and help clear toxins.
- Manage or relieve stress, to help reduce high cortisol levels that create a yeast overgrowth.
- If SIBO is present, you'll need to wipe out pathogens in the small intestine first. *See Chapter 28.*
- Avoid overeating and late night eating, as this creates an environment where candida thrives.
- Cleanse your liver to help flush the body of excess estrogens that candida may be feeding on.
- Use bentonite clay to help surround the toxins and efficiently remove them from your system.

TESTING FOR CANDIDA

There are tests available from pathology clinics that will confirm the presence of candida, although in my opinion this is not always necessary, as your symptoms will tell you if you have an overgrowth or not. If you decide you'd like confirmation via a test, then contact one of the clinics below. In some cases, you'll need a practitioner to order the kit for you.

For information about testing for candida, check out the following websites:

- www.greatplainslaboratory.com
- www.FunctionalPathology.com.au
- www.Healthscope.com
- www.Nutripath.com.au

chapter twenty
BATTLING ENDOMETRIOSIS

Without the knowledge once passed down by our foremothers, we women and girls go to work while on our moon cycle, unwittingly use tampons made from GM cotton, bleach and cancer-causing estrogens in our vagina, pop a painkiller, wear synthetic tight clothing and off to work we go, trying hard to smile. Then we wonder why we're depressed and anxious, feeling lonely, in pain, pissed off and sick, sedating ourselves with chocolate, chips, wine, pot, ciggies, Thai takeaway, Netflix or Tinder.

Endometriosis is becoming increasingly common in a world that has denied the sacred feminine* for far too long. According to Ayurveda, during our moon cycle there is a downward flow of prana (life force), so it is a time of introspection for women, a withdrawal from daily life. It's when we can pull back from the world to recharge and reconnect with our silent, spiritual centre.

It's estimated that over 176 million women worldwide suffer from endometriosis. Once thought to affect only women above thirty and those who hadn't had children, now it affects 3–20% women of any age (likely much higher though), while around 10–50% of infertility

---

* *Worship of feminine beauty, the cycles of the moon, and the power of sexual reproduction, intuition and healing.*

is thought to be caused by endometriosis. Some women with endo-metriosis may be symptom-free, but the majority suffer.

Two-thirds of women with period pain go on to be diagnosed with endometriosis. It can affect women of any age after their first period. Conventional medicine recommends 'having a baby young'. If you've had your babies, it recommends a hysterectomy or laparoscopy, with the pill or an IUD for the time in between. It seems ludicrous to give such recommendations to any female, let alone a teenager, but they are often suggested.

I was diagnosed with endometriosis (endo) via laparoscopic surgery at age 18, as was my younger sister soon after. Many women with this dreadful disease remain undiagnosed, while trying to live with the chronic pain and the unsettling hormone craziness it involves.

WHAT CAUSES ENDOMETRIOSIS?

Endo is no longer considered a hormonal condition as much as a chronic, inflammatory disease, where our body is attacking itself. Yes, it's an autoimmune disease, so it's probable leaky gut is also present and needs to be treated as well. This (usually) very painful and debilitating disease occurs when tissue similar to the lining of the uterus grows in places where it shouldn't, including ovaries, outside the uterus, fallopian tubes, pelvic sidewall, bowel, bladder, peritoneum, gastrointestinal tract, uterosacral ligaments and in the pouch of Douglas.

The hormones that trigger our period also trigger the shedding of these growths. Each month, this displaced tissue also responds to the hormonal changes that regulate our cycle. That means they grow larger throughout the first half of our cycle; during the second half they will often release small amounts of blood, causing even more irritation and scarring. These spiderweb-like lesions stick organs together, contributing to the pain and infertility. Much of the intense pain may also stem from the deep scar tissue that results from the numerous laparoscopies performed on endo sufferers.

Recently we've seen endometriosis being associated with high levels of a nasty type of environmental toxin called dioxin, a by-product of industrial practices. These estrogen-like chemicals (known as xenoestrogens) mimic our own estrogen, causing hormone disruption due to an excess of estrogen. Autoimmunity plus emotional stress plus chemical stress (excess estrogen) is looking like equalling endometriosis, making life hell for many.

Progesterone promotes calmness and is important for fertility and a regular and divine moon cycle. It is associated with 'rest and digest' whereas cortisol, as a stress hormone, is associated with 'fight or flight'. Both hormones are produced from pregnenolone, which decides where it diverts its energy. If we're in an anxious state, we will make cortisol, to help us through the crisis. So you can see how chronic stress leads to a deficiency in progesterone. This is referred to as 'the progesterone steal'. Why would our bodies want us to get pregnant when we're living in the middle of a crisis like war, famine, opening bills or listening to the gyno telling us we'd better hurry up and have a baby or we might miss out? The progesterone steal is the leading cause of low progesterone.

ENDO SYMPTOMS

Time and time again, I have seen endo symptoms all but disappear with the right diet, medicinal herbs and changes in lifestyle and mindset. I'm living proof! The only trouble I have now with my reproductive and digestive organs is from the scar tissue left from all the laparoscopies I unwittingly endured, and the severe endo I suffered for years.

Endo symptoms are many and varied, as is the case with any autoimmune disease. Pain in the uterus at any time of the month is common, as is lower back, gut and pelvic pain; pain during sex; full-on bloating; large, dark clots during your period; bleeding intermittently throughout the month, as well as with sex; nausea, vomiting and/or constipation during your period (and sometimes all month); infertility;

mood swings from anxiety, resentment, isolation and depression, then back again. Iron deficiency is often a side issue due to heavy periods, as is a kind of 'drawing down' ache in your legs.

Currently, the only way to accurately diagnose endometriosis is via a surgical excision, known as a laparoscopy. This requires at least an overnight hospital stay, a two-week recovery time at home, and many thousands of dollars. As well, it's not without long-term side effects. During the procedure, the surgeon inserts several thin viewing tubes into the abdomen to view the pelvic organs, then removes the adhesions. The tissue that's removed frequently and quickly grows back, requiring repeated laparoscopies and creating more scar tissue.

Only consider surgery if you're desperately trying to get pregnant, and/or living with unbearable pain. But remember, you will have scar tissue to deal with later. If you're not in a huge rush, then three months on a wholistic program (including the right diet, new headspace and exercise regime) is the preferred first option. Following the 40-Day Reset Program is the perfect start.

TREATING ENDO

There is much we can do to help reduce the symptoms of endo and it starts with your diet. You need to reduce as many toxins as you can from your food, reduce excess estrogen coming into your body, and lighten the load on your liver. Next, go for foods that contain lots of flavonoids—pretty much all fruits, vegetables and herbs. Particularly good are green and red vegetables such as broccoli, kale, onions (red, yellow and spring), red chili, spinach and watercress. Chocolate, tea, wine, as well as some legumes, lentils and seeds are also good sources of flavonoids.

Foods high in vitamin E will help keep your blood 'slippery', reducing the chance of clots. Include nuts and seeds, plus their oils and butters, in your diet. Vitamin B will help reduce stress and an estrogen dominance by boosting progesterone. Eat wild Alaskan salmon, bananas, walnuts, organic chicken, organic prunes and sweet potatoes. To reduce cramps and spasms and help progesterone production, eat magnesium-rich foods such as cashews, leafy greens, kale, raw cacao, brown rice, black beans and lentils. Foods rich in progesterone, including organic fermented soy products like tamari, tempeh and natto miso, as well as coconut products, eggs, olives and yoghurt can help balance your hormones.

Zinc is really important in helping boost progesterone levels and also for a healthy immune and reproductive system. Include oysters, prawns, red meat, pepitas and cashews. For bowel health and a progesterone boost, eat lots of fibre especially from flax, quinoa, amaranth, millet, gluten-free oats, nuts, seeds and vegetables. For improved immunity and circulation, include foods rich in vitamin C like sweet potato, kiwifruit, strawberries, oranges, papaya, pumpkin, broccoli, mustard greens, tomatoes, brussels sprouts and lemons.

------- ------- ------- -------

Women who drink more than 4–5 cups of coffee per day
have 70% higher estrogen levels than other women.

------- ------- ------- -------

Food speaks to your genes, sometimes not helpfully. Avoid cow's milk; it contains the A1 casein protein, which may cause immune problems. Most endometriosis sufferers improve when they exclude this protein from their diet. Goat and sheep dairy (A2 casein) don't usually cause the same problems. They're even better when cultured into yoghurt, kefir, quark and lubne. Sugar and other high carb foods need to be reduced, as does gluten and potentially eggs, as they can increase autoimmune symptoms. Studies show you will have a dramatically increased risk of having endo if you eat red meat or ham. When it comes to organic soy products, keep them in your diet a few times a week, as they are mildly estrogenic and will have a positive effect on your health.

I'm generally not a big fan of supplements, but in cases of endo-metriosis I believe specific nutraceuticals will be of great benefit in the short term, until you can make the necessary changes to your lifestyle. Endo sufferers often have higher levels of estrogen than progesterone, so take vitamin C to increase your progesterone.

——————— ——————— ——————— ———————

Studies have shown that Vitamin C also reduces endometrial cysts and inflammation.

——————— ——————— ——————— ———————

Gubinge and camu camu are two foods very high in vitamin C, or use a wholefood supplement. Omega-3 essential fatty acids help to bring down inflammation, so include sustainably caught salmon, anchovies and sardines a few times a week, as well as hemp seeds and algae-like chlorella and spirulina. Take an omega-3 supplement, if that's easier for you. Just be sure to get a wild-caught (not farmed) fish. N-acetylcysteine (NAC) protects and improves liver function, can lift you out of a bad mood and helps with fertility. NAC is not found naturally in food sources, but its precursor cysteine is present in high-protein foods. Diindolylmethane (DIM), a phytonutrient found in cruciferous vegetables, including broccoli, brussels sprouts, cabbage, cauliflower and kale is effective at helping our liver remove unwanted used hormones. You can't really eat enough of these veggies to get the right dose you need, so in this case you'll need to take DIM as a supplement.

Good ol' turmeric is a powerful anti-inflammatory and immune-modulating medicine. A 2012 animal study demonstrated that turmeric can 'promote regression of endometriosis lesions', and in another study in the same year, prevent the onset.[*] Include it regularly in your diet; for a medicinal dose, you can get it as herbal medicine in liquid or tablet form. Magnesium is recommended for cramping, together with zinc, B6 and B1; all are important in regulating hormones. Magnesium

---

[*] Jana, Sayantan & Rudra, Deep Sankar & Paul, Sumit & Swarnakar, Snehasikta. 'Curcumin delays endometriosis development by inhibiting MMP-2 activity.' *Indian journal of biochemistry & biophysics, no. 49* (2012):342-8.

also helps remove excess estrogen and lessens PMT. Zinc helps to correct leaky gut associated with autoimmunity, an imbalance in gut flora, as well as your sex organs. Your zinc level should be between 9–15, ideally 11 or 12.

Herbal medicine is essential when treating endo. Expect to be taking it for 3–6 months at least. More realistically, you'll be taking it on and off until after menopause. My go-to herbal medicines are chaste tree to balance hormones; gingko biloba to increase circulation to reproductive organs and decrease scarring; turmeric to reduce inflammation and excess estrogen, as well as improve liver function; calendula to increase lymphatic detox; barberry to encourage normal cell growth, liver health and hormone balance; peony for its positive effect on ovaries and reproductive health in general; skullcap to reduce anxiety and an overworked liver; cramp bark for menstrual cramping; withania, rhodiola and holy basil as adrenal tonics; and rehmannia for adrenal health and to help balance the immune system.

Avoid alcohol, as it's only going to stress your body more, making sleep more difficult, and your weight harder to control. The sugar it contains isn't helpful either, plus alcohol affects how we process estrogen, thanks to its effect on the liver. Body fat is a secondary production site for estrogen, so being overweight usually means excess estrogen.

A review of 27 studies found that acupuncture may alleviate menstrual cramps better than drugs or herbal medicine, by stimulating the production of feel-good endorphins and serotonin.[*]

Candida is also involved here, as many women with endometriosis have an overgrowth of yeast. By reducing the overgrowth (and your weight), symptoms tend to be less debilitating. Endometriosis frequently occurs with other autoimmune conditions such as Hashimoto's disease and inflammatory bowel disease. Vitamin C and herbal medicines

---

[*] Lena Seippel, Torbjörn Bäckström. 'Luteal-Phase Estradiol Relates to Symptom Severity in Patients with Premenstrual Syndrome'. *The Journal of Clinical Endocrinology & Metabolism*, vol 83, no. 6, (1 June 1998): 1988–1992.

can help to regulate this response. Try organic tampons and pads, to avoid putting toxic xenoestrogens into your body and allowing them to build up each cycle. Better still, a menstrual cup or even a sea sponge tampon. Meditate on your (orange) sacral chakra, responsible for the organs of reproduction which are affected in endometriosis.

Keep your liver healthy, so it can help remove excess estrogen from the body, preventing it from recirculating. Women who exercise regularly suffer fewer symptoms than those who don't. However, choose gentle exercises such as yoga, brisk walking, tai chi, qi gong, swimming and bushwalking. When pain is present, be extra kind to yourself by not pushing through it to get to the gym or go for a run. During these times, a gentle approach is best. Mainstream medicine will recommend the pill, and this will probably decrease or even halve your symptoms, but behind the scenes it will make things worse. Make yourself familiar with the serious side effects of synthetic estrogen and progesterone before making a decision.

Traditional Chinese medicine (TCM) refers to the group of symptoms we know as endometriosis as 'blood stasis', so the acupuncture points chosen aim to help move your blood. Moxabustion is also wonderful. In this heat therapy, dried plant materials or 'moxa' are burned on or very near particular points on the body, to warm and wake up the flow of Qi (energy and blood) in the body and remove harmful influences. Pelvic massage and manipulation or osteopathy that works deeply on our organs are wonderful to help undo the stickiness of the organs, reducing scar tissue and freeing organs up.

The role of dysbiosis (an imbalance in our gut microbes) is interesting: one gram-negative bacteria, in particular lipopolysaccharide (LPS), is known to bring on both autoimmunity and endo.

Bioidentical progesterone is fairly popular and usually prescribed as a cream or capsule to boost low progesterone levels, but side effects (heart palpitations, sleepiness and nausea) can be awful. It can build up in fat tissue and take three to six months to clear. Bioidentical progesterone may be needed after a hysterectomy, or chronic and continual stress. Over-the-counter non-steroidal anti-inflammatories such as Ibuprofen may help ease menstrual cramps, but ongoing use contributes to a candida overgrowth, leaky gut and dysbiosis. In severe cases, your gyno may recommend a hysterectomy (surgical removal of your uterus plus maybe your ovaries). This is usually, but not always, effective. It is not recommended as a first or even second option.

There is a correlation between women with endo and unresolved emotional problems, especially those that have occurred at a young age within the family of origin. Dealing with those issues is just as important as the right diet and lifestyle changes. Kinesiology is very effective to help work through the emotional blocks. Louise Hay (a pioneer of modern-day body/mind medicine) says endo sufferers are blamers and generally have blood sugar issues. When I read this in her life-changing book *You Can Heal Your Life*, my first reaction was to get defensive and then a little bit ashamed, as I knew it was probably true in my case.

Looking honestly at yourself and your patterns, without judgement, isn't easy at first. But it does get easier and the rewards of living an authentic, fearless and pain-free life are endless.

chapter twenty-one
EXCESS ESTROGEN

Let's look a little closer at this hormone. Something happened after World War II that has affected our health like nothing else in history. That was when we started to use the chemicals left over from World War II to grow our food, to add to our water, cosmetics, cleaning products and home furnishings. The toxic chemicals, genetic engineering and antibiotics our food is grown with are making us seriously sick, and destroying the environment. This is why I am a great believer in organic food, as well as non-toxic cleaning and body products. Yes, most of us **can** afford them; it really is a matter of priority.

We're being affected by constant exposure to chemical toxins, and it ain't good news. There are about 70,000 registered chemicals with hormonal effects, in addition to being toxic and cancer-causing. The link is strong between pesticide residues and chronic diseases such as Parkinson's, some cancers and gut issues. Yet most of us have no idea to what extent they are present in our soil, water, air, food supply, and everyday personal care and household products.

We all carry toxic chemical residue in our bodies, including newborns. Even the breastmilk of women living in third world communities, far from the developed world, contains pesticide residues. And it's not just us humans; wildlife in remote places and oceans aren't safe either.

REDUCING EXPOSURE TO EXCESS ESTROGEN

To reduce your exposure to excess estrogen, eat organic wherever you can; use organic pads and tampons or a menstrual cup; choose chlorine-free products and unbleached paper products like toilet paper, paper towels, coffee filters and tissues. Avoid toxic weedkillers and growth enhancers in your garden, and chemicals to clean your car or your pets. Use non-toxic paint, and natural soap instead of sugar soap.

Use chemical-free, biodegradable laundry and household cleaning products whenever possible, along with chemical-free soaps and tooth-pastes, face creams and cosmetics. Avoid nail polish and nail polish removers, unless non-toxic.

Sunscreens typically include a combination of two to six active and toxic ingredients (oxybenzone, avobenzone, octisalate, octocrylene, homosalate and octinoxate). So if you have to use sunscreen, look for straight zinc oxide or another non-toxic sunscreen from your health food store or online; or DIY at home using coconut or carrot oils.

Avoid X-rays, ultrasounds, MRIs, CT and PET scans whenever you can. Don't spend excess time hanging around the security screening point at airports, photocopiers, fax machines, printers or the pump at petrol stations, as they all emit noxious gases, namely ozone, nitrogen dioxide and radiation.

Fire retardants are made up of compounds called polybrominated diphenyl ethers (PBDEs). They are also found in dozens of products in our homes: in carpet underlay, bedding, soft furnishings, couch, computer, mobile phone and television screen. Keep an ioniser, filter or vaporiser going in your home, to help detox it of these chemicals. Air fresheners and insect repellents are also a major source of xenoestrogens, so steer clear and choose essential oils instead.

Reduce the use of plastics whenever possible. A cocktail of chemicals are added to plastics to increase flexibility, transparency, durability and longevity, and these seriously need to be avoided. Plastic wrapped foods, heated in the microwave, contain some of the highest levels of xenoestrogen. Avoid drinking coffee or eating meals or other hot substances out of plastic. Take care not to leave plastic containers, especially your water bottle, in the sun. If you do, then throw it out. Avoid refilling plastic water bottles and avoid freezing water in plastic bottles to drink later. Use glass or ceramics whenever possible to store food. Sex toys are made with plastics, so can cause irritation and add to our toxic load as well. Read the labels on condoms and diaphragm gels as well.

Avoid toxic cookware made of aluminium and other toxic substances, cleaning products and sunscreens. The birth control pill and hormone replacement therapy contain synthetic hormones that interrupt our natural hormone balance. There are effective birth control alternatives without the side effects of these pills and creams.

_____ _____ _____ _____

It's shocking that our internal environment is more toxic than the external, but it is. Higher temperatures inside our homes result in higher concentrations of phthalates in the air. Let these toxins out by opening the windows, and let the healthy microbes in!

_____ _____ _____ _____

As we lose weight, pesticides are released from the fat tissue, so effective detox is important while losing weight. Xenoestrogens are in your jeans and anything else made from GM cotton (which is almost all cotton available to us), so buy organic jeans, pads and tampons, and get an organic mattress and sheets if you can.

REMOVING EXCESS ESTROGEN

Below are the 6 elimination channels that our body uses to remove toxic residue, in this case the excess estrogen that has built up in our body. These 'free radicals' contribute to the oxidative stress that create the right environment for disease to flourish. Here are some easy ways at home to encourage their exit.

- Liver—herbal medicine and tea, lemon water, chlorophyll, Epsom salts, castor oil pack
- Skin—skin brushing, sweating, avoiding toxic body products
- Lungs—deep breathing, exercise, hyperbaric oxygen chamber, time in nature, meditation, herbal medicine and tea
- Bowel—adequate fibre in the diet, herbal medicine, aloe vera, colonic irrigation, enemas, psyllium husks, slippery elm bark, bentonite clay, Epson salts
- Kidneys—a steady intake of clean water, herbal medicine and tea, meditation
- Lymphatic system—Rebounding, exercise, skin brushing, massage, zen chi machine

A lymphatic massage is one way, as is time in a float tank or oxygen chamber. Have some lemon water first thing in the morning. Squeeze half a lemon into ½ glass of (preferably) warm water. Add a little raw honey if you like. You can also add the smallest pinch of Himalayan crystal salt for an extra hit of alkalinity. Lemon water will kickstart your liver; over time it will start to flush out toxins and balance your pH levels. DIM, a phytonutrient in broccoli, cauliflower, cabbage and kale, promotes estrogen metabolism and aids in healthy hormone balance. Calcium D-glucarate occurs in fruits and vegetables and helps remove toxins and excess (used) hormones. Skin brushing will help increase the release of toxins via the skin (our largest organ), by promoting tighter and smoother skin. Use a soft bristle brush with natural fibres to brush your dry skin for a few minutes before you get in the shower.

An excess of estrogen (and other hormones and toxins) need to be removed from our bodies to prevent build-up, and our major organ of detox' is our liver. Castor oil packs are used to improve liver detoxification, so will be great here. Apply two to four drops of either clary sage, eucalyptus, lavender, and/or cypress essential oil over your abdomen. Lightly soak a piece of cloth in castor oil (it has a rather strong smell) and place it over your abdomen with a heat source like a wheat pack or hot water bottle on top. (Placing the pack over the whole torso helps support the liver and digestive organs.) Lie flat in bed and perhaps cover your eyes with an eye pillow. Leave it on for twenty minutes, using this time of quiet relaxation to go within. Castor oil packs can be messy. I wrap my piece of cloth in a compostable, leak-proof bag. Aim to do this three times a week. Avoid doing it during or close to your period, as it's going to be more effective to apply the pack when your pelvis is less congested.

Infra-red saunas help our body to release environmental chemicals by matching the frequency of the water in our cells, causing toxins released into the bloodstream to be excreted via our sweat. Start out with 4-minute sessions at 70–80°C (160–180°F), slowly working your way up to 30-minute sessions.

Colonic irrigation helps remove built-up waste from our bowel by hydrating and toning the large intestine. Seek out an experienced practitioner. I wouldn't recommend having more than six treatments over a month, and a course like that no more than once a year. The first couple of treatments probably aren't going to be much fun, but after the water has softened the poo somewhat, watch the 'release' flow!

Hyperbaric oxygen therapy, a well-known treatment for decompression sickness, is a personal favourite. It involves breathing pure oxygen in a pressurised room (or tube). You lie down, fully dressed, in a sealed chamber (with a see-through lid) and just relax for 40 minutes. (You're not going to like this if you're claustrophobic.) In the chamber, the air pressure is increased to three times higher than normal, so your lungs can gather more oxygen. This helps fight bacteria and stimulates the release of growth factors and stem cells, which promotes healing.

Perhaps the easiest and most enjoyable way to help the body eliminate harmful toxins is by being around the negative ions found in nature, especially around waterfalls, at the beach, in mountains and forests, as well as after a storm. Negative ions release endorphins, the feel-good hormones. At a large waterfall you might find over

100,000 negative ions, in large cities less than 100 negative ions. Indoor air isn't necessarily great either. If you can't get out into nature easily, have your bare feet touch the earth as often as you can (this is called earthing) or get some indoor plants. Salt lamps are great way to encourage negative ions in your home and/or workplace.

When we aren't carrying around a whole lot of toxic built up in our bodies, we won't feel so much like a big sewage tank. Plus it'll give us a better chance of living with balanced hormones, which means we once again feel motivated, focused, calm and sexy, whilst enjoy being a healthy weight and have an easy menstrual cycle, or menopause. Our hair, eyes, nails and skin look and feel great, and we get a good night's sleep. If our hormones are out of balance, life can be harder than it needs to be. So go ahead and start to remove those hormone disruptors, and before long you'll be looking, feeling and thinking in a much healthier way.

chapter twenty-two
DEALING WITH PREMENSTRUAL TENSION

Did you know that around 80% of menstruating women will experience premenstrual syndrome (PMS)? While painkillers and antidepressants are standard treatments in Western medicine, this is a normal and temporary imbalance, forcing us to look at ourselves and our lives.

The good news is that seven out of ten of us goddesses first look for natural ways to help with our symptoms. With changes to our way of life, specific natural remedies, tweaking our diet, finding a way to better handle emotional stress and reducing chemical stress, we can reduce the symptoms of PMS.

Typically, most women in the 21st century suffer for 7–14 days before their period. When you consider we're now menstruating more than our ancestors, the pieces of the puzzle start to join.

On average, the modern woman will menstruate 450 times in her life—triple that of our foremothers. Previously, women spent more time pregnant and on average lived shorter lives. PMS seems to be related to our disturbed hormones, especially estrogen and progesterone. Another cause is our modern diet, low in whole organic foods and good oils but with too much meat and trans fats. Issues with our thyroid are related, as is estrogen dominance from exposure to toxic chemicals.

A less than happy liver plus insulin resistance from too much sugar compounds it all into one messy fortnight.

Our symptoms can range from mild to brutal. Feeling really tired is not unusual before your period, nor is having trouble sleeping. Headaches and migraines are very common, in addition to feeling bloated, having skin issues, tender and swollen breasts, weight gain, feeling very emotional, back pain, hot flushes, changes in bowel movements, food cravings and cramps. But it needn't be this way. There is plenty we can do to help bring us back into harmony with our natural feminine rhythms.

TREATING PMS

Eating a mostly plant-based diet is effective for reducing PMS. Currently, calcium is among the most science-backed nutrients helping this particular condition, so include quinoa, spirulina, kefir, cooked kale, broccoli, seaweeds, sardines and some goat or sheep yogurt in your diet.

Fibre will help maintain a proper hormone balance, by binding to excess estrogen and carrying it out of the body. It'll also keep your blood sugar balanced, helping you say 'no' to chocolate, wine and chips. This will increase your vitality and reduce your irritability. Green leafy vegetables are a good source of calcium, magnesium, and vitamin K and will reduce period cramps. Eat kale, spinach, rocket, radicchio and Asian greens. Flaxseeds help promote healthy estrogen levels and balance, so grind them into flax meal or blitz them in a smoothie.

Go for omega-3 oils like wild-caught salmon, sardines and anchovies; they help reduce PMS pain and inflammation. Try to eat avocados regularly, as they're full of nutrients: healthy fat, fibre, magnesium, potassium and vitamin B6. Fennel seeds help reduce PMS. Add one teaspoon to curry spices and stir-fry veggies, or have as a tea. (They're also good for blood sugar balance, bloating, weight loss and to promote breastmilk.) Turmeric is a plant source of estrogen. It helps stop synthetic estrogens taking hold, is good for the liver and is a strong anti-inflammatory.

What makes PMS worse is conventional dairy, although organic A2 milk should be okay, as should be organic butter and full-fat cream. Avoid these foods initially if you have endometriosis. Salt causes water retention, especially during menstruation, making everything worse. Processed and junk food disrupts your hormones and causes gut problems that will affect your metabolism and hormones. Trans fats, hydrogenated fats, high-fructose corn syrup and refined sugar are also in processed foods and can make PMS symptoms worse. Excess estrogens make more histamine, and histamine stimulates your ovaries to make more estrogen, causing headaches, anxiety, insomnia, brain fog, blood sugar chaos and worsening mood swings. Drinking too much alcohol in the second half of your cycle (and for some people any) makes PMS symptoms worse and may increase the risk of bad cramping during menstruation. Antibiotics make PMS even worse, (and disrupt your cycle, and effectiveness of the Pill) one to two months after taking them. A specific group of microbes called estrobolome, determine how estrogen is used in our body. This job of this bacteria is to break down the estrogen that the liver sends to the gut, allowing the body to remove it via one of our elimination channels. These being our bowel, kidney, liver, lungs, skin and lymph glands. *See Chapter 21, Excess Estrogen.* But when the estrobolome is disrupted, the broken down estrogen is turned back into active estrogens which are then reabsorbed into the blood stream, creating estrogen dominance.

Your supplements of choice for correcting your estrogen metabolism are vitamin B6 (I recommend taking a wholefood B complex, or food, rather than an isolated vitamin) and DIM to help detoxification of estrogen via the liver. A deficiency in magnesium could be the main cause of your PMS, as it's required for the proper metabolism of estrogen; it can also help relieve cramping. Aim for 150–300 mg/day. Zinc is required for a proper balance of our sex hormones. Dosage is 15–20 mg.

According to a large, double-blind, placebo-controlled study published in a 1998 issue of *American Journal of Obstetrics and Gynecology*, Calcium (carbonate or citrate) supplementation produced significant improvements in PMS symptoms in double-blind studies. Symptoms including mood swings, headaches, food cravings, and bloating were halved over a period of three menstrual cycles by taking the recommended dosage of 600 mg 2×/day

An iron deficiency has been linked to PMS. Have your levels checked and if you are below the ideal range, supplementation will be necessary until your levels are back up. (You can check levels by swirling around 10mls of Zinc Drink, available from your health food store; otherwise from a blood test ordered by your GP.)

When it comes to medicinal herbs, chaste tree (vitex agnus-castus) is essential for dealing with an estrogen/progesterone imbalance. Take 2.5ml of the liquid or as directed on the tablets. Take it in the morning as early as you can, before your hormones decide where to go on their own. In trials with women suffering from premenstrual dysphoric disorder (a more severe form of PMS), chaste tree worked just as well as prescribed drugs in relieving symptoms.[*] Motherwort works well to reduce cramping and strengthen the uterus. It is also used to reduce stress and heart palpitations stemming from anxiety. Motherwort is among the Chinese herbs found to help relieve PMS, according to a Cochrane Systematic Review.[†]

Withania and holy basil are two herbs that reduce cortisol, balance hormones and reduce PMS symptoms. The polyphenol in turmeric (curcumin) has proven capable of improving symptoms of PMS. Cramp bark, as the name suggests, is extremely helpful for relieving muscle spasms and premenstrual cramps. Traditionally, cramp bark is said

---

[*] Dante, Giulia, and Facchinetti, Fabio. 'Herbal Treatments for Alleviating Premenstrual Symptoms: a Systematic Review.' *Journal of Psychosomatic Obstetrics & Gynecology*. Taylor & Francis, March 1, 2011.

[†] Zhu X, Proctor M, Bensoussan A, Smith CA, Wu E. 'Chinese herbal medicine for primary dysmenorrhoea.' Cochrane Database of Systematic Reviews 2007, Issue 4. Art. No.: CD005288.

to be particularly useful for cramps that radiate to your lower back or thighs.

Essential oils like clary sage and ylang-ylang applied to the lower abdomen will aid in hormonal balance.

Mix five drops with a carrier oil (like almond oil) and then rub on the lower abdomen and/or the back of your neck. Apply a warm compress to the area for two to five minutes.

Other practices that may provide temporary relief for premenstrual pain and discomfort are placing a hot water bottle or wheat pack on your lower abdomen, and soaking in a warm bath. Add in a few drops of one of the essential oils above or magnesium oxide bath salts, to help reduce the cramps.

DOES PMS CAUSE STRESS, OR IS IT THE OTHER WAY AROUND?

Let's now look at lifestyle habits that may be causing discomfort each month. If you're emotionally stressed during the first two weeks of your cycle, you're 25 times more likely to experience PMS in the second two weeks, due to the effect cortisol has on your hormones. High levels of cortisol (a stress hormone) can block your progesterone receptors, causing low progesterone levels, leading to PMS.

A connection between the overgrowth of candida yeast and PMS has been made. The natural rise and fall of estrogen throughout the month may help to explain changes in the severity of PMS symptoms, such as bloating, thrush, foggy head and nausea. For information on how to reduce overgrowth: *See Chapter 19, The Thing About Candida.*

We know that estrogen dominance causes hormones to be less available and low thyroid function can reduce progesterone levels, causing PMS symptoms to flare. Have you had your hormones checked to determine whether hyperthyroid or hypothyroid symptoms are interfering with the balance of your hormones and contributing to PMS?

How about your iodine levels? If they're on the low side, then include more iodine-rich foods in your diet, and remove fluoride, chlorine and bromine wherever you can. Low iodine is related to breast pain, as well as other symptoms.

The time before our period is related to our shadow (the subconscious or hidden away parts of ourselves). Listen to your shadow. Something is out of balance physiologically if you're suffering from PMS each month. *See Chapter 4, Your Shadow Self.*

Research shows that PMS is more likely if you're obese,[*] and/or if you don't exercise enough.[†] Moving your body will also help balance your wayward hormones and reduce stress, which can reduce the symptoms of PMS. Exercise raises endorphin levels, which are chemicals in your brain associated with pain relief. Hatha yoga (at least weekly) is at the top of the list here.

Non-steroidal anti-inflammatory drugs containing ibuprofen (brands include Nurofen and Ponstan) are the most commonly used conventional medicine options for PMS symptoms. These drugs will help reduce symptoms for two-thirds of women, but they come at a price. Ibuprofen warns of serious gastrointestinal side effects, like stomach bleeding and increased chance of heart attack. And yes, an ibuprofen overdose is possible. Your cramps might stop, but you'll likely be left with a whole new set of more serious health issues. The contraceptive pill is the other medication often prescribed for PMS. Please try to avoid this option unless absolutely necessary, especially as there are herbal medicines and other natural alternatives readily available that work well to reduce and even eliminate the symptoms and cause of PMS.

---

[*] Masho, Saba Woldemichael, Adera, Tilahun, and South-Paul, Jeannette. 'Obesity as a Risk Factor for Premenstrual Syndrome.' *Journal of Psychosomatic Obstetrics & Gynecology 26*, no. 1 (March 1, 2005): 33–39.

[†] Zeinab Samadi, Farzaneh Taghian, Mahboubeh Valiani. 'The effects of 8 weeks of regular aerobic exercise on the symptoms of premenstrual syndrome in non-athlete girls.' *Iran J Nurs Midwifery Res.*, vol 18, no. 1 (Jan-Feb 2013): 14–19.

chapter twenty-three
GETTING HELP WITH FIBROIDS

M ost women suffer from fibroids at some point in their lives, but not all are aware of it. Fibroids are non-cancerous growths within the wall of the uterus that cause annoying, sometimes painful symptoms. Some women have no symptoms at all; it depends a lot on where the fibroid is in the uterus. They can range in size from a few millimetres to the size of a watermelon. Usually a woman finds out she has fibroids when her periods get longer and heavier, sometimes never seeming to end. 'Flooding' is a term I hear very often to describe this extreme, often embarrassing condition.

Every year in Australia, around 30,000 women, (600,000 in the United States) have a hysterectomy, and most of these are performed due to uterine fibroids. In fact, it's the most common major operation performed in Australia after Caesarean section. According to a report published in the *New England Journal of Medicine* fibroids are 'the most frequent indication for major gynecologic surgery'.[*]

The uterus contains two types of tissue but is mostly made up of muscle tissue (myometrium). An overgrowth of the myometrium causes fibroids. There are several different types of fibroids, and the location, size and number of fibroids will influence how you're affected.

---

[*] Clark, NM et al. 'Uterine-Artery Embolization Versus Surgery for Symptomatic Uterine Fibroids.' *The New England Journal of Medicine*, vol 356, no. 4 (January 25, 2007): 360–370.

While 70–80% of women will have fibroids by the age of fifty, it's rare to see them in women under 20 years of age or after menopause, suggesting it's another case of hormone disruption. Heavier women are more likely to have fibroids, probably due to the increase in estrogen levels in fat cells. So keeping a steady and healthy weight reduces your chances of developing fibroids.

Another factor that increases the likelihood of developing fibroids is how much alcohol we drink. Too much alcohol burdens our liver, making it harder to detox excess estrogen, so the trapped hormones recirculate causing all sorts of havoc. Seven or more alcoholic drinks a week is said to be too much.

High blood pressure seems to increase a woman's risk of fibroids too, especially in perimenopausal women. Herbal medicine, supplements and lifestyle changes help most women keep blood pressure around 120/80.

And it's no surprise that a sluggish thyroid is linked to an increased risk of fibroids. Taking the pill can make fibroids grow faster, because of the extra estrogen in the body. Putting a young woman on the pill before she's sixteen increases the chances of her suffering from fibroids later on. In one study, an earlier age at menarche (first period) increased the risk of uterine fibroids, attributing this to higher estrogen levels starting earlier.[*]

Common annoyances are pain in your pelvis, along with a feeling of pressure. Constipation, gas and abdominal bloating are not unusual either. Sex can hurt, and you may find yourself needing to urinate often, but then have trouble going. Fibroids can create backache or pain in the back of the legs. There are often reproductive issues, including infertility and miscarriages. Fibroids can cause complications during pregnancy and labour, including a six times greater risk of needing a caesarean section to deliver.

Fibroids can grow anywhere in the uterus. When they grow closer to the centre of the uterus, they're linked to a greater chance of infertility.

---

[*] Laughlin SK, Schroeder JC, and Baird D. *New Directions in the Epidemiology of Uterine Fibroids. Seminars In Reproductive Medicine*, vol 28, no. 3 (2010):204-217.

TREATING FIBROIDS

When it comes to mainstream medicine, a few treatment options are recommended:

- medications that lower hormone levels
- non-steroidal anti-inflammatory drugs
- surgically removing the fibroids
- removing the uterus via hysterectomy (fibroids are the leading reason for hysterectomies)
- uterine embolisation, the latest medical approach, where substances are injected into the uterine arteries to cut off blood supply

Applying a castor oil pack to your abdomen helps increase circulation to that area. Apply one of the essential oils to your abdomen first for a deeper healing (see previous chapter for more detail.)

Regular exercise helps our circulation and assists our lymphatic system to pump out toxins. It also helps to keep our weight down, thereby reducing estrogen levels. Numerous studies have been done on the correlation between exercise and fibroids, including this one done in 2006 by The National Institute of Environmental Sciences in Washington DC. They found that women who did the most physical activity (more than 7 hours a week) were significantly less likely to develop fibroids than those who did the least amount of exercise (less than 2 hours a week). Exercise at a comfortable level for you.

Estrogen's starting place is the gut, so intestinal bacteria play a big role when it comes to shrinking fibroids. Eat fermented foods if you can handle them, and take oregano oil mindfully, for two to three weeks. A dodgy gut flora causes estrogen excess, so avoid antibiotics and xenoestrogens. *See Chapter 21, Excess Estrogen.*

Eating an organic diet, and using natural cosmetics and cleaning products, helps to prevent estrogen levels getting out of control, allowing fibroids to grow. Eating plant-based estrogens (some whole grains, seeds, legumes, veggies and organic soy) will be beneficial.

For children and men, plant-based estrogens will increase estrogen a little; for women, plant-based estrogens block xenoestrogens and help detox them, promoting an anti-estrogenic affect.

Research shows that eating loads of broccoli, cabbage, tomato and apples seems to protect against uterine fibroids.* Again the cruciferous family is recommended, due to their ability to help support liver detoxification, helping to create healthy estrogen levels. Studies show that eating this family of veggies regularly—broccoli, cauliflower, cabbage, kale, kohlrabi and brussels sprouts—reduces the incidence of uterine fibroids. Green leafy vegetables are high in vitamin K, which encourages proper clotting, discouraging fibroids and heavy bleeding. Include Asian greens, chicory, rocket, baby spinach, English spinach, kale and dandelion leaves in a daily salad.

Essential fatty acids, from eating sustainable, oily fish a few times a week or by adding two tablespoons of flaxseed to your daily diet, are known to balance out your hormones too. Fibroids soak up iodine, so be sure you are getting enough, preferably from your diet. Include foods high in iron, like organic spirulina, sea vegetables, legumes and occasionally some organic grass-fed beef if you like, to replace the loss of iron from heavy bleeding. Women who eat highest amounts of lignans, a type of phytoestrogen found in flaxseed and whole grains, had less than half the risk of fibroids, compared with the women who generally didn't include these foods. Flaxseed is also a wonderfully healing source of phyto (plant) estrogen, which helps to balance your estrogen levels, shrinking fibroids. Have two to three tablespoons a day. Grind or soak them first, to make them easier to digest.

Processed, non-organic meats can increase inflammation and estrogen levels, as they contain chemical additives and antibiotics. In addition, the animals are fed GM crops. Studies have shown that eating poor quality beef or **any** type of pork is linked to a higher risk

---

* Shen Y, Wu , Lu Q, Ren M. 'Vegetarian diet and reduced uterine fibroids risk: A case-control study in Nanjing, China.' *J Obstet Gynaecol Res., vol 42, no. 1* (January 2016):87–94.

of fibroids.* Likewise, processed dairy is very high in xenoestrogens and other chemicals that disrupt hormones and encourage the growth of fibroids. A small amount of organic cultured dairy should be fine though, especially made from goat or sheep milk.

Refined sugar and carbohydrates cause a spike in blood sugar, linking these foods with a higher risk of uterine fibroids. Drinking more than two cups of coffee daily may increase estrogen levels, due to the effect it has on the liver. Avoid soy products, unless they're organic and preferably fermented. Eating this type of quality soy a few times a week is linked to a reduction in fibroids.†

One study has linked non-organic soy formula given to babies with uterine fibroids in adult women.‡

Another study reported in the *NIEHS Study of Environment, Lifestyle, and Fibroids (SELF)* found that 50 percent of women who were fed non-soy formula as babies were more likely to have experienced moderate or severe menstrual discomfort between the ages of 18 and 22, and 40% more likely to have used hormonal contraception to help alleviate menstrual pain.

The supplements to consider here are similar to those for any reproductive issue. DIM and CDG to remove excess estrogen; iron for the reason stated above, and consider an infusion if your levels are really low; natural vitamin E to keep your blood slippery and clot-free; essential fatty acids like fish, hemp or flaxseed oil to reduce inflammation in your body, which may play a part in fibroid growth. Take a vegan source of DHA/EPA if you prefer, plus B complex to aid the liver in balancing estrogen levels.

---

* Chiaffario, Francesca ScD, and Fabio Parazzini MD, Carla La Vecchia MD, Liliane Chatenoud ScD, Elisabetta Di Cintio ScD, Silvia Marsico MD. 'Diet and Uterine Myomas.' *Journal of Obstetrics and Gynaecology Research*, no. 94 (1999): 395–398

† Atkinson, Charlotte, and Johanna W Lampe, Delia Scholes, Chu Chen, Kristiina Wähälä, Stephen M Schwartz. 'Lignan and isoflavone excretion in relation to uterine fibroids: a case-control study of young to middle-aged women in the United States.' *The American Journal of Clinical Nutrition*, no. 84 (2006): 587–593

‡ Upson K, Harmon QE, Baird DD. 'Soy-Based Infant Formula Feeding and Ultrasound-Detected Uterine Fibroids among Young African-American Women with No Prior Clinical Diagnosis of Fibroids.' *Environ Health Perspect.*, vol 124, no. 6 (June 2016):769–75.

My favourite herbs to use when treating fibroids include chaste tree, to reduce estrogen levels and boost progesterone. Chaste tree takes somewhere between a week to a month to show its effect, and sometimes up to three months, so be patient. Shepherd's purse and American cranesbill are also both incredibly effective at reducing the heavy bleeding caused by fibroids. Use liver herbs like dandelion root, burdock and St. Mary's thistle to help remove excess estrogen. I like to use kudzu to reduce excess estrogen (plus it's known to help reduce cravings for alcohol). Peony cools the blood, moves stagnating (stuck) blood, and relieves pain. I also use uterine tonics like raspberry leaf or lady's mantle.

Rub two drops of clary sage essential oil over your lower abdomen twice daily. If you have sensitive skin, you may want to first mix it with one teaspoon of a carrier oil like jojoba, hemp, coconut, almond or olive oil. Clary sage oil has a positive effect on our reproductive organs. Thyme and frankincense are the best to use in treating fibroids, as they help balance hormones naturally. And most importantly, send love to your second (orange) chakra, responsible for the sex organs affected by fibroids. There are many online meditations that focus on this area of your body.

The women I see with fibroids have a terrible time with flooding, during their period or all month long. Understandably, many can't handle this. Their resulting iron deficiency makes them feel even worse, so eventually they have a hysterectomy.* Seeking out natural treatment before you get to that stage is preferable. And as I've outlined above, there are lots of positive steps you can take.

---

* As many as 50,000 Australian women have this procedure done each year, one in three women by 60yo, and most of these have been deemed unnecessary. To make things a bit scarier, a recent survey of 258 gynaecologists from across Australia found that only 16.7% of those surveyed rated themselves as 'highly skilled at conducting a total laparoscopic (keyhole) hysterectomy'. So 'open hysterectomies' are still being performed, because they are experienced in these. Essentially, 'they were comfortable doing what they've always done' the survey stated. In both private and public systems, a lack of surgical skills was identified as the biggest

barrier to practising total laparoscopic hysterectomy. There is overwhelming evidence that a laparoscopic hysterectomy is associated with a shorter hospital stay, equivalent survival rate as 'open hysterectomies', quicker recovery, better quality of life and less cost to the health care system. And let's not forget about the scar tissue, and living with that particular kind of ongoing discomfort. Plus losing your reproductive organs and all that goes with that. A hysterectomy is a pretty serious decision and one with potentially long-lasting repercussions, so why not try a natural and wholistic approach first?

The University of Queensland's surgeon Professor Andreas Obermair led the 12 year trial at the 'Centre for Gynaecological Cancer Research'. It involved 760 patients and 27 surgeons.

chapter twenty-four
MENOPAUSE DOESN'T HAVE TO BE HARD

Before I hit menopause, I regularly saw clients going through this change of life, complete with weight gain, mood swings, anxiety, tears, hot flushes, night sweats, insomnia, zero sex drive, and tiredness from being everything to everyone. It wasn't something I looked forward to. I thought menopause would be challenging, as I had never had an easy run of anything to do with my reproductive organs. But here I am two years into menopause—the definition being twelve months straight without a period—and it hasn't been the nightmare I thought it would be. Most women dread this time of their lives, but I've actually found it rather liberating, thanks to some specific herbal medicine and supplements, as well as new attitudes and beliefs.

We hear menopause horror stories from older women, but it doesn't have to be that way. It can realistically be the time in a woman's life that renowned yoga teacher B.K.S Iyengar called the 'forest dweller' stage. A time to be free of social and familial obligations. A time to turn inwards, to withdraw from the external world to pursue your own spirituality, creativity and … your authentic, essential self. Hooray for that!

Menopause is a natural part of life, not something that needs to be cured. Not a punishment or curse. It can and should be the beginning of an easier and healthier time in a woman's life, especially if she's been suffering throughout her thirty-five odd years of menstruation with too much estrogen and conditions like endo, polycystic ovarian syndrome, fibroids, adenomyosis or debilitating PMS.

This is the time to step into the **crone** phase of your life. The word 'crone' means 'disagreeable old woman' (and anyone who has gone through it without emotional or physical support will get my drift here). But in times gone by in matriarchal societies, it meant the end of a cycle and was defined in a positive light as 'powerful and wise old woman'. In new age, spiritual and feminist circles, 'croning' is a ritual rite of passage into an era of wisdom, freedom and personal power.

Each woman's attitude toward this 'change of life', as well as her view on ageing, will largely determine the intensity of the change. That, and how hard she's been living until now. Young women, take note!

So, if we can educate our 21st century daughters in the ancient principles of the Sacred Feminine, we may be able to prevent menopausal concerns in women currently in their fertile years. For example, if there's too much yang or do-ing, too many CrossFit classes and excessive activity, our adrenal glands release stress-fighting cortisol at a time when we're meant to be moving inward. Over time, this kind of adrenal stress during our moon cycle can and does affect the health of our menses, leading to nasty PMT and a challenging menopause.

Menopause can begin any time in a woman's life after about 35 years. Usually the symptoms appear in the late forties and last approximately five years. For others, menopause comes earlier due to health conditions, including a history of eating disorders, Western treatments for cancer, some medications, adrenal fatigue or surgical removal of the ovaries.

PERIMENOPAUSE

Thinking you're probably too young for menopause, but feeling a little unhinged, with a new muffin top and a strange and constant fatigue?

Before you go into full-blown menopause (12 consecutive months without a period), you'll be in perimenopause.

It can start as early as the mid-thirties but most women start to notice it around 45–47 years of age, when your jeans don't fit so well anymore, and you're caring less about what others think. Around this time your periods can come and go, plus they may get much heavier, or lighter at times. Perimenopause begins about five to ten years before menopause technically starts, so follow some of my recommendations from the first sign of 'the change', to help your chances of gliding through to the next stage.

Night sweats are common, but they decrease over time and often completely disappear without any treatment. Hot flushes, headaches/migraines, sleep problems and weight gain (especially around the abdomen, waist and triceps) are all common symptoms.

All three different types of estrogen in our system (estrone, estridiol and estriol) start to decrease during perimenopause, and this is when you'll likely start to notice emotional and physical symptoms of your hormones changing. Due to less estrogen, you'll feel less likely to 'people please', look pretty, be over generous, or feel the need to secure a partner to father a child. Your biological clock is slowing down and so is the urgency and anxiety around these matters.

Exercise during the perimenopausal years is vital, as is meditation and having a positive attitude about moving into the next stage of your life. Yes, it's kinda hard when you feel fat, tired and anxious, with zero interest in sex or exercise—which is why it's essential to be on the right diet, herbs and supplements.

Exercise will help you control blood sugar levels, improve bone density and mood, and decrease muscle wasting and chronic stress. Start now, even if you've been prone to a sedentary life. Engage in some form of aerobic activity most days for 10–30 minutes (if you don't have chronic fatigue issues, that is). Interval training has been shown to be helpful, but don't forget to practise a gentler form of exercise like qi gong, tai chi or yoga for a more peaceful mind. Try also to get plenty of time outdoors; walking, taking a slow jog, ocean swimming, bushwalking, horseriding and cycling are all perfect ways to get to the other side of menopause in one piece.

Estrogen can also double during perimenopause, so check out some of my recommendations to help balance it now. *See Chapter 21, Excess Estrogen.*

POSTMENOPAUSE

After menopause women have fewer ovarian follicles, so there's not as much estrogen or progesterone being released from our ovaries each month. Once our ovaries stop producing these hormones, our possibly already overworked adrenal glands will pick up some of the task of providing the energy you used to get from your ovaries. This is why it's not uncommon for women in their peri-menopausal years to start to crash with adrenal fatigue. Both the ovaries and adrenal glands clock off.

Decreased estrogen needs to be addressed, as it's been linked to cardiovascular disease and osteoporosis. Once thought of only as a sex hormone, we now know estrogen receptors are in the bladder, breasts, arteries, heart, liver, bones, vagina, brain and skin, as well as the ovaries. Estrogen is also necessary to maintain proper functioning of our body's own thermostat, to keep skin healthy and bones strong. You may notice you're suddenly urinating a **lot** more and your bras don't fit, as your breasts are now smaller, larger, or not as full as they once were. Hair may be thinning and skin becoming drier. And when it comes to sex drive, we'd much rather garden, sleep, read, binge on Netflix or wash the car! The walls of our vagina start to thin, caused by a drop in estrogen levels. 40% of postmenopausal women have vaginal atrophy, creating redness, itching, and a dry yoni (external female genitals). This can also lead to pain during intercourse and urination.

Mood swings may leave us more anxious, irritable, depressed and forgetful than normal. We care a little to a lot less about how we look.

Think wearing track pants to the shop, and forgetting all about your lipstick ... and purse!

Another thing I want to address is how we release dark energy after our menopausal years. During our monthly bleed, we can automatically shed unwanted feelings of attachment, shame, sadness and irritability. But after that particular lunar cycle ceases forever, we need to find new ways to do this. Meditation is one way. Swimming in natural water bodies like lakes or the ocean is another, as is kundalini yoga or having an energy clearing from a trusted, experienced energy worker.

With the right natural and/or integrative practitioner prescribing you appropriate herbal medicine, supplements, along with appropriate exercise, quality social interactions, a creative outlet, joy, good nutrition, sleep and positive thoughts, there is no need for menopause to be an unwelcome or annoying time. In Japan, the word for menopause loosely translates to 'second spring', where women are stepping into their own—into being an elder and 'wise woman'.

TREATING MENOPAUSAL SYMPTOMS

To counter menopausal symptoms, it's essential we eat a well-balanced diet including healthy fats and fibre from sources other than grains during this transition. Flax is a plant estrogen known to reduce menopausal symptoms, and sunflower seeds and almonds are high in healthy plant steroids known to lower cholesterol. Two grams of these plant sterols a day may help lower your LDL cholesterol (bad cholesterol) by 10%.

Add one teaspoon of maca root to your smoothies. This root veggie has been used for thousands of years to lessen the effects of stress and ageing on the body by decreasing cortisol levels. It can also help reduce hot flushes, restlessness and weight gain, while improving sex drive, stamina and endurance.

Phytoestrogens are plants that can mimic the effects of our body's natural hormones. They have recently been proven to reduce some women's menopause symptoms, by making the decrease in natural estrogen feel less drastic. Include organic soy products, lentils, flax, sesame seeds, carrots, alfalfa, fenugreek and licorice. Turmeric is an all-round winner during menopause. It helps reduce the inflammation associated with menopause, has estrogenic properties, plus it aids your liver and helps you sleep.

To help regulate appetite-controlling hormones like insulin, ghrelin and leptin, regularly include foods high in probiotics; they'll also boost immunity and reduce change-of-life brain fog. Beetroot juice has proved to be more permanently helpful than drugs or synthetic hormones during menopause.[*]

It's also known to balance high or low blood pressure (in a matter of minutes), help move your bowels, and build your blood due to it's iron content. It should be taken in smallish quantities of 60–90ml, three times a day. Carrot seeds are also valuable for reducing menopausal symptoms. Simmer a teaspoon of the seeds in a glassful of (your choice of quality) milk, for a tasty hormone-balancing medicinal milk. Boron is a mineral used to help reduce the signs of ageing skin, poor memory and recall, preventing osteoporosis, increasing bone density and balancing estrogen levels.

Include wholefoods in your diet, especially beans, nuts, some whole grains and avocados, as well as fruits like berries, plums, oranges and grapes. Matcha, the green tea powder from Japan, is very helpful for menopausal symptoms (but don't buy the cheap stuff). Have your zinc levels checked; if they are too low, you may need a supplement for three months. Take it outside of meals for best absorption. If your levels are borderline, boost your zinc by eating pepitas, oysters, mushrooms and sea vegetables to help reduce moodiness, poor immunity and premature ageing.

Now let's look at foods that are just going to make everything worse. You guessed it, refined sugar and carbohydrates, processed

---

[*] Clifford, Tom, Howatson, Glyn, West, Daniel J. and Stevenson, Emma J. 'The Potential Benefits of Red Beetroot Supplementation in Health and Disease'. *Nutrients* vol 7, no. 4 (April 2015): 2801–2822.

foods and trans fats, because they increase our estrogen to abnormal levels (as much as twice the normal), making menopausal symptoms much, much worse. *See Chapter 21, Excess Estrogen*

Even a moderate amount of alcohol seems to be an issue for many menopausal women. It worsens hot flushes and leads to faster weight gain. Fizzy drinks contain too much sugar or artificial sweeteners, both of which are hormone disrupting and dangerous to our health. Most also contain caffeine, which may exacerbate anxiety in the menopausal years, and bromine which will reduce iodine levels, negatively affecting your thyroid. Omega-6 oil is needed in the right amounts. *See Chapter 52, Fats and Oils.*

Supplementation may be necessary for some women during this hormonal change, but keep your routine simple. Vitamins B and C may stimulate the body's production of estrogen or enhance the effect of existing estrogen. Supplementation of GLA oil helps to reduce bone loss, with calcium, vitamins D3 and K2 plus fish oil to improve a cranky mood, nerve pain, headaches, anxiety, fluid retention, irritability, breast tenderness and hot flushes, and to increase sex drive and bone density. Like other fatty acids, GLA is thought to help to elevate levels of serotonin, a brain chemical that contributes to the feeling of fullness, so it's going to be helpful in controlling your appetite and weight. Magnesium works best when it's balanced with calcium, so take them together for a bad mood, insomnia, headaches, cramps, restless legs and heart health. Vitamins D3 and K2 are good for bone health, or get ten minutes of sunlight daily (in your birthday suit, if possible). Eat fermented foods that are loaded with vitamin K2. Vitamin E helps to regulate estrogen production, so your need for this vitamin increases dramatically during menopause.

When it comes to bioidentical hormones, discuss using these with a naturopath or integrative doctor. I don't personally recommend them to my patients, but in some cases they may be needed. You'll need a prescription from a medical doctor to obtain them.

When I'm treating patients who are experiencing really challenging menopausal symptoms, I'm so glad I'm a herbalist with access to some incredibly effective herbs. Briefly, there are two classes of herbs that exist for the relief of menopausal symptoms:

phyto-estrogenic herbs such as ginseng, soy, red clover and dong quai, whose compounds are similar to human hormones; and

non-estrogenic herbs like black cohosh, that stimulate the body's own hormonal production.

Both are effective at easing our hormones to a level that makes this whole change much easier.

My favourites are chaste tree for its balancing effect on the hormonal changes that occur during menopause; black cohosh for hot flushes, weight management, mood swings and sleep disturbances; shatavari as an adaptogen for increased energy and a better mood, to balance estrogen and progesterone, and to improve libido and reduce vaginal dryness; adaptogenic herbs like withania, rhodiola and holy basil for energy and mood, and also for a better night's sleep; sage and zizyphus for flushes; nigella and gymnema for weight management; lion's mane and ginkgo for forgetfulness; motherwort and St. John's wort for anxiety and a bad mood in general; and finally, nut grass to help reduce liver and lymph stagnation, thereby better supporting the body's own detox pathways, rather than reverting to hot flushes or night sweats.

Essential oils are a gorgeous way to ease through menopause. Clary sage is your first choice here. It's used for balancing hormones, reducing anxiety, cramps and hot flushes. Peppermint helps cool the body from hot flushes; rose geranium and cinnamon are helpful to ease cramps, nausea, flushes, fatigue, fluid retention and mood swings.

Jasmine is a natural remedy for all things menopausal. It'll help improve sexual desire (as will ylang ylang), calm heart rate, control body temperature, minimise stress and improve alertness, blood pressure and breathing. This sexy oil has been used for centuries to help reduce anxiety, emotional stress and insomnia. Finally, carrot seed oil nourishes, tightens and rejuvenates tired and grey skin and is also useful for reducing stress and anxiety.

The most important thing you can do for yourself now is reduce stress in your life. Better still, learn a technique that will help you handle it better. Mindfulness and meditation are going to be very beneficial, so find a technique that suits you. When it comes to personal relationships, it's especially important that you nurture healthy connections. Get more rest than you would normally. *See Chapter 6, Are You Stressing Yourself Out?*

When it comes to your diet, remember we are not growing now, so we don't need as many calories as we did when we were children. Plus our metabolism has slowed and we most likely sit more than we did then. All of these factors can add up to an extra few kilos a year/week, if we're not mindful of portion control.

The quality and quantity of your sleep is essential during this transitional period, so do whatever you need to make this happen. *See Chapter 25, When You Just Can't Sleep.*

'Legs up the wall' pose is a restorative, relaxing and gentle yoga inversion that has many benefits. It eases anxiety and emotional stress by calming the mind, plus it's good for relieving headaches, blood pressure issues and insomnia. It will help ease the symptoms of menopause, and relieves tired or cramping feet and legs, as well as reducing lower back pain. Roll up a big towel and put it under your lower back. Shimmy your bottom against a wall, then swing your legs straight up the wall. Try to do this pose for 10–15 minutes a day. (I often put gentle healing music on at the same time, and cover my eyes with an eye pillow. Heaven!)

If you've never tried acupuncture, this might be the time to start. The practice of 'needling' can safely treat many symptoms of menopause, so find a respected and experienced practitioner you feel good with. Deep breathing can reduce hot flushes by almost 50%, so breathe deeply for 20 minutes twice a day (inhale for 5 seconds, hold, then exhale for ten seconds). Exhaling stimulates progesterone production, making us feel safe and calm.

As estrogen decreases, orgasms may feel like a long-lost dream. Even if you have the desire, getting there is another matter; if you do, they may be hardly noticeable. Regular physical connection will help keep the blood flow to your vulva (outer) and vagina (inner) flowing and sensitive. Or practise regular massage yourself or with a partner.

For over 5,000 years, Asian women have been using stone eggs called 'yoni eggs', even after menopause, to increase natural lubrication, balance estrogen levels, tighten the vaginal wall and stimulate tissues, organs and muscles, promoting new nerve growth, helping strengthen pelvic floor muscles and increasing overall sensitivity. Yoni eggs are also known as jade eggs or love eggs. Yoni is a Sanskrit word meaning 'sacred womb'. The eggs are used for spiritual and physical awakening and to align the chakras.

If you've undergone surgical menopause by having a hysterectomy before natural menopause, it's most likely you'll need to replace the hormones your body can no longer produce. The bioidentical hormone estradiol is all you'll probably need. However if estrogen is used, it is usually wise to use it in conjunction with natural progesterone.

chapter twenty-five
WHEN YOU JUST CAN'T SLEEP

Does it seem to you that many people you know just aren't sleeping well? Most of my clients aren't getting enough quality sleep, and then they start to unravel. This is usually when they come to see me—when their body is inflamed, their adrenals are drained, and they're gaining weight.

I wonder why we don't see lack of sleep as a sign that our body is out of balance? Good, uninterrupted sleep is essential for our wellbeing and is defined as seven to ten hours a night, dropping to nine hours after age 65. Six hours is not enough sleep and over ten hours is too much. Lack of sleep increases our risk of dying from **any** cause, not to mention accidents, poor decision-making, days off work and resulting healthcare costs.

Cutting your sleep down from 7.5 to 6.5 hours a night increases your vulnerability to inflammation, immune issues, heart disease, diabetes, cancer and stress. For adults over 50, lack of sleep is also the **strongest** predictor for pain. Sleep deprivation can increase your cortisol (a stress hormone), resulting in fewer new brain cells being created. It also reduces the brain's ability to detox, rejuvenate and repair.

And you've probably noticed you're hungrier the day after a bad night's sleep. Often (but not always) we'll eat more, because we're in a state of insulin resistance that makes us feel hungry, even after we've just eaten. We'll likely head towards sugar for a quick burst of energy. So we eat more food, then crash. Even an hour's less sleep a night can cause us to gain as much as five kilos in a year, without changes to any other part of our lives. Lack of sleep makes us feel old and we look it too, as human growth hormone (HGH) is released during deep sleep.

In general, women make sleep more of a priority, sleeping about 30 minutes per night more than men. However, about half of all women experience problems sleeping during their menstrual cycle, and three-quarters throughout pregnancy. Many more experience terrible sleep during perimenopause, due to their hormones being on the move, as well as during menopause, due to hot flushes at night.

Our sleep patterns are hugely disrupted these days. Your to-do list dictates what time you go to bed, but your internal clock is what wakes you up or sends you to sleep. The Spanish have the world's latest bedtime, possibly because they still have a siesta in the middle of the day. We're biologically programmed to nap in the middle of the afternoon for somewhere between 10–20 minutes, to avoid entering the deeper levels of sleep which can leave us feeling groggy.

WHAT KEEPS US AWAKE?

Australians get to bed earlier than the rest of the seven billion plus people on the planet. Yet a long, sound sleep is often elusive for people with anxiety, autoimmune disorders, chronic pain and fatigue, as well as hormonal issues. What else is keeping us awake?

Cortisol, one of our stress hormones, naturally rises and falls throughout a 24-hour period. It is typically at its highest around 8am, peaking 40 minutes after waking. It's at its lowest between midnight and 4am, or three to five hours after getting to sleep. Both high and low cortisol levels can interrupt your sleep, and even more so for those with depleted adrenal glands. This is due to the connection between cortisol and melatonin, our sleep hormone.

Melatonin is made from serotonin, one of our feel-good hormones. We release it at night to help make us sleepy. Melatonin starts to be produced when the sun goes down around 9pm, depending on the time of year and where you live. Melatonin levels in the blood rise sharply, so theoretically you start to look forward to bedtime. Melatonin levels are supposed to stay elevated throughout the night, for about 12 hours. They fall back to their low daytime levels by about 9am.

However when the stress hormone cortisol is rising, melatonin declines and vice versa. So when your eyes are exposed to lights, your pineal gland (the tiny organ regulating hormones in your brain) won't secrete the melatonin you need for a good night's sleep, as it thinks it's daytime.

Basically, cortisol and melatonin can't exist together. Why would we want to fall asleep (melatonin), when we need to get moving and get through the day? We need cortisol to navigate our days, but hopefully not so much that we are stressed out.

PROMOTING SOUND SLEEP

If you've had a stressful day (or life) and every light in the house is on, sleep can seem impossible, even though you're exhausted. So around 8pm, dim your lights. Turn off all screens, as enough blue light is emitted from these devices to suppress your melatonin. You can also install blue light-blocking software, which automatically alters the colour temperature of your screen as the day goes on, pulling out the blue wavelengths as it gets late. On Apple computers, it's called Nightshift. Another option is to use amber-coloured glasses that block all blue light, available on Amazon for less than $10.

------- ------- ------- -------

Waking between 1am and 3am in a state of panic is not unusual
in cases of adrenal fatigue. This could be caused by a blood
sugar crash, low adrenal function, high cortisol or all three.

------- ------- ------- -------

To turn off our melatonin, we need to increase morning daylight, particularly bright, morning sunlight, which tells our body it's time to wake up and get going. Use a sunlamp on cloudy days, if necessary. If you are in relative darkness for most of the day, you won't produce enough melatonin to sleep properly at night.

Reducing stimulants like caffeine, cannabis, alcohol, nicotine, cacao and even maca may help. Addressing restless leg syndrome, insulin resistance, high blood pressure and cholesterol will help. Some medications (antidepressants and heart medications) may also keep us awake.

Interrupted night breathing (sleep apnoea) is the most common reason insomniacs seek help. This annoying and disruptive pattern affects 10% of middle-aged men and 5% of women, though the true figures are more like 30%. Partners are affected as well, of course.

Emotional stress, attempts at self-medication, eating or drinking too much in the evening, and late night screen time all contribute to terrible sleep. Before you turn to medications to help you sleep, try a few lifestyle changes, herbal medicine and specific supplements, and see how these help.

According to traditional Chinese medicine, the heart not only regulates the circulation of blood, it's also responsible for our consciousness, sleep, spirit, memory, and is where the mind is seated. So do whatever you need to find joy. Stop thinking, by bringing energy down to your heart or looking between your eyebrows (third eye). To meditate on your heart chakra, use music as the focus. I like using the apps *Chakra Balance Meditation* and *Insight Timer*.

If you want your sleep to improve, stick to a regular, daily schedule and create a relaxing bedtime routine. Have a regular time to shower or bathe. Pull down the blinds. Apply essential oils and set your room up for sleep. Exercise regularly and moderately, in the early morning if possible; the importance of exercise in getting a good night's sleep cannot be overstated. But try to avoid exercising late at night, as this will only increase your cortisol.

If your liver needs cleansing you can overheat, creating feelings of frustration, aggressive behaviour and insomnia. So avoid alcohol, tobacco, coffee, junk food, sugar and chemicals in your food and cosmetics, as they allow unresolved emotions to fester, by creating more heat and allowing those emotions to rise.

Eating a light dinner and avoiding TV snacks three hours before bed really helps prevent your body being busy digesting food, when it should be recharging. Your bedroom temperature should be on the cooler side; around 18°C is ideal for sleep. Try to have a bath an hour before bedtime because four hours after you fall asleep, your body's internal temperature drops to its lowest level. A warm bath increases your core body temperature; it then drops abruptly when you get out of the bath, signalling to your body that it's sleep time.

Avoid screens in your bedroom, let alone having them turned on at bedtime. Keep bedroom energy flowing and clear, by avoiding clutter and dirt. Check out the feng shui of your bedroom: ideally, your feet shouldn't face the door and your head should point north. A comfy bed and pillows (preferably made from organic materials) will aid slumber. A fan or another form of white noise may help to drown out distracting noises.

Cognitive behavioural therapy (CBT) helps people change their thoughts and behaviours around sleep and is often more effective than drugs.

Some foods sedate us, others are stimulating. Knowing a bit about food as medicine will help you make the right choices here. The amino acid tryptophan stimulates the production of serotonin which makes us sleepy, so include organic turkey or chicken, figs, dates, almonds, chocolate, yoghurt, goat milk or nut butters in your diet. Complex carbs such as butternut pumpkin, sweet potatoes, carrots and peas will also help with the production of serotonin, so include them in your evening meal. Magnesium relaxes the body and is found in green leafy vegetables, raw cacao, almonds, tofu, sesame seeds, sunflower seeds and oats. B vitamins also help calm our system and digestion and are abundant in spirulina, nuts, seeds, quinoa, avocado, sweet potato, most whole grains, organic meat, brewer's yeast and green leafy veggies. You'll especially need foods containing B12, from animal products or a supplement.

A lack of blood can cause insomnia, according to the ancient modality of traditional Chinese medicine, so include such blood-building foods as leafy greens, pumpkin, beetroot, kidney beans, coconut milk, chestnuts, and organic Chinese red dates. Chamomile has sedative effects that have helped millions sleep over the years. Sip a warm cup prior to bedtime, perhaps with a little honey or maple syrup, to help control your blood sugar overnight. Add dill or basil for their calming effect in your (light) evening meal, or have them as a tea before bed.

Avoid caffeine after midday, or avoid altogether if you are having difficulty sleeping. Caffeine lingers in our body, blocking the brain chemical adenosine that helps us sleep. Blood sugar issues can also make falling asleep a lost dream or wake us during the night. So avoid anything with refined sugar, especially in the evening. As fats take longer to digest, avoid heavy, fatty food before bed also. The amino acid tyramine stimulates the brain, so avoid potatoes, cheese, bacon, sugar, sausage, tomatoes and wine, especially close to bedtime. Avoid alcohol for at least two hours before bed, and drink sparingly. If possible, get organic, sulphur-free alcohol.

If you're still tossing and turning into the wee hours after implementing some of these changes, try these herbal medicines and supplements:

- *Chamomile.* Daily supplements improve daytime functioning and sleep.
- *Melatonin.* You can only get this on prescription in Australia, or else homeopathically from your health food store. It's best for short-term use only, as excessive supplementation can cause depression, insomnia, irritability and agitation.
- *Calcium and magnesium.* You'll see better results if you take these together (500 mg calcium/400 mg magnesium chelate or citrate).
- *Vitamin B12.* A deficiency can cause insomnia.
- *Magnesium.* Relieves restless leg syndrome, muscle pain and anxiety.

Herbal medicine is very effective when taken before sleep and in the morning, to nourish the adrenal glands and reduce anxiety. I make up a liquid blend for clients, using any four of these herbs: Californian poppy, chamomile, passionflower, Mexican valerian, skullcap or valerian root. Take 10ml an hour or so before bed, then another 10ml at bedtime. If you wake during the night, take another 5–10ml. You'll find these herbs in tablets, capsules, tea and tinctures at your health food store or online.

Essential oils are also very effective. Put a few drops of lavender in your diffuser by your bed at night, or rub a few drops into the back of your neck. Try a small drop on each brow or on your pillow or eye pillow. Have a lavender bath 60–90 minutes before bed. Rub 10–20 drops of lavender oil diluted in three tablespoons of carrier oil over your body, then get into a warm bath with one cup of Epsom salts for 20 minutes. After your bath, read in bed for 30 or so minutes before turning off the lights. Practising this ritual helps remind your body of its natural rhythms. Chamomile, cedar wood and valerian are also known to induce sleep. Dab a drop between your brow and one on each wrist (or big toe), or use a diffuser in your bedroom. You could also mix a couple of drops with one teaspoon of coconut or jojoba and rub on your chest.

Sleep blends are easy to find and buy online. Be sure to get quality therapeutic grade oils, **not** fragrant oils.

chapter twenty-six
DEALING WITH REFLUX

Reflux happens when the lower oesophageal sphincter, designed to prevent food from moving back up into the oesophagus (food pipe), is weakened or damaged. This can be caused by candida, emotional stress, fatty foods, SIBO, leaky gut, fructose malabsorption, weight gain, an imbalance in gut flora, smoking, too much alcohol, or if the oesophageal sphincter weakens with age. Prolonged use of antibiotics greatly contributes to acid reflux. Certain medications, including ibuprofen, aspirin, muscle relaxants and those for blood pressure can also cause acid reflux.

When there is prolonged inflammation and irritation, reflux is the result. Symptoms include feeling hoarse, a burning and irritated throat, nausea, coughing, wheezing, asthma-like symptoms, food getting stuck in the throat, hiccups and eroded tooth enamel. There could also be a hiatus hernia present, causing the stomach to push up into the oesophagus, allowing acid to creep up and a feeling of something being stuck in there, rather than a feeling of acid rising.

Antacids are commonly used to reduce symptoms, but prolonged use can lead to nutrient deficiencies and other health conditions. These proton pump inhibitors (PPI) are designed to stop the production of stomach acid, but in most cases acid reflux is caused by **underproduction** of acid. PPIs also come with side effects.

We **need** our stomach acid, as it protects us from dangerous bacteria, parasites and other microorganisms in our gut. Reflux should not be ignored or its symptoms suppressed, so try to work out what's causing it, and treat that.

Chronic reflux can put you at risk of Barrett's esophagus. In this condition, stomach acid damages the lining of the oesophagus and can lead to oesophageal cancer.

TREATING REFLUX

Avoid fatty (junk) foods as well as high acid fruits and vegetables, including pineapples, citrus, tomatoes and their sauces, and potentially garlic and onions. Introduce a few raw almonds a day, sauerkraut, beans, broccoli, cauliflower, lettuce, ginger, oats and healthy fats like avocado, walnuts, flaxseed, hemp and olive oil.

Mint and peppermint essential oils are really helpful here also. Rub a few drops on your chest where it hurts, or use naturally flavoured mint gum and mints. Improvement will also come with a healthy weight, mindful eating and not overeating.

Exercise regularly and meditate on your third (yellow) chakra at the solar plexus, as it supports digestion.

There are very effective natural alternatives to synthetic antacids. Betaine hydrochloride (HCL) with pepsin is available over the counter or online, and is brilliant for treating reflux. When you supplement your stomach acid, you're preparing the pancreas to produce its own enzymes (once again) and trigger the necessary bile secretion needed to properly digest your meal. Take one 650mg capsule with the first bite of your meal, or just before. If symptoms don't improve, increase the dose by half a tablet, and continue to do so until you feel 'pressure' in your stomach. In some cases, you may need three tablets. Cut back by half a tablet once you feel that pressure. You'll know you have the right dose when you feel no pressure or heartburn after eating. Plan on taking this HCL supplement from two weeks to several months, depending on how severe your symptoms are. You'll know acid production is increasing when the betaine HCL supplement can no longer be comfortably tolerated. At that time, wean yourself off it over a couple of weeks.

Digestive enzymes may be of benefit. Take them fifteen minutes before meals, and look for a vegan option. Slippery elm will reduce inflammation in your digestive tract by giving it a protective coating, It's available in capsule, powder or lozenge form. Take a multi-strained probiotic. Low magnesium levels can also lead to malfunctioning of the oesophageal sphincter that prevents acid from escaping. Aloe vera twice a day on an empty tummy will also work wonders.

Apple cider vinegar is wonderful for balancing the acid in our gut. Have one tablespoon in as much water as you need to make it palatable, or add raw honey to help the medicine go down.

My favourite herbs here are meadowsweet (a great antacid), ginger, chamomile, peppermint and barberry. Have them as either a tea or herbal supplement.

Essential oils to use are peppermint, ginger, turmeric and lemon. Add two drops of one oil to a cup of warm water and sip throughout the day. Or add it to a teaspoon of apple cider vinegar. Another option is to mix an oil with one teaspoon of a carrier oil and rub into your chest from your stomach to your throat. Rubbing this into your thoracic spine on your back will also help relax the often tight muscles there.

A great way to improve digestion after a meal is to kneel on the floor, with your calves under your hamstrings and your feet touching your bottom. You could always eat your meals like this, as the Japanese have traditionally done. (There are more centenarians in Japan than any other country!) It's not an easy pose for everyone at first, but gets easier the more you do it. Stay in the pose for at least five minutes after you eat.

chapter twenty-seven
NON-ALCOHOLIC FATTY LIVER DISEASE

Non-alcoholic fatty liver disease (NAFLD) is estimated to affect almost a third of adults in developed countries and is becoming increasingly common in Asia as well. I'm seeing a lot more people with raised liver enzymes, indicative of a fatty liver. The liver is our most important organ of detoxification. It's also responsible for fat metabolism and fat burning in the body, as well as proper digestion.

A 'fatty liver' is diagnosed when fat makes up more than 10% of the liver. This happens because the liver is unable to break down fat at its regular rate, so there's a fatty build-up in liver tissue. As more fat is continually being consumed, a backup results. This is an increasingly common condition in those who are overweight and over thirty, but is sadly affecting an increasing number of young children as well. It will become the number one reason for liver transplants, if left untreated.

Fatty liver is intimately entwined with obesity, diabetes, metabolic syndrome, high blood pressure and cirrhosis. The most promising treatments are correcting the diet, appropriate exercise and weight loss. Herbal medicine is also very helpful, as is appropriate vitamin supplementation. There is little evidence that any drug is effective in slowing down the progression of this disease.

There is no one way to treat fatty liver; it needs to be a wholistic approach, specific to each patient. If the cause is obesity, then reducing weight is key; if the issue is medication, then that has to be addressed; if high fructose corn syrup is the culprit, then it needs to go.

Excess fructose in the diet is possibly the leading cause of fatty liver. This is the sugar found in high-fructose corn syrup (HFCS), fruit juices, agave syrup, fake honey and most processed foods you'll find in your supermarket, even soy sauce and tomato sauce. Fructose behaves in a similar way to alcohol in the liver and can **only** be metabolised by this organ. This means that all fructose we consume ends up burdening our liver, in the same way alcohol and other toxic substances do.

Besides a poor diet high in fructose and long-term medication, other causes of NAFLD are: gastric bypass surgery, cancer therapy, chronic illness, high (bad) cholesterol, metabolic syndrome, polycystic ovarian syndrome, sleep apnoea, type 2 diabetes, underactive thyroid (hypothyroidism), and underactive pituitary gland (hypopituitarism).

There are three stages in the progression of fatty liver disease:

- *Non-alcoholic fatty liver.* This causes excess liver fat and is a very common condition.
- *Non-alcoholic steatohepatitis.* This occurs when excess liver fat causes inflammation in the liver. This reduces the liver's ability to function and leads to scarring of the liver (cirrhosis).
- *NAFLD-associated cirrhosis.* With time, scarring can become so severe that the liver no longer functions adequately (liver failure), necessitating a transplant.

PREVENTING AND TREATING NON-ALCOHOLIC FATTY LIVER DISEASE (NAFLD)

It is possible to completely regenerate the liver if this condition is caught early enough, before the scarring has done too much damage. The first thing is to clean up our diet to one low in processed foods (or none at all), especially those containing HFCS, alcohol, white flour, sugar, meat (especially processed), trans fats in takeaway food, and vegetable oils. A diet high in plant foods is essential to prevent and also treat NAFLD. Quality oils are essential, plus some fruit and lean protein if desired. Foods high in potassium like bananas and sweet potatoes are also helpful, but don't overeat them as they're high in sugars. Follow the 40-Day Reset Program.

Vitamin E deficiency may be linked to liver disease and fatty deposits, so it may be necessary to supplement with this vitamin. Medicinal herbs that contain berberine help reduce the build-up of fat in the liver and protect against NAFLD. These are herbs like barberry (my favourite here), phellodendron and Oregon grape. Nigella will really help control your appetite; turmeric has a positive effect on the liver, reduces inflammation and boosts immunity. Peppermint is extremely beneficial in 'cooling' down a hot liver, which you will have with NAFLD.

Ginger essential oil significantly reduces fat accumulation in the liver, and garlic essential oil protects the liver from further fat accumulation, inflammation, toxicity and metabolic disease. The liver loves peppermint, so this is a good oil to use here also. A castor oil pack is a great old remedy that has a really positive effect on our liver. See *Chapter 21, Excess Estrogen.*

A sedentary lifestyle is seriously bad for our health. Sitting too much, especially with our shoulders hunched, leaning over a desk. A quiet, slow, morning walk outdoors for half an hour is a perfect start to the day.

Man-made chemicals, particularly xenoestrogens like bisphenol A (BPA) and phthalates could contribute to fatty liver disease later in life, if exposure occurs shortly after birth. So avoid plastic, canned foods and drinks, and the docket you get after purchase at retail stores and ATMs. Eat organic food and use natural cleaning products and cosmetics. Drink fluoride and chlorine-free water at room temperature, and of course avoid soft drink and alcohol. *See Chapter 21, Excess Estrogen.*

Emotionally, the liver is associated with anger, resentment, frustration and a sense of being held back in life. It's important to deal with underlying, unresolved emotional issues (current or past) that trigger these feelings.

chapter twenty-eight
COULD YOU HAVE SIBO?

21st century health conditions are complex. Small intestine bacterial overgrowth (SIBO) is one of these recently named conditions I'm seeing a lot more of. It may be just the diagnosis you're looking for, after years of searching and terrible gut pain.

This was the case for me. After I figured out that SIBO was playing a huge part in my gut problems, I went to work figuring out the best way to treat it. Immediately I started treatment, I had a massive decrease in gut pain. I had been suffering for almost four years with the same intense symptoms. I thought it was candida, so dealt with that particular nuisance, but the symptoms remained. This continued until I had VEGA testing done, which confirmed the issue was with my stomach and small intestine and that it was a bacterial infection. Yep, SIBO alright.

It's thought that around 25% of the world's population have SIBO. It's the main reason for IBS (85% of the reason), and some suggest that up to 15% of 'healthy' people without symptoms have SIBO. It is largely underdiagnosed, because many don't seek medical attention and because many practitioners aren't aware of just how common SIBO is, or what it is.

SIBO is a chronic bacterial infection of the small intestine (SI), which is not supposed to be home to bacteria—the large intestine is.

When lots of bacteria do inhabit the SI, these little guys consume the nutrients the small intestine would otherwise absorb, causing us to become malnourished. The issue here is about the **location** of the bacteria, rather than the type of bacteria.

The breakdown of these bacteria can lead to gas, pain, bloating and constipation or diarrhoea. Proper digestion of food by stomach acid, pancreatic enzymes and enzymes found in the intestinal 'brush border' (fuzzy microscopic protrusions that aid in absorption, likened to the bristles of a paintbrush) breaks food down into particles small enough to be absorbed by our body. If this 'cleansing wave' or 'sweeping' isn't efficient, bacteria can easily take over in the small intestine, producing toxic secretions. If left untreated, it can cause long-term damage to our intestines.

The SI, which connects the stomach to the large intestine (LI), is approximately seven metres long. Although bacteria are normally present in the entire gastrointestinal tract, relatively few bacteria live in the SI. And the types of bacteria in the SI are different from those in the LI. The microbiome living our gut (parasites, yeast, bacteria and viruses) should be living in a happy balance. If they're out of balance, they interfere with how well we absorb and digest food, then they go on to damage the lining of our SI, which leads to leaky gut syndrome. *See Chapter 9, What You Need to Get About Your Gut.*

Bacterial overgrowth can produce lots of hydrogen and/or methane gas, not normally produced by us humans, as a result of carbohydrates fermenting in intestinal bacteria in our SI, causing flatulence, belching, pain, bloating, constipation and diarrhoea. So it's not actually **us** making those embarrassing noises and smells, it's the displaced bacteria living in us!

Larger particles of food that haven't been fully digested sit fermenting in the SI, then enter into our bloodstream through the damaged lining of our SI. This creates leaky gut which the immune system reacts to, as they shouldn't be there. There is now much evidence suggesting leaky gut syndrome is a major cause of autoimmune diseases.

The immune system treats these particles of fermented food as dangerous substances, causing food allergies and sensitivities, among other things. It's not just the larger, undigested particles that can leak out into the bloodstream, but the bacteria. When this happens the immune system gets very upset, causing chronic fatigue and intense 'all over' body pain. It also burdens an already overworked liver.

The act of chewing physically starts the breakdown of our food, then the enzymes are supposed to do the rest. But when larger particles of food aren't digested, only the very small molecules can be absorbed. SIBO can be the underlying cause (or after-effect) of many dis-eases.

How do we get SIBO? These days it's pretty easy, which is probably why so many of us have it. Common reasons include low stomach acid (reflux), irritable bowel syndrome, inflammatory bowel disease, previous bowel surgery, diabetes types 1 and 2, multiple courses of antibiotics, processed foods, any medication including the contraceptive pill, IUDs, steroids, and organ dysfunctions including liver cirrhosis, chronic pancreatitis and kidney failure. Of course, chronic stress plays havoc on our gut too.

One of the more common symptoms here is anxiety, which is twice as common as depression in SIBO sufferers. Then there's extreme abdominal bloating, pain and cramps. A feeling that food is stuck in your oesophagus. A tight, full feeling in your stomach, along with belching and flatulence. Constipation, diarrhoea or both. Heartburn/reflux (a burning sensation anywhere in your gut) is also commonly experienced, as is nausea, food sensitivities, headaches, joint and all-over body pain, crazy fatigue, new skin issues, mood and brain disorders, fatty stools, anaemia (iron or B12) and changes in weight.

DIAGNOSING SIBO

It's still early days, so diagnosing SIBO isn't always 100% accurate. The most common method of assessing SIBO is a hydrogen and methane breath test (these gases are produced by bacteria, not by humans), because it offers the most precise, detailed information, while being non-invasive and inexpensive. It measures these two gases on your breath, specifying which gases are present, as well as the location and severity of the SIBO. Many tests come back as 'false negatives', meaning the test results have come back negative but you actually do have SIBO. You can imagine how frustrating that is.

Testing can also be done by an endoscopy, but that involves a mild general anaesthetic and a tube down your throat into your small intestine. Neither a stool nor an organic acid test (OATS) is able to diagnose SIBO.

The following labs in Australia offer hydrogen/methane breath testing:
- SIBO Test (07) 3368 1300
- Gastrolab 1300 624 771
- Stream Diagnostics (03) 9890 2666

TREATING SIBO

Once you get a positive test result, what next? The lining of the small intestine needs to be healed. This will happen once the bacteria are reduced, when you take away their food source. The aim is to feed yourself, while starving the bacteria. Bacteria primarily eat carbo-hydrates, so you'll find all the recommended diets decrease these. The only carbohydrate that bacteria do not eat much of is insoluble fibre. *See Chapter 38, Understanding Fibre.*

There is so much conflicting information out there about what to eat for SIBO, often because we all have different symptoms. It's also likely you have other health issues going on, such as food sens-itivities, thyroid issues, adrenal fatigue, candida, hiatus hernia, leaky gut and estrogen dominance. I recommend following the 40-Day Reset Program, removing any of the foods you know you presently don't digest well. These will likely be high FODMAP (Fermentable

Oligosaccharides Disaccharides Monosaccharides and Polyoils) foods and those high in histamines, but not always.

Dietary treatments for SIBO should only be followed for two weeks after becoming symptom-free, depending on the severity of the infection. Many of the foods you'll be avoiding are healthy foods, so you'll want to get them back into your diet as soon as you can. The restrictions are about healing the SI, not changing your entire way of life, nor driving you and your family crazy.

SIBO can cause poor absorption of the nutrients you're consuming, particularly fat-soluble vitamins and iron, so you'll need to consider supplementation.

Oregano oil is very effective here as an antibiotic, but it can be a bit hard to take at first, potentially making you feel a bit queasy. And yes, you do taste and smell a bit like a pizza for the first few days, so take it easy to begin with. The recommended dosage varies, as this is a very strong medicine. Take 1–5 drops, 1–3 times a day. Be sure to mix with a little water or add to your herbal formula, and have after food. Work up to the maximum dose, if your body allows. Otherwise just stay at the level comfortable for you. If you find you can't tolerate even a drop of oregano oil right now, hold off taking it until after you finish the 40-Day Reset Program.

Slippery elm is a lovely mucilage that will help heal your entire gastrointestinal tract. Put one teaspoon in a little hot water to make a slurry, then drink 1–2 times a day to reduce inflammation in the gut. Aloe vera is another mucilage that will cool and coat the gut. It's also antiseptic, so will work on a number of levels. Drink 30mls morning and night on an empty stomach. Digestive enzymes are helpful to take before you eat, to aid in breaking up large particles of food. Don't forget to add B complex, preferably from a wholefood source or in powder form, to encourage absorption.

You may need a hit of vitamin B12, due to your decreased ability to absorb nutrients. Add a green superfood powder to your diet, one that contains microalgae like spirulina, chlorella, barley grass and wheatgrass. Put a teaspoon or two in your smoothie, to ensure you're getting adequate nutrition despite malabsorption. Plus, microalgae kill harmful, toxic organisms.

After a month of healing with the above herbs and supplements, take a multi-strained probiotic, meaning not just *Acidophilus* or *Bacteroides*, but a supplement containing many different bacteria. This is the **seeding** after the weeding (killing off the misplaced bacteria with diet, oregano oil and barberry). Supplement with a vitamin D spray if you are deficient.

You're going to need a few different actions from your herbal medicine now, to deal with your own individual symptoms of SIBO. An antacid will likely be needed, and my favourite is meadowsweet. A digestive tonic like chamomile, peppermint, kawakawa, fennel or ginger. Such herbs as skullcap, St. John's wort, withania or chamomile help ease anxiety and irritability. Antibacterials are essential here, to take the place of antibiotics; my favourites are any with berberine, a chemical found in herbs like Oregon grape, barberry and phellodendron.

Demulcent/mucilaginous herbs (licorice and marshmallow) are traditionally used to heal mucosal lining. However their use post-SIBO is controversial, as they could encourage bacterial regrowth. Add immune-boosting herbs like astragalus, holy basil or echinacea. There's withania, rhodiola, holy basil and reishi to help nourish your adrenal glands, and I always add a liver herb to my formulas, such as dandelion root, St. Mary's thistle, schisandra or burdock. A sample SIBO formula contains barberry, echinacea, skullcap, meadowsweet, withania, ginger and burdock.

Essential oils will help reduce the bacterial infection and associated symptoms more quickly. Ideally, we want to use those that help get our gut back into balance, while still protecting our beneficial bacteria. The essential oils caraway, lavender and bitter orange come out on top here. Lemon oil is also really helpful in reducing nausea, as is a combination of peppermint and ginger. Lavender is good for reducing emotional stress; ginger and chamomile for bloating; and peppermint for any gut issue at all.

Tarragon, frankincense and clove oils help reduce bloating and gas, as well as other digestive upsets. These 'hot' oils can burn your mouth and/or tummy, so put them in a veggie capsule first, or add a drop or two to a glass of water before a meal. Naturally, use only high-quality, food-grade essential oils.

When it comes to gut issues, we need to consider what's going on in our lives. As well as looking at what we're eating, drinking, thinking, feeling and doing, we need to look at who we're spending our time with. Surround yourself with people and practitioners who give you hope and support, not doom and gloom.

On average, it can take two years to properly heal from SIBO. So it's a good idea to treat this infection with a combination of diet and the remedies listed above. Don't give up! Reducing gut inflammation is vital, as is having adequate stomach acid and enzyme activity. *See Chapter 26, Dealing with Reflux.*

On the practical side, try to eat three smaller meals a day, 4–5 hours apart. However, don't wait that long between meals if you have blood sugar issues, are malnourished, have adrenal fatigue and/or are underweight. In these cases, eat 5–6 smaller meals a day to allow the food to be digested sooner, rather than having a big meal sitting in your gut fermenting. Good bacteria thrive on properly digested food, while undesirable bacteria thrive on undigested foods such as FODMAPs. (Foods that aren't absorbed in the small intestine, but continue down to the large intestine/colon.)

Overeating is one of the worst things you can do when you have SIBO. The 'cleansing wave' of the small intestine kicks in a few hours after eating and sweeps undigested food and bacteria from the stomach to the colon. These waves only occur when the body is **not** digesting, so eating often, grazing or snacking will decrease this process and promote growth of bacteria in the small intestine. It's important to drink lots of clean water, to stimulate the vagus nerve that connects our brain to our gut, as this aids proper digestion.

When it comes to exercise, try to practise ahimsa (non-violence). In other words, be nice to yourself. Movement should be gentle, focusing on mindfulness, stretching and opening the torso up, thereby relaxing the organs of digestion. Yoga is perfect for this, especially lying on the floor, with a bolster or rolled up towel under shoulder blades, arms stretched out. *See Chapter 7, Too Much Exercise?*

chapter twenty-nine
UNDERSTANDING AUTOIMMUNE ISSUES

Over millions of years we have been evolving as a species, as a result of interactions between our genes, our immune system, our diet and the environment. Over time, this process ensured that our bodies were as best suited as possible to our surroundings. But lately something has gone terribly wrong.

Autoimmunity occurs when our body attacks itself, when our immune system produces antibodies against our own tissue, organs and joints. This happens when it senses danger from ingesting, absorbing or inhaling an allergen, food, infection or toxin. Basically, if your immune system is in overdrive, it responds by attacking your joints, brain, thyroid, gut, skin and sometimes your whole body.

Autoimmune disorders (AID) occur almost exclusively in modern cities. You just don't see them in places without running water, flush toilets, antibacterial wipes, washing machines and concrete backyards. Statistics tell us you're far less likely to have an AID if you grew up on a farm with animals, getting dirty, and being exposed to bugs and infections.*

---

* Ege MJ, Bieli C, Frei R, van Strien RT, Riedler J, Ublagger E, Schram-Bijkerk D, Brunekreef B, van Hage M, Scheynius A, Pershagen G, Benz MR, Lauener R, von Mutius E, Braun-Fahrländer C; Parsifal Study team. 'Prenatal farm exposure is related to the expression of receptors of the innate immunity and to atopic sensitization in school-age children.' *J Allergy Clin Immunol.*, vol 117, no. 4 (April 2006):817-23.

------- ------- ------- -------

Since the 1950s, rates of multiple sclerosis, Crohn's disease, type 1 diabetes, and asthma have soared by 300% or more. Conversely, due to the introduction of vaccines, antiseptic wipes, antibiotics, and improved hygiene, the decline in the incidence of mumps, measles, tuberculosis, and other infectious diseases in developed countries mirror the increase in AIDs. Good-bye to one set of problems (infections), and hello to the incoming (compromised immunity). In the 1990s scientists began to suspect that these two trends might be connected, suggesting that perhaps the decline in infections was causing human immune systems to malfunction in some way.

------- ------- ------- -------

Over the past decade, a theory has gained support to the effect that if you're healthy, exposure to bacteria and viruses can serve as a 'natural vaccine', strengthening your immune system and providing long-lasting immunity against disease. The answer is not to eat food off the floor, but to eat food that has been grown in healthy soil that contains beneficial bacteria. This is incredibly important, as exposure to different microorganisms trains your immune system to recognise the difference between an invader and 'you'. Presently, in many cases, it's getting it wrong.

Autoimmune diseases include Hashimoto's disease, Graves' disease, rheumatoid arthritis, lupus, multiple sclerosis, inflammatory bowel disease, psoriasis, coeliac disease, and some of the many other hard-to-classify syndromes of the 21st century. Over a hundred distinct autoimmune diseases have been identified, and at least forty other diseases suspected of having an autoimmune component, such as endometriosis, fibromyalgia, chronic fatigue, Alzheimer's disease, and type 2 diabetes. Common symptoms include inflammation, musculoskeletal pain and fatigue.

More than 700 million people now have an AID—around one in ten people worldwide—putting it in the top ten causes of death in women and the elderly. Being female means your immune system is three times more sensitive than that of a male, making us three times more likely to get an AID. If you already have an autoimmune disease, you are three times more likely to get another.

Western medicine usually prescribes steroids and other immunosuppressants, because steroids suppress the immune system, which is usually overactive in autoimmune disease. The problem is that steroids suppress the **entire** immune system.

Autoimmune diseases like type 1 diabetes, IBS, MS and scleroderma are prevalent and still on the rise, and it looks like environmental factors, rather than genetics alone, are to blame.

Another (related) reason for the increasing rates of autoimmunity is thought to be intestinal permeability (leaky gut). About 80% of our immune system lies under the thin lining of our gut, which is like thin tissue paper. If this layer is permeated, the immune system becomes overexcited, thinking pretty much everything entering your body is dangerous, so it goes on the attack. Damage to the gut lining and leaky gut syndrome are considered pre-conditions for autoimmunity.

Removing these triggers can often lead symptoms to disappear, even if the mechanism for autoimmunity is still in the body. The main culprits are our pasteurised, irradiated and sterilised modern diet, environmental toxins, the overuse of antibiotics, hand sanitisers, antibacterial soaps, wet wipes, treated water and refrigeration, along with long-term stress, sleep deprivation and vitamin D deficiency.

TREATING AID SYMPTOMS

There's much we can do to help reduce AID symptoms. Once your symptoms start to reduce, then you'll find making changes to your diet, lifestyle and headspace so much easier. Leaky gut must also be healed at the same time. *See Chapter 9, What You Need to Get About Your Gut.*

Firstly, remove inflammatory foods during the 40-Day Reset Program, then slowly reintroduce (some of) them to see how they're affecting you. These include all junk and processed foods, also amines, sulphur, GM foods, palm oil, oxalates, processed dairy, gluten, grains, sugar and red meat. Start adding in prebiotic and probiotic foods, to improve your gut health and immunity; immune-boosting foods like garlic, shiitake mushrooms and organic red, green, yellow and orange veggies (but not nightshade initially); and vitamin D to control and prevent autoimmunity, by differentiating between dangerous invaders and 'you'. Include ethically-caught fatty fish, and 10–20 minutes of morning sunshine on your skin each day, of course.

The areas of your body affected will dictate what foods, herbs and supplements to take. What you will likely need is magnesium, which is found in cacao, dark leafy greens such as spinach and bok choy, and also in nuts, figs, fish, avocado and bananas. Zinc will help increase the production of white blood cells (immunity) and is found in oysters, alfalfa, pepitas and seafood. Don't forget omega-3 oils, found in hemp, chia and flax oils, fatty fish and sea vegetables, as they lower inflammation and help our immune system fight off pathogens (the bad guys). Yucca plant extract is thought to decrease stiffness and pain in muscles and is also used for skin/dermatology-related autoimmune diseases, internally and topically. Chlorella or spirulina are commonly used to ease lupus symptoms. Green tea contains polyphenolic compounds, which possess anti-inflammatory properties.

––––––– ––––––– ––––––– –––––––

Vitamin K2 is effective at reducing inflammation in the spinal cord, brain and immune system in MS sufferers. Natto, a Japanese condiment made from non-GMO fermented soybeans, is especially high in K2, as are fermented veggies.

––––––– ––––––– ––––––– –––––––

When it comes to effective supplementation, first try to get enough of the nutrients listed here from your diet, together with sunshine. If you're still deficient, consider a wholefood supplement. B vitamins help to control immune function, hormones, mood, sleep, nerves, circulation and digestion. Vitamin B12 is involved in white blood cell production. Vitamin C is proven to control autoimmune disease and allergy. Probiotics help calm down our immune response. Selenium has been shown to be essential for regulating extreme immune responses and chronic inflammation. Magnesium deficiency raises the overall level of inflammation in our bodies, contributing to autoimmunity. Vitamin D3, together with Vitamin K2, is effective for improving bone health, by helping our bones absorb calcium. Iron deficiency anaemia (IDA) is linked to autoimmune diseases, because ferritin (which helps store iron) is absorbed in the intestines. So if there's damage to the gut lining, iron will likely be low.

From the herbal medicine dispensary, I use echinacea, rehmannia, astragalus, sarsparilla and yarrow. You can get them made up into a formula, or as a tablet or powder. Remember that our whole self needs to be treated, not just the disease, so also include herbs that will address your individual symptoms.

Avoid essential oils that might boost your immune system, such as palmarosa, rosalina and thyme. Instead focus on oils to help relieve your symptoms, whether that's pain, swelling, emotional stress, insomnia, gut issues or any other symptom specific to you. To treat this dis-ease wholistically, we must address our day-to-day habits. Exercise is a natural anti-inflammatory, if we don't overdo it. Get enough time outside in the sun, preferably barefoot and on the earth. Ten minutes a day is usually enough for healthy vitamin D levels. Why not combine your exercise and time outdoors?

Stress worsens our immune response, so regularly practise some form of relaxation like meditation and deep abdominal breathing. Get a regular massage and/or facial. You need to sleep for at least eight hours at night and take a daytime nap. Try to have fun and remove as many toxins as you can from your life—diet, cosmetics, cleaning products, as well as toxic people and places!

By initially making a few small changes, and noticing the benefits from these, you'll be more likely to make significant changes in the future. Our bodies respond well to a balanced life and mind, so watch how quickly you start to improve. *See Chapter 21, Excess Estrogen.*

TESTING FOR AID

Testing options include:

- *For coeliac disease.* Get tested using either a stool test (not definitive) or endoscopy. Modern medicine will suggest you eat loads of gluten for three days prior to testing. This is counter-intuitive, and just plain dangerous!

- *For heavy metals.* You may have a toxicity, as mercury and other metals can cause autoimmunity. *See Chapter 54, Avoid Heavy Metals.*

- *For thyroid.* Have your antibodies tested, to see if there is autoimmunity present. *See Chapter 31, Understanding the Thyroid.*

- *For leaky gut.* This is a leading cause of autoimmune disorders, as it causes our immune system to overreact. If you suspect you have this, then treat it by following the 40-Day Reset Program.

chapter thirty

GETTING TO GRIPS WITH YOUR WEIGHT

Australia is ranked as one of the fattest nations in the developed world, just behind the US. The cost to our collective wellbeing has been estimated at $120 billion. For those of us who have struggled to keep our weight stable, it's hardly ever about money and so much more about our quality of life. If you are overweight, you are twice as likely to be depressed, and are at higher risk of suffering type 2 diabetes, non-alcoholic fatty liver disease, menstrual and fertility issues, heart disease, cancer and Alzheimer's. This is pretty shocking, and the fact that our girth is continuing to grow is even more of a concern.

I have struggled with my weight for as long as I can remember. This has shaped my life, professionally and personally. I have been on an absolute mission to find out why I gained weight literally by looking at food, while my sisters have never struggled with their weight. My diet and portions are healthy; I exercise and sleep well; I'm happy, healthy, fulfilled and grateful to live in the most beautiful part of the world where I can swim, fish, grow my own produce, meditate, keep bees, and be creative in nature. Despite much formal study and ongoing research, the reasons for my weight issues were a mystery to me until I discovered the undeniable connection between this and past trauma, current emotional stress, and our own individual gut microbiota. Mostly though, we're overweight because we eat too much crap food, and sit for too long in front of a screen. Often at the same time.

My interest in the gut, weight, immunity, hormones and mood are now hot topics in health care. But do we know more than we did ten years ago? The answer is 'yes', we do:

- We **don't keep weight off** if the loss has been achieved by **eating less short term**, because not only do we put all the weight we've lost back on, we gain 10%-30% more! How much more evidence do we need that eating less and moving more just doesn't work? While dieting, our body tries to compensate for the reduced calorie intake by shutting down various processes in order to survive; by reducing thyroid and reproductive function, for example. With anorexia nervosa, we grow a fine layer of hair over our entire body, to keep us warm.

- **When you eat** is another important factor in achieving a healthy weight. Unlike our grandparents, we've become used to snacking. By eating often, without regular fasting, our body forgets how to burn fat as a fuel. It has the food we've just eaten to use for fuel first, so the fat gets stored.

- **Low fat foods are not healthy.** Saturated fats are, in moderation. Grains are not healthy in excess, especially refined carbs like white grains and sugar. In the US, they have recently reversed nearly four decades of disease-causing nutritional advice by finally admitting that healthy dietary fats have no impact on cardiovascular disease risk. And that cholesterol in food has no impact on cholesterol in the blood. The old low-fat, high-carb recommendations were wrong, and have made too many of us very fat and very sick.

- **Our ancestor's lives affect our own.** One theory says that those of us who had ancestors living through leaner times store our calories, just in case we need them for when food is scarce again. This blends in nicely with the studies done on trans-generational trauma, and how up to three generations on, the descendants of victims of terrible trauma don't process emotional stress as well as others; instead, they become highly stressed with small stressors.

From this we can see how our emotions, and how we digest them, affect the way we digest and use our food.

Another interesting theory potentially explains why the leaner of us use only what we need for energy from the food we eat, then pass the rest, while the heavier of us use what we need then store the rest as fat. Our ancestors evolved to survive long winters with little food around. Longer winter nights mean more sleep, which means more leptin (a hormone telling us we're full) and less ghrelin (telling us we're hungry), both telling our brain it's time to burn those calories we stored during summer, when we had more food available to eat plus shorter nights. With less sleep, we have more ghrelin, making us want to eat everything in sight, storing those calories for the long winter ahead. Our problem is that **we don't have a scarcity of food** at any time of the year anymore.

The challenge for some of us is determining cause and effect. Which came first? The weight or unhealthy gut flora? Does a less than perfect microbiome due to a premature or traumatic birth, a lack of breastfeeding or a C-section set you up for obesity? Does eating a low-fibre junk food diet or taking too many antibiotics change our bacterial composition so much that we now eat and drink more of everything, and store what we don't use as fat?

Transferring the gut flora from an obese person into a lean mouse induced obesity in the lean mouse.* And then we saw that a long-term, high-fat diet given to rats saw major shifts in gut microbiota, causing weight gain and additional fat, plus changes to important hormones that regulate metabolism, such as insulin. There are 16

---

* Ellekilde, Merete and Ellika Selfjord, Christian S Larsen, Maja Jakesevic, Ida Rune, Britt Tranberg, Finn K Vogensen, Dennis S Nielsen, Martin I Bahl, Tine R Licht, Axel K Hansen, Camilla H F Hansen. 'Transfer of gut microbiota from lean and obese mice to antibiotic-treated mice' *Scientific Reports*, vol 4 (2014):5922

messenger chemicals or gut hormones that travel from your intestines to your brain telling you how much to eat. Genes will in part determine **when** we eat, as well as **what** we eat. *See Chapter 13, Digesting Emotions.*

Diversity in your diet helps maintain a healthy weight. The more species of food you have in your microbiome, the more nutrients they'll get out of that food. This means you'll enjoy a stronger immune system with less chance of needing to go up a size with your jeans and bra next year.

The good news is our own personal microbiome can change relatively quickly, so a healthier lifestyle will improve intestinal health almost immediately, especially after eating processed foods. Eating a healthy diet of organic, unprocessed wholefoods, including lots of fibre, limiting alcohol and sugar, and getting enough exercise and sleep are all going to play a role in determining your weight. We also need to consider how much stress is (or was) in your life; the toxic chemicals you're exposed to in your internal and external environment; and how many medications you take or have taken.

Your gut microbiome changes when you lose weight, looking like that of a lean person. However, further studies (and lifestyle changes) are needed before we all start getting faecal transplants from a lean person with heaps of bacteroidetes to spare, or consider surgery. (Obese people had *more* firmicutes and *fewer* bacteroidetes, compared to normal-weight people.)

HUNGER HORMONES

Knowing you're putting on weight but finding yourself ravenous all the time (even after a big meal) and feeling just too exhausted and achy to exercise is a frightening state to be in. Many dis-ease states cause us to crave sweet, fatty and salty foods with high calories. These foods decrease cortisol, tricking us into feeling we're not in danger, so it's no wonder those potato chips, ice cream, brownies and wine look so appealing.

Wayward blood sugar, often caused by high cortisol levels, together with grehlin and leptin, the hormones in charge of our appetite, are most likely the causes of our never-ending hunger.

Grehlin is a hormone secreted in our stomach when it's empty, so we don't starve to death. We're like a bear coming out of hibernation. But today we're the most overfed people ever living. When we're asleep, our grehlin levels decrease because we don't need as much energy. However, those of us not sleeping enough end up with an excess of grehlin. At the same time it stops us burning calories, because it thinks we don't have enough. So sleep deprivation impacts on our weight, and also leads to an increase in stress hormones and a resistance to insulin, neither of which help us lose weight.

On the other hand, the hormone **leptin** (made by fat tissue) tells the brain we have enough fat. This helps to regulate our appetite and metabolism, as well as burn calories, by creating energy for our body to use.

When we don't get enough sleep our leptin is low, and our brain thinks we don't have enough energy for our needs; so it stores the calories we eat as fat for when we do need more energy. These hormones get all messed up once our adrenal hormones are out of whack, creating an insatiable appetite, especially late at night. At the same time **dopamine**, a hormone that stimulates pleasure and reward, wants sweet and salty foods. Dopamine also likes alcohol, and other things that (often pretend to) satisfy us.

––––––– ––––––– ––––––– –––––––

Leptin influences both the total amount of thyroid hormone released and how effectively we convert inactive T4 to the active T3. All of which dictate our weight and metabolism.

––––––– ––––––– ––––––– –––––––

LIFESTYLE CHANGES FOR WEIGHT LOSS

If you want to lose weight, make a decision to **eat a little bit less** by monitoring your portions, and leave around five hours between your last meal and the next. Then after your weight reduces, keep your portions at that size.

Regular exercise is a key component in weight loss. All activity is effective, but interval training (aka burst training) is the fastest way to promote fat loss (that's if you're not already exhausted or have adrenal fatigue). But remember, exercise alone will not help you drop the kilos, not without addressing your diet. They're more effective together than alone.

Avoid xenoestrogens. A theory gaining traction is that rising rates of obesity in humans are related to the increasing number of toxins and pollutants we're exposed to, through our environment and food. Try to leave 12–15 hours between your evening meal and breakfast. Meditate, to reduce stress. Prolonged stress hormones make us think we're in danger, so prompt us to hold onto every bit of fat we can. Stress does contribute to weight gain, and it makes it very hard to get it off. Maybe you're overeating to suppress a past emotional trauma? After all, high calorie foods do increase serotonin and dopamine, making you feel better temporarily. If this is the case, address the unresolved hurt first.

Besides tweaking your diet, **some supplements can be helpful.** Studies have shown that probiotics may help women lose weight. The same effect wasn't found for men.[*] Green tea extract (1,500mg daily) seems to increase our body's ability to burn energy; and chromium

---

[*] Marina Sanchez, Christian Darimont, Vicky Drapeau, Shahram Emady-Azar, Melissa Lepage, Enea Rezzonico, Catherine Ngom-Bru, Bernard Berger, Lionel Philippe, Corinne Ammon-Zuffrey, Patricia Leone, Genevieve Chevrier, Emmanuelle St-Amand, André Marette, Jean Doré and Angelo Tremblay. 'Effect of Lactobacillus rhamnosus CGMCC1.3724 supplementation on weight loss and maintenance in obese men and women.' *British Journal of Nutrition*, no. 1 (2013).

(500 mcg daily) helps reduce cravings for sweet foods and can maintain blood sugar control.

Eating and exercise will both increase cortisol levels, so at the end of the day you'll be tired but also wired, and finally feeling a little better than you have been all day. Remember that promise you made about going to bed early, and not eating or drinking anything naughty while bingeing on a Netflix series!

Like many, you probably thought losing weight was going on a diet—about exercising more and eating less for a period of time. Not anymore, and actually it never was. Nor was it about eating a low fat diet. Quite the opposite. Perhaps it's time we also consider how efficiently we digest emotions, feelings, information, and not just what goes into our mouth and onto our skin. What goes into your mouth does play a huge part in what numbers you see on the scales, but it's not the only part.

The bulk of your diet should come from high-fibre plant food, including some whole grains, lots of vegetables, nuts, seeds, and low-carb fruit. **Eat unprocessed wholefood**, meaning food in the most natural form you can find it. Ideally eat mostly whole, organic fresh produce, and organic animal products. Toxic chemicals from our modern diet create hormonal changes that lead to weight gain, so we really want to be eating and drinking less chemicals. *See Chapter 21, Excess Estrogen.*

Include lots of fibre, both soluble and insoluble, and eat a small amount of protein and fat with each meal, to help control your appetite. Most of your calories should really come from fat, but that's only going to be a small amount of food, as fat is very nutrient-dense. *See Chapter 38, Understanding Fibre; Chapter 52, Fats and Oils.*

Being overweight increases inflammation, so reduce weight by **including healthy fats** like wild salmon, hemp and flax seeds, avocado, olives, tahini, coconut and nuts. Getting enough healthy fats in your diet reduces (but doesn't eliminate) the need for carbohydrates to cover your energy needs. Coconut oil and coconut milk contain medium-chain fatty acid (MCFA) that your body can easily burn as fat, and are less likely to be stored compared to other fats. Coconut contains 20% MCFA, or you'll find 100% pure MCFA (called MCT) in the fridge of your health food store.

Don't forget to include seaweed in your diet a few times a week. The iodine in seaweed will give your thyroid and metabolism a boost, aiding weight loss.

Resistant starch, the new kid on the block when it comes healthy eating, appears to have several beneficial effects that may contribute to weight loss, including less blood sugar spikes after meals, less appetite, and decreased fat storage in fat cells. *See Chapter 49, Prebiotics.*

There is some confusion around what foods are good for us and which ones aren't, so I'm going to simplify it. There is no shortage of research linking excessive sugar consumption with obesity. Sugar and refined carbs tell our hormones not to use the fat for fuel, but to store it as fat. This 'sweet poison' feeds yeast, causing you to crave more sugar and carbs; it encourages 'bad' bacteria, creating a vicious cycle. And forget about artificial sweeteners, as we're likely to get sicker and heavier from them. One sugar-sweetened drink a day increases our chances of being overweight by 27% percent. Fruit juice has too much fructose, so avoid this too.

Processed and junk foods are masterfully designed with the golden ratio of sugar, fats and carbs (not found anywhere naturally in nature) to create the perfect obesity bomb, leaving you wanting more. Trans fats are very harmful, highly-refined oils that contribute to hormone imbalance, diabetes, heart disease and weight gain. *See Chapter 52, Fats and Oils.*

Refined carbohydrates like white bread, pastry, pasta and sugar need to be avoided also. They turn to sugar, leading to overeating and weight gain. Manage your carbohydrate intake, by following the 40-Day Reset Program. Aim to eat only 3–4 servings of whole grains a week, and for breakfast or lunch only.

The essential oils to use now are grapefruit and cinnamon, as they are the most effective in supporting weight loss and reducing hunger and cravings. Take two drops of grapefruit oil and one drop of cinnamon oil internally, while on the 40-Day Reset Program. Peppermint will relax your gut, helping proper digestion to take place, and that means weight loss. To reduce cortisol use lavender; to increase your mojo, so you'll want to get out and move your body, use orange, lemon, eucalyptus and grapefruit oils.

When I'm making up a formula for weight loss, I use something to control blood sugar like nigella or gymnema. I always add in a liver herb, like dandelion root, schisandra, burdock or St. Mary's thistle. Also the adaptogen rhodiola, as this adrenal herb can help with long-term fat loss by lowering cortisol and helping our body burn fat for energy. And something to help create a happy digestive environment, like chamomile, barberry, peppermint, ginger and/or kawakawa.

chapter thirty-one
UNDERSTANDING THE THYROID

There's been so much talk about the thyroid gland over the past few years that it's more than possible you're aware of this small, butterfly-shaped gland, located below the larynx at the base of the neck. The thyroid secretes hormones that regulate almost every process in our bodies, including our weight, growth and how we store energy. If it's not functioning properly, our overall health suffers. Far too many of us are currently dealing with long-term thyroid disorders, but many remain undiagnosed, often due to incorrect testing.

Our thyroids have taken a hit in recent times thanks to a lack of minerals in the soil (such as iodine and selenium); a diet of nutrient-deficient, highly processed foods grown with toxic chemicals; chronic stress; and environmental toxins.

Diagnosis can either be hypothyroidism (too little) or hyper-thyroidism (too much) hormone production:

Hypothyroidism (not enough thyroid hormone) can lead to feeling sluggish, depressed, thinning or coarse hair, weight gain, constipation, lack of concentration, dry skin, muscle pains, cramping, fluid retention and sensitivity to cold. Hypothyroidism isn't always caused by lack of iodine, as was once thought. If you're taking iodine or kelp and feel like you're getting worse, make sure you get all four hormone levels (T4, T3, T2, T1) rechecked. *See Testing and Diagnosis* later in this chapter.

Hyperthyroidism (too much thyroid hormone) may lead to unexplained weight loss, sleeping difficulties, increased heart rate, sensitivity to heat, irritability, nervousness or anxiety and diarrhoea. According to the American Thyroid Association, the number one cause of hyperthyroidism is Graves' disease. However, lumps on the thyroid or taking too much T4 in tablet form can also contribute to hyperthyroidism.

Women are ten times more likely to have a thyroid problem. These conditions are not too difficult to treat and a full recovery is possible with a few changes to lifestyle and mindset. But if an autoimmune disease is causing the issue, it's not so easy to get on top of. These are Hashimoto's disease (thyroid is underactive) and Graves' disease (thyroid is overactive).

The function of our thyroid begins with the hypothalamus, the part of our brain responsible for overseeing the level of thyroid hormones in our body. It releases thyrotropin-releasing hormone (TRH), which stimulates the pituitary gland to produce thyroid-stimulating hormone (TSH). In turn, TSH tells the thyroid gland to produce thyroid hormone T4 (thyroxine). We then need T4 to convert to thyroid hormone T3 (triodothyronine). The ratio of T4 to T3 is about 17:1.

TESTING AND DIAGNOSIS

If you're wanting to know how your thyroid is functioning, there is a standard TSH test ordered by your GP, but it won't give you a definitive answer to your thyroid question. Often TSH levels are found to be within 'normal' range, but health issues continue undetected. Prescriptions are often antidepressants, the pill or hormone replacement therapy.

You may need to insist thyroid tests are done, as many mainstream doctors don't see them as necessary. If your GP won't order these tests, find a good naturopath or an empathetic 'integrative' or 'functional' GP.

Remember that medications like corticosteroids, aspirin and lithium can interfere with your result, as can a recent X-ray that used iodine dye, or other radioactive tests. Pregnant women in their first trimester also need to ask questions about the right timing to have their TSH tested.

The seven tests you need to ask for are:

- *Thyroid-stimulating hormone (TSH)*. TSH goes up when thyroid function is low. The ideal level for TSH is between 0.3 and 2.5 milli-international units per litre. The higher your level of TSH, the higher the likelihood that you have hypothyroidism.

- *T3*. The majority of thyroid hormones produced by our thyroid gland are T4, however T3 is the most useable form, so the conversion of T4 to T3 is vital. Your T3 level should be between 240 and 450 picograms per decilitre. T3 levels suffer from chronic stress, poor diet, toxic body, allergens and infections.

- *Free T3 (fT3)*. FT3 is the amount of T3 that is not bound by globulins, proteins that carry the thyroid hormones to tissues in the body. When T3 is 'bound up' it can't be helpful, so we'll probably end up feeling the effects of low thyroid function or hypothyroidism. Conversely, if our body doesn't bind enough T3, we will experience symptoms of hyperthyroidism. Free T3 levels should be between 2.0–4.4 pg/ml. It's better in the top half of the normal range.

- *Free T4 (fT4)*. This tests for the active form of thyroxine, a more accurate reflection of our thyroid hormone function. In most cases, it has replaced the 'total T4 test'. It's used to detect too much or too little thyroid hormone (hyperthyroidism and hypothyroidism). The normal level of Free T4 is between 0.9 and 1.8 nanograms per decilitre (ng/dl), and of Total T4 is 4.6–12 micrograms per decilitre (ug/dl).

- *Reverse T3 (RT3)*. In some cases, the body conserves energy by converting T4 into RT3, an inactive form of T3. Elevated RT3 can be triggered by adrenal fatigue, chronic emotional stress, a long-term disease or short-term illness, low ferritin (stored iron) levels and injury. RT3 can also become elevated in response to heavy metal toxicity; in such cases, treatment must include detox, using 'chelation therapy'. Reverse T3 has no thyroid action except that it binds to T3 receptors, blocking the action of T3. The normal RT3 range is 1.06 to 2.2. Keep in the lower half of normal range.

- *Thyroid antibody test.* This looks for antibodies and anti-thyro-globulin antibodies to determine if your body is attacking your thyroid, as in cases of an autoimmune disease like Hashimoto's or Graves' disease. This is rarely automatically tested.
- *Thyrotropin releasing hormone (TRH).* This test helps identify a rarer hypothyroidism, caused by a problem with the pituitary gland. This 'basal body temperature' test helps give an indication of what our thyroid is up to, but is not definitive.

Reduced thyroid function often shows up in variations in our body temperature. If your average temperature over three days is less than 36.6°C (97.8°F), it could be that your thyroid is underactive. On the flip side, if it's consistently above 37°C (98.6°F), this could indicate an overactive thyroid. It's important to know that our body temperature changes slightly at certain times of the month, so avoid taking your temperature when you're menstruating or ovulating. Other factors such as alcohol, illness, a bad night's sleep and stress can also interfere with the readings.

CAUSES AND SYMPTOMS

A number of factors can cause thyroid dysfunction. A deficiency in iodine, selenium or zinc, the three key nutrients that support thyroid function, along with poor diet, emotional stress and dodgy gut health. Some medications can impact on the thyroid, like those often used to manage autoimmune disorders, cancer, surgery, mental disorders or heart disease. Environmental toxins and sleep issues are another cause of thyroid dysfunction. Problems can also be due to a genetic pituitary disorder, or a lack of the pituitary gland. Occasionally during pregnancy, women produce high levels of thyroid hormones; this is known as postpartum thyroiditis and usually disappears after giving birth.

Menopause can also affect our thyroid function. For 20% of women, menopause is associated with hypothyroid symptoms, so managing symptoms during this change of life is important for a healthy thyroid, and easier transition. *See Chapter 24, Menopause Doesn't Have to Be Hard.*

Many thyroid symptoms are the same as other diseases, which is why your health will start to improve when you find an experienced natural health practitioner or integrative GP or by following my guidelines outlined in this book. Some issues may include dry skin, hair loss (including the outer third of your eyebrows and/or eyelashes), dry/lifeless hair, fatigue (particularly in the morning or all-day lethargy), goitre (enlarged thyroid), sensitivity to cold, brittle/ridged fingernails, depression or moodiness, constipation or not eliminating properly, sleep problems, headaches, muscle and joint pain, fluid retention and/or swollen ankles, trouble losing weight, high cholesterol, tingling in your hands or feet, brain fog, slow reflexes, trouble falling pregnant or holding a pregnancy, issues with your moon cycle, a slow heart rate of less than 60 beats per minute, difficulty swallowing and a swollen tongue.

REGAINING AND MAINTAINING A HEALTHY THYROID

The good news is that there are many things we can do to maintain and regain a healthy thyroid gland. Iodine is essential for the production of thyroid hormones, which in turn are important for normal growth and development. I hear a lot about supplementation, but not much about chemicals called halogens (fluorine, chlorine, bromine, iodine and astatine), which can displace iodine in your thyroid gland. These chemicals need to be removed before iodine can be absorbed and do its work. Be guided by a natural health professional if you're on thyroid medication or have hyperthyroidism, as most people haven't been deficient in iodine since the Western world started adding iodine to salt. *See Chapter 58, Bromines.*

We're now seeing an increased prevalence of Hashimoto's disease (autoimmune thyroid disease), recognised as somewhat due to adding iodine to table salt. Have your levels checked before including more iodine-rich foods. If your levels are low, include more oysters, spirulina, all sea veggies, Himalayan salt, cranberries, organic yoghurt, navy beans, potatoes and strawberries in your diet. If you're on a supplement, the recommended dietary allowances (RDAs) are 150ug/day for adults, 220ug for pregnant women and 270ug during lactation.

Selenium is another important mineral when it comes to iodine, as it converts T4 (inactive thyroid hormone) to T3 (active). Some of the best sources are Brazil nuts, wild salmon, sunflower seeds, organic beef, poultry, game products, mushrooms and onions. Soil concentration of selenium varies widely and affects the levels in plant food. As Australian soils are known to be selenium deficient, consider a supplement if your levels are very low.

The third important mineral for thyroid health is zinc. Include oysters, mushrooms, pepitas and organic red meat in your diet. If you decide to use a supplement, take it away from foods containing phytic acid (nuts, seeds, grains, legumes and beans). Perhaps leave it by your bed and take it before you go to sleep.

We also need to be getting enough healthy fats and oils in our diet for good thyroid health. Fibre again is essential here. Aim to include 30–40g/day. Fermented foods will reduce the amount of environmental toxins you'll absorb, which will help maintain a healthy thyroid (but avoid these if you have a histamine intolerance). *See Chapter 51, Fermented Foods.*

Eat a low-carb diet, to reduce estrogen that can negatively affect our thyroid. Coconut oil will help raise the basal body temperature, which is important for those of us dealing with low thyroid function.

Avoid gluten and A1 casein, as these are the most common allergens and can cause leaky gut, which in turn will cause inflammation of the thyroid. *See Chapter 44, Is Dairy Good for You?*

As is always the case, avoid GM foods, as they can send signals to the body to create antibodies to rid it of the invader. This is a chronic inflammatory response that interferes with thyroid function.

Too much soy in your diet may inhibit thyroid hormone absorption, though we're not entirely sure about this yet. So you can either eliminate it altogether, or limit it to organic fermented soy a few times a week. Never include processed forms of soy like shakes, powders, bars, soy milk and isoflavins.

There are a few supplements to consider for the health of your thyroid. High selenium yeast has recently emerged as the preferred option for selenium supplementation, because it is natural and contains a wide range of organically bound selenium-rich proteins. It's important to note that selenium may be toxic in high doses, so adults should take no more than 150mcg daily. Take it in the morning on an empty tummy, and with vitamin E (if you're not on blood-thinning medication) for better results. And if you're also dealing with candida, consuming yeast is rarely a good idea.

Our thyroid loves iodine, but as with most things, the dosage needs to be right. So before you start eating loads of seaweed, have your iodine levels checked. Be sure you get the right dosage for you, otherwise you could be soon dealing with hyperthyroidism. If you do decide to supplement, only take 250mcg per day and monitor your levels regularly.

Many people with hypothyroidism don't produce enough hydrochloric acid (HCL) in the stomach, which in turn can cause a wide range of nutrient deficiencies, including iron. Supplement if you have symptoms of GERD (gastroesophageal reflux disease). *See Chapter 26, Dealing With Reflux.*

Omega-3 oils are good for increasing the uptake of thyroid hormones, and they also fight inflammation and increase immunity. Be sure to get an ethical source of sustainable fish oil, or get the vegan type that contains ALA and GLA oils. Dosage is 3g/day. A deficiency in vitamin D has been consistently linked to an increased risk of autoimmune disease. This vitamin is important, because it drives thyroid hormones into your cell nucleus, where they're needed. Keep your level above 52, but it's much better to have levels of 70–90. If you need a supplement, look for a combination of vitamin D3 and vitamin K2.

To improve thyroid function by balancing our hormones naturally while supporting metabolism, B vitamins are essential. They also help to treat accompanying conditions such as chronic fatigue, chronic stress and digestive issues.

The herbal medicines to use here are withania and holy basil, both known to lower cortisol levels and improve thyroid function. Withania helps both hypothyroid and hyperthyroid conditions. You'll also need herbs to deal with individual symptoms like insomnia, anxiety, digestive problems, weight issues, emotional stress and blood sugar issues.

For an underactive thyroid use essential oils with stimulating properties; use spearmint, lemongrass, peppermint, clove, frankincense, myrrh, cedarwood and rose geranium. For an overactive thyroid, use oils with sedating and calming properties. Any blue (especially midnight blue) oil will be good here, as that's the colour of the throat chakra; use wintergreen, lemongrass, sandalwood, frankincense, myrrh and black spruce.

You could make a blend with 3–5 drops of each of the first four oils below, and mix with a base oil such as rosehip, jojoba or coconut oil. Put in a vaporiser or a bath, or pour it into a rollerball bottle. Apply topically to the base of the neck where your thyroid is, tracing the infinity sign (horizontal figure 8) every morning, or whenever you feel like you need it. You can also roll it onto the reflexology point for your thyroid, which is located at the base of the foot in the fleshy area below the big toe.

The following essential oils support thyroid function:

- Geranium supports adrenals and brings on a good mood.
- Lemongrass is relaxing and supports thyroid health.
- Peppermint reduces inflammation.
- Frankincense balances hormones and is anti-inflammatory.
- Turmeric, black pepper, bergamot, lemongrass, coriander and frankincense reduce inflammation and encourage detoxification.

Adrenal fatigue is usually present with thyroid issues, so the way you handle stress has a direct effect on these two glands. When any stress becomes long-lasting, the flood of stress chemicals produced by your adrenal glands interferes with your thyroid hormones, contributing to such health issues as obesity, high blood pressure, high cholesterol, and wayward blood sugar levels. Cortisol that is either higher or lower than normal can negatively influence your thyroid functioning.

------- ------- ------- -------

When it comes to sleepless nights, remember that our thyroid's hormone production is dependent on several hormones, in particular the right amount of cortisol, melatonin and growth hormone. In other words, sleep more, stress less and vice versa.

------- ------- ------- -------

Avoid perfluorinated chemicals (PFCs), commonly used to manufacture fabrics, carpets, cosmetics and paper coatings, as these chemicals break down very slowly and take a long time to leave the body, causing changes in thyroid function.

Heavy metals from amalgam fillings and vaccines have an affinity for the thyroid and can disrupt your hormone balance and thyroid function. Remove leaking amalgam fillings, but seek out a wholistic dentist who uses the 'rubber dam' protocol for safe removal of your amalgams, and can guide you through a proper detox program as well.

Use herbal medicine like St. Mary's thistle, turmeric and dandelion root, along with chlorella, and eat heaps of coriander to aid their detox. *See Chapter 54, Avoid Heavy Metals.*

Clean water helps your metabolism function more efficiently. It can help reduce appetite, water retention and bloating; improve digestion and elimination; and combat constipation. If you find it difficult drinking plain water, add a squeeze of fresh lemon or some liquid chlorophyll.

Try to keep your blood sugar balanced for good thyroid health. Being out of breath is often a symptom associated with low ferritin levels and thyroid function, so check serum ferritin (your body's storage of iron). Levels should ideally be between 70–90. This is not usually a problem after menopause, due to decreased blood loss. Also manage gut issues like SIBO, reflux, fructose malabsorption, candida and leaky gut, as they can all contribute to poor functioning of the thyroid, as can our blood sugar levels. Something many of us don't realise is that a hiatus hernia is connected to Hashimoto's disease, so treat this too if present.

Exercise directly stimulates our thyroid gland to secrete more thyroid hormone; it also increases the sensitivity of all our tissues to thyroid hormone, so it's important to have a regular routine, preferably outdoors. Activities like walking your dog in the park or a brisk walk or jog in the morning are enough, incorporating strength training and other core-building routines. It doesn't have to be extreme—on the contrary. Yoga works on the body, spirit and mind to improve adaptability and strength, creates core stability, builds an increased sense of positive thinking, is extraordinarily relaxing and revives your whole being.

While you're in the park, why not sit under a beautiful tree and meditate? It slows down biological ageing, (both being under the tree **and** observing your thoughts), and the even better news is that beginners enjoy the benefits too. If you find this way too difficult at the moment, then listen to some healing music especially designed to work on your throat chakra. There are plenty of apps that can help you with this.

Take your thyroid meds at night before bed, to increase absorption. Keep them away from caffeine. Always wait 30–60 minutes after eating or drinking, or after taking a supplement of calcium, magnesium or iron.

chapter thirty-two
SUPPORTING YOURSELF THROUGH CANCER

Sooner or later, cancer seems to touch someone in our lives. Western medicine offers drugs that have brought hope but some concerns, in terms of their wider effect on the patient's health. One issue is that these drugs don't address the underlying causes of cancer; also the damage done to healthy cells while destroying the cancerous ones is of massive concern.

More and more we have come to understand that the cause of cancer is complex and that genes don't have a big part to play in whether we get cancer or not. Rather, it's looking like the cause is anything that puts us into an acidic or inflammatory state for too long, thereby decreasing oxygen in the body. In other words, anything that causes stress in our system.

In 1924, Otto Warburg was awarded a Nobel Prize for discovering that 'low oxygen was characteristic of cancer cells'. *Cancer Metab.* 2016; 4: 5. In his later years, he suggested 'prolonged exposure to toxins, especially in combination with cells that haven't been properly nourished, oxygenated, hydrated and cleansed is **the** primary cause of cancer. Over time, the stress and inflammation that result from a toxic build up leads to a dysfunction in the cellular mitochondria.' Meaning, prolonged inflammation can damage our body, weakening its immune system and setting up the right acidic environment for cancer (and other diseases) to thrive. Obesity, emotional stress, long-term illness, poor diet, environmental toxins, overexercising, lack of sleep, pollution, smoking, and lack of movement all contribute to this.

Warburg became convinced that illness resulted from pollution. Half a century earlier, this had been suggested by the great French scientist, Antoine Bechamp, who believed that illness is the result of a combination of toxins *and* an unhealthy terrain. Germs (microbes) have no influence on healthy cells. The condition of the host organism (us) is the primary cause of disease. Disease is built by unhealthy conditions. To prevent and heal disease we have to create health.

We do not catch diseases. We build them.

ANTOINE BECHAMP (1814–1908)

BOOSTING THE IMMUNE SYSTEM

To give our immune system a boost, it's vital we eat an organic diet including garlic, mushrooms, ginger, oysters, paw paw, kale, wild Alaskan salmon, anchovies and sardines; lots of broccoli and cabbage plus foods rich in vitamin C. Add in a microalgae like spirulina or chlorella, and herbal medicine such as echinacea, reishi, cordyceps, astragalus, holy basil and turmeric. Make sure you have enough vitamin D by getting out in the sun. Eat fermented foods. Work less. Love more. Judge less. Have a purpose. Connect with others. Be of service.

At least two-thirds of your plate should consist of clean (organic), plant-based foods. Limit processed foods by including whole, fresh foods. Limit red meat and avoid processed meats, such as deli meats, bacon, sausage, hot dogs and pepperoni, as they are known carcinogens. If you eat meat, buy organic, grass fed meat only. However, replace some of the red meat you eat with wild fish and organic chicken, pulses and hemp seeds, which are lower in protein.

Our gut bacteria may be one of the most important factors determining our health and longevity, so encourage the growth of 'good' bacteria in your gut by feeding it fibre and fermented foods (if there isn't a histamine intolerance present), and by reducing sugar, chemicals and emotional stress. *See Chapter 9, What You Need to Get About Your Gut.*

Cancer cells are fuelled by burning sugar, so avoid it altogether. Avoid soft drinks, sport drinks and other sugary beverages (including fruit juices) as these contain too much sugar. Without sugar, most cancer cells won't survive.

The beneficial bacteria in fermented foods are particularly effective for suppressing colon cancer, but may also inhibit cancers of the breast, liver, small intestine and other organs. Fermented foods using raw milk containing *Lactobacillus* and *Bifidobacterium* are especially helpful for a couple of reasons: they increase carbohydrate metabolism and remove toxins such as bisphenol A (BPA) and others. *See Chapter 21, Excess Estrogen.*

The *Lactobacillus* strains bind to and excrete heavy metals from the body. Indeed, fermented foods have been shown to reduce the toxicity of heterocyclic aromatic amines (HCA), the cancer-causing compounds in charred meats.[*] *See Chapter 56, Red Meat.*

Kimchi (a Korean condiment made from fermented cabbage) contains probiotics shown to help detoxify pesticides and break down nitrates, a food preservative associated with increased cancer risk.[†] *See Chapter 51, Fermented Foods.*

Butyrate, a short-chain fatty acid created when microbes ferment fibre in the gut, has been shown to destroy colon cancer cells. The Commonwealth Medical College, Pennsylvania; Michael Bordonaro *See Chapter 41, Butyrate.*

And when it comes to fat in the diet, you basically need to balance your omega-3 and omega-6 ratio, by reducing the amount of omega-6 you're eating. Omega-6 is found in hydrogenated oils, as well as processed and packaged food. These oils destroy the membranes of

---

[*] Stidl, Reinhard et al. 'Binding of Heterocyclic Aromatic Amines by Lactic Acid Bacteria: Results of a Comprehensive Screening Trial.' *Molecular nutrition & food research* 52.3 (2008): 322–329.

[†] Park, Kun-Young et al. 'Health Benefits of Kimchi (Korean Fermented Vegetables) as a Probiotic Food.' *Journal of Medicinal Food* 17.1 (2014): 6–20.

our cells, causing inflammation and toxicity in our body. Replacing these toxic oils with healthy unsaturated/saturated fatty acids gives our cells a chance to heal. At the same time, increase your omega-3 intake by including more flax oil, fatty fish low in mercury and other contaminants, such as wild-caught Alaskan salmon, anchovies and sardines, mackerel, hemp seeds, walnuts, seaweeds and chia seeds. Essential fatty acids (EFAs) from avocados are rich in cancer-fighting antioxidants as well. *See Chapter 52, Fats and Oils.*

Vegetable juicing is recommended as a good way to get concentrated nutrients delivered to our body, without relying too much on our digestion to do all the work. Without fibre to digest, the nutrients can go straight to work. I recommended you include only vegetable juice, as fruit will provide too much fructose (sugar). Aim for one cup of juice (200ml) four times a day between meals. Have a green juice once a day and a coloured juice the other three times. For green juice, include assorted green leafy veggies like endive, lettuce and spinach. Add some cabbage, celery, mint, cucumber, rocket, parsley, dandelion leaves (if around), coriander and green capsicum. Fill half a glass with this juice, then top up with clean water. Add one teaspoon of a 'green' powder that has a combination of spirulina, chlorella, wheatgrass and barley grass. For the other three glasses, juice a combo of carrot, beetroot, red cabbage, red capsicum, celery, ginger, turmeric, mint and parsley. If you use a cold-pressed juicer, you can make enough to last for 72 hours, as the enzymes will stay intact that long after juicing. Use the pulp to make veggie patties.

Fat-soluble vitamin D may be a highly effective way to help prevent cancer. Your vitamin D3 levels should be at least 40–60 ng/ml, better still if they're closer to 75 ng/ml. Aim to get 20 minutes of sun exposure every day. This is best done by exposing 40% of your body to the sun between 10am and 2pm. If your levels are really low, consider taking a supplement containing around 5,000–10,000 IU of vitamin D3 daily. Try to get D3 with K2 as a spray, in a fat-soluble oil.

Turmeric (more specifically curcumin, the active constituent in turmeric) has been widely researched, especially when it comes to cancer. Wungki Park, A.R.M Ruhul Amin, Zhuo Georgia Chen, and Dong M. Shin It seems to be able to fight cancer cells and prevent more from growing, and is most effective against breast, bowel, stomach and skin cancer cells. A combined treatment of curcumin with chemotherapy may eliminate more bowel cancer cells than chemotherapy alone.

Traditional Chinese medicine has long known the value of medicinal mushrooms, and now science is catching up. Look for cordyceps, reishi, lion's mane and shiitake in your health food shop or online, available as a herbal medicine or as a powder that you can add to smoothies. Research on cordyceps and reishi in particular shows they help to shrink tumours, boost immunity and reduce side effects of radiotherapy and chemotherapy, such as nausea and hair loss. Shiitake mushrooms are also known to be of great benefit to our immunity, so add these to your meals often. PDQ Integrative, Alternative, and Complementary Therapies Editorial Board.

We frequently hear that we should add protein powders to our smoothies and eat protein with every meal. But we are all eating way too much, and this can have a great impact on cancer growth. Consider at least reducing your protein levels to one gram per kilogram of lean body weight (unless you are an extreme athlete or pregnant). *See Chapter 56, Red Meat (mTOR pathway).*

In 2015, the cancer research arm of the World Health Organization (WHO) reported that glyphosate, the world's most widely used herbicide, is 'probably carcinogenic to humans'.* According to the American Cancer Society, more research is needed to assess the potential long-term health effects of genetically-modified foods. So avoid this toxin

---

* Kogevinas, Manolis. 'Probable Carcinogenicity of Glyphosate.' *British Medical Journal (Clinical research ed.),* no. 365 (April 8, 2019): 1613.

and the GM crops they use it on, by eating organically or locally grown spray-free produce. *See Chapter 57, GM Foods.*

Probiotic supplementation may stop tumour growth. Considering its effect on our immune system, that makes sense. It will also improve digestion and help heal a leaky gut, which we know are other ways to prevent and heal from cancer. *See Chapter 50, Probiotics.*

Enzymes are necessary for most healthy cells to function properly. In the 1920s, Otto Warburg discovered that cancer is caused by a defect in this functioning, caused by enzyme deficiency.[*]

There are three types of beneficial enzymes:

1. **Digestive** enzymes break down food and eliminate waste.
2. **Metabolic** enzymes are involved in energy production and detoxification, and help keep our cells healthy. Fasting is a good way of allowing metabolic enzyme production, while conserving our digestive enzymes.
3. **Food-based** enzymes are contained in raw, uncooked or unprocessed foods and/or supplements. For example, bromelain in pineapple and papain in papaya are beneficial enzymes for proper cellular function.

Astragalus, echinacea, barberry, cat's claw, reishi, cordyceps, pomegranate, skullcap, pau d'arco and St. Mary's thistle are the most effective herbal medicines when dealing with cancer. It's best to use practitioner-only grade herbs. I believe liquid is best, but not always palatable at first. Ask your naturopath or herbalist about these, or enquire in your health food store.

Frankincense essential oil is potentially effective in both cancer prevention and treatment. Rub Indian frankincense (*Boswellia serrata*) oil on your neck three times daily. Dilute in a carrier oil, if you have sensitive skin. You can also drink three drops in a glass of clean water, three times daily. Be sure to get therapeutic grade oil.

---

[*] Otto, Angela M. 'Warburg Effect(s)—a Biographical Sketch of Otto Warburg and His Impacts on Tumor Metabolism.' *Cancer & Metabolism*, vol 4, no. 4 (2016): 5.

To achieve optimum health, detoxify your body and your life. One way to do this is by vitamin C chelation—yet another way to remove toxic chemicals from the body. Chelation therapy grabs onto toxins and expels them, and appears to have an anti-inflammatory effect, destroying tumour cells. Ask your health practitioner about this.

Cancer cells cannot survive in high levels of oxygen, as that's far too alkaline a state for them to survive. This is where oxygen therapy and hyperbaric chambers can play a healing part. The air pressure inside a hyperbaric oxygen chamber is about 2.5 times greater than in our atmosphere, thereby carrying more blood to the organs and tissues in your body. Google to find your nearest hyperbaric oxygen chamber.

> *Deprive a cell of 35% of its oxygen for*
> *48 hours and it may become cancerous.*
>
> OTTO WARBURG,
> WINNER OF 1931 NOBEL PRIZE IN PHYSIOLOGY

Finding peace by reducing stress really should be top priority. It is so important to allow our body, mind and spirit to have time out, as stress puts us in an acidic state. Green juices or not, if you're highly stressed, you're healing will be prolonged or even thwarted. Twenty minutes of meditation a day is really key here. Twice a day is even better. Check out a local tai qi, qi gong or restorative (also called Hatha or yin) yoga class. Practise mindful walking, ocean bathing, dancing, charity work, no work, playing music, listening to music, enjoying a creative outlet, and deciding who stays in your life, or not. It's time for you and whatever makes you happy, as much as possible. Full stop!

chapter thirty-threee
ANXIETY AND DEPRESSION

The ability of disease-causing bacteria to influence behaviour has been recognised for decades. This means our gut bacteria can influence how prone to anxiety and depression we are. Strains of two bacteria, lactobacillus and bifidobacterium, reduce 'anxiety-like behaviour' in mice. Both of these microbes seem to be very important in the gut-brain axis, not least because studies have now also shown that certain microbes can activate the vagus nerve.[*] This pathway is possibly the most obvious physical representation of the mind-body connection; the main line of communication between the gut and the brain (liver, heart, stomach, lungs), and back again.

Gut bacteria produce neurotransmitters such as serotonin, dopamine and gamma-Aminobutyric Acid (GABA), all of which have a major role in our mood. For this reason antidepressants are designed to increase levels of these same compounds. Current evidence now shows that the microbiome is intertwined with the immune system, which itself influences mood and behaviour.[†]

---

[*] Javier A. Bravo, Paul Forsythe, Marianne V. Chew, Emily Escaravage, Hélène M. Savignac, Timothy G. Dinan, John Bienenstock, and John F. Cryan 'Ingestion of *Lactobacillus* strain regulates emotional behavior and central GABA receptor expression in a mouse via the vagus nerve.' PNAS September 20, 2011 108 (38) 16050-16055

[†] El Aidy, Sahar, Dinan, Timothy G, and Cryan, John F. 'Immune Modulation of the Brain-Gut-Microbe Axis.' *Frontiers in microbiology* 5 (2014): 146.

It's all very exciting stuff! And it gets even better. Gut bacteria also generate chemicals from the food we eat, that have been linked to reduced anxiety and depression. In particular, one called Butyrate, so it's worth include foods rich in this. *See Chapter 41 Butyrate*

People who have the best quality diet have the lowest risk of developing depression and anxiety. Foods containing omega 3 fatty acids help improve mood disorders and brain functioning. B complex vitamins are beneficial during anxiety and panic because they promote healthy nerve function, helping the body to manufacture brain chemicals such as serotonin, essential for the body to cope during times of stress. Magnesium rich foods are calming as they nourish the nervous system and help prevent anxiety, fear, nervousness, restlessness and irritability. Take before bed with calcium to help promote a restful sleep. Foods to include are pumpkin seeds, raw spinach, avocado, legumes, quinoa, nuts, brown rice and other whole grains, sea vegetables, bananas, organic dried fruit, dark chocolate. Zinc makes neurotransmitters, and an imbalance in these can cause symptoms of anxiety. Animal based foods like beef, lamb, oysters, and scallops are high in zinc, and plant-based sources include like pumpkin seeds, pecans and garlic. Calcium is a relaxing mineral, which can help reduce anxiety. Try unsweetened organic yogurt, almonds, sea veggies and wild-caught salmon as good sources. If you're having trouble getting enough of these nutrients though your diet, consider wholefood supplements.

What to avoid:
- Gluten and too much of any grain
- A1 Casein in cow's dairy
- Chemicals in your food. GMO and pesticide use creates less tryptophan in our plants. We can't make serotonin without tryptophan. Go organic!
- Too many animal products
- Processed and packaged foods. Avoid all junk food
- Too much alcohol, if any for some people

- Aspartame and other artificial sweeteners
- Excessive sugar consumption (including refined grains). This increases blood lactate levels, which increases inflammation.
- Too much caffeine, especially instant coffee. Organic (and fair trade) coffee is much less acidic yet may still contribute to mood fluctuations in some of us
- Processed and refined salt

Supplements to consider are prebiotics.* *See Chapter 49 Prebiotics.*

Stephen Collins, a gastroenterology researcher at McMaster University in Hamilton, Ontario, transferred gut bacteria from anxious humans into "germ-free" mice, (animals that had been raised so their guts contained no bacteria at all). After the transplant, these animals behaved more anxiously. Some of the mice were fed 5.5 grams of a carbohydrate known as galactooligosaccharide, or GOS. Others were given a placebo. (Previous studies in mice by the same scientists had shown that this same carbohydrate fostered growth of Lactobacillus and Bifidobacteria.) The mice who were administered the GOS showed lower levels of the stress hormone cortisol, and many signs of peacefulness. They noted that the results were similar when the mice were given anti-depressants or anti-anxiety medications. Another study was conducted with humans, and the results were similar.†

Yogurt is a probiotic, meaning it contains live bacteria, in this case strains of four species—bifidobacterium, streptococcus, lactococcus, and lactobacillus. There is a well-known study involving 25 healthy women over 4 weeks, whereby 12 of them ate a cup of commercially available yogurt twice a day, and the other 13 didn't. The results, published in 2013 in the Journal of Gastroenterology,

---

* Schmidt, Kristin, Cowen, Philip J., Harmer, Catherine J., Tzortzis, George, Errington, Steven, and Burnet, Philip W. J. 'Prebiotic Intake Reduces the Waking Cortisol Response and Alters Emotional Bias in Healthy volunteers. (Original Investigation)(Report)' 232, no. 10 (May 1, 2015): 1793–1801.

† Desbonnet, L., Garrett, L., Clarke, G., Kiely, B., Cryan, J.F., and Dinan, T.G. 'Effects of the Probiotic Bifidobacterium Infantis in the Maternal Separation Model of Depression.' *Neuroscience* 170, no. 4 (2010): 1179–1188.

showed significant differences between the two groups; the yogurt eaters reacted more calmly to negative images than the control group. Probably the bacteria living in the yogurt changed the composition of the subjects' gut microbes, which changed brain chemistry. As we learn more about how the gut-brain microbial network operates, it is being suggested it could be used to treat psychiatric disorders, the same way we now use Prozac or Valium. It's a whole new way to alter brain function, and it's really very exciting.*

Herbal medicines to include are St John's wort (not if you're on prescription anti-depressants), lemon balm and skullcap and also immune-modulating herbs, one of the best being echinacea. We know about the strong relationship between depression and inflammation, so consider anti-inflammatory herbs like turmeric and willow bark. The antibacterial herb barberry is going to be great to balance your gut flora. The adaptogenic herb rhodiola due to its ability to increase the activity of our good-mood chemicals serotonin, dopamine, and norepinephrine.

Essential oils to use regularly are bergamot, Roman chamomile, lavender, frankincense and vetiver.

When it comes to changes to your lifestyle, those of us who are the most physically active seem to have the lowest risks of developing depression and anxiety. Exercise reduces levels of inflammation. One of the best ways to feel at peace is to meditate 20 minutes 1-2 times a day. In severe cases of anxiety and depression use a guided mediation, instead of trying to sit there, not thinking. Eight hours quality sleep regularly a night is so important, and a 20 minute daytime nap is highly recommended. I hear you laugh at this, but it's ideal. Any less than the eight hours a day is likely to be adding to your toxic load, leading to oxidative stress and inflammation. *See Chapter 25 When You Just Can't Sleep.* It's also very possible that in some cases anxiety

---

* Tillisch, Kirsten, Labus, Jennifer, Kilpatrick, Lisa, Jiang, Zhiguo, Stains, Jean, Ebrat, Bahar, Guyonnet, Denis, et al. 'Consumption of Fermented Milk Product With Probiotic Modulates Brain Activity.' *Gastroenterology* 144, no. 7 (June 2013): 1394–1401.e4.

and depression will stem from Adrenal Fatigue, so look after these glands and your kidneys upon which they sit. See *Chapter 16, Could You Be Suffering With Adrenal Fatigue?*

You may also decide to test for Pyrrole Disorder: Having this condition may be preventing you from holding onto your zinc and B6, causing all sorts of mood issues.

part three
TURNING THINGS AROUND

chapter thirty-four
MORNING RITUAL

Starting your morning with ritual helps set you up for the day ahead, and reminds you to stay mindful about your intentions. Commit to making this time for yourself each morning and enjoy the benefits it will bring. You'll be glad you did.

Here's a six-step routine to follow:

1. *Meditate.* Best practised early in the morning. Decide for yourself if it's better for you as soon as you wake up, or a bit later.

2. *Brush your teeth.* Do this before having anything to eat or drink, to avoid washing down built-up bacteria that has accumulated in your mouth overnight. Or you can 'oil pull' if you prefer. *See Chapter 37, Oil Pulling.*

3. *Drink a large glass of warm water.* This will help your digestion immensely. If you like, squeeze ½ lemon (about two tablespoons) into warm water, to stimulate your liver. The sour flavour helps the liver to better eliminate toxins. You can add sliced or grated ginger, turmeric, cayenne or manuka honey. Substitute lemon with apple cider vinegar, if that's more convenient for you.

4. *Aloe vera.* Take 30mls of the juice on an empty stomach, twice a day. First thing in the morning before eating, and again just before bed.

5. *Exercise.* 20–40 minutes first thing on an empty stomach is ideal. The level of intensity depends on what condition your body is currently in, your health, goals and age.

6. *Breakfast.* Have something small, but nutrient-dense. A smoothie is ideal, or a few mouthfuls of yoghurt with hemp seeds. It is important to feed your body within a few hours of waking, especially when you are tired or run-down.

chapter thirty-five
ALOE VERA

Aloe vera produces at least six natural antiseptics, which can kill mould, bacteria, fungi and viruses. So is it any wonder aloe vera is one of nature's most gentle, yet potent, digestive healers? In fact, the plant is so powerful that researchers and scientists are looking into its potential for fighting AIDS and cancer.

While it has many topical uses, I'm a huge fan of its ability to soothe and heal the gut lining, which has a big effect on our skin, mood, weight and overall health. Here are just some of its benefits:

- relieves gastrointestinal disorders such as leaky gut, indigestion, reflux, heartburn, bloating and constipation
- reduces symptoms of irritable bowel syndrome, including bloating and discomfort
- eases stomach ulcers, colitis, haemorrhoids, urinary tract infections and prostate problems
- reduces gum disease
- speeds up healing
- helps maintain healthy gut bacteria
- reduces cholesterol and triglycerides for a healthy heart
- balances blood sugar levels and blood pressure
- reduces arthritis and rheumatic pain
- helps with detox

chapter thirty-six
PSYLLIUM HUSKS

When water is added to psyllium husks a soft gel forms, helping matter to move through the colon smoothly. As it is a resistant starch (RS), it encourages natural bacteria in the bowel. Psyllium is a simple and inexpensive way to get a good part of your recommended daily intake of fibre, not to mention butyrate.

To further increase RS production in your colon, try combining half a teaspoon potato starch with psyllium husk fibre. Start slowly, and be sure to drink a big, clean glass of water after it, otherwise it may get 'stuck' and cause constipation.

Psyllium contains both soluble and insoluble fibre. Taking one serving of 7g (one heaped teaspoon) three times a day could add as much as 15g of fibre to your diet. You'll still need to include lots of other plant foods to get your full recommended dietary intake (RDI) of fibre.

Try to buy only organic psyllium husks, as otherwise they will be contaminated with pesticides, herbicides and fertilisers, being a heavily sprayed crop. Also check the ingredients to make sure you're buying 100% psyllium husks. Lots of brands will add artificial sweeteners, colouring and other creepy additives, which restrict the full benefit of the husks.

chapter thirty-seven
OIL PULLING

An ancient Ayurvedic remedy for improving health, oil pulling uses pure oils to extract toxins that have accumulated in your mouth overnight. It's a very effective activity to do first thing in the morning. The benefits include whitening your teeth, detoxifying, promoting clearer skin and improving energy. It assists in drawing out damaging bacteria, fungi and other harmful organisms from your mouth, teeth, gums and throat.

Use one tablespoon of coconut, olive, hemp, pumpkin seed or macadamia oil. Vigorously swish warmed oil around your mouth for 5–20 minutes, then spit into your bin or garden.

Try mixing up a 100ml glass bottle of coconut, pumpkin seed and hemp oils, then add a few drops of an essential oil* such as peppermint, lemon, tea tree or clove, or a combination of these. If using coconut oil, store in a wide-mouth jar during the cooler months, to prevent the oil from solidifying.

---

* Ensure you always use food-grade quality essential oils

chapter thirty-eight
UNDERSTANDING FIBRE

Fibre is the indigestible portion of plant food that moves food through your gut, absorbing water as it goes and making bowel movements easier to pass. When it comes to what we eat, fibre is the most important dietary factor in determining our gut flora composition. Again, we need to eat a variety of plant foods so we have a greater diversity of microbes in our gut. And that's looking like a very good thing.

------- ------- ------- -------

Because vegetables are so high in fibre, they're very low in total carbs. And it's the fibre content that differentiates the good carbs from the bad.

------- ------- ------- -------

We've long known that many disorders of the lower gastrointestinal tract such as IBS, diverticulosis, colon cancer, polyps, Crohn's disease and ulcerative colitis are almost non-existent in societies that consume large amounts of plant foods each day (fruits, vegetables, nuts, whole grains, legumes and seeds). Typically, most fibre in our modern diet comes from the wheat bran in most breads and cereals, but this is far from ideal for myriad of reasons. It's been refined to remove the fibre for one, many of us are allergic or intolerant to wheat products, plus our bodies really do like variety.

No fibre is digested by the small intestine; in fact all of it should arrive into the colon (large intestine) unchanged. From there, insoluble and soluble fibres behave differently. Almost all plant food, which is where fibre comes from, contains both soluble and insoluble fibre, in different proportions. For instance, wheat is about 90% insoluble fibre, oats are 50/50 and the psyllium plant is mostly soluble fibre.

Insoluble fibre **does not** dissolve in water and is not fermented by the gut's bacteria. However, it does hold lots of water, adding bulk to your stools, helping to make them softer, thus allowing foods to leave your system faster. The result is an easier, more regular bowel movement. You'll find this type of fibre in such foods as whole grains, wheat bran and vegetables.

Soluble fibre **does** dissolve in water, turning into a gel during the digestive process. The gel slows digestion, allowing for greater absorption of essential nutrients. The gel is fermented by the colon's microorganisms or bacteria, then used as a food source. Furthermore, certain soluble fibre (such as inulin, oligofructose and fructooligosaccharide) causes remarkable changes in the bacterial mix in the colon. These are called **prebiotics**. Foods high in soluble fibre include oat bran, nuts, seeds, beans, lentils, barley and peas.

The recommended daily amount of fibre is between 20–30 grams daily, but I believe more like 50 grams per 1,000 calories is ideal. Unfortunately, most people are getting only half that or less. Your best source of dietary fibre comes from vegetables, and most of us are simply not eating enough veggies.

chapter thirty-nine
JAMU

Jamu is an Indonesian word, loosely translated as 'tonic'. It is a medicinal drink made by infusing various fresh and dried herbs, spices, barks and roots of plants. This is an age-old remedy that these days contains mainly turmeric, yet you may never find the same two Jamu recipes. Turmeric contains hundreds of compounds found to have anti-oxidant and anti-inflammatory properties, and needs pepper to do its work. Jamu shots are usually taken daily in the morning as a health boost, then more frequently if we're run-down or sick with a cold or flu.

An interesting fact is the discovery of *Curcuma longa* or curcumin, dating to around the early 1800's when the isolation of 'yellow colouring-matter' from the rhizomes of *Curcuma longa* (turmeric) was reported, and named curcumin. Later, we learnt this substance to be a mixture of resin and turmeric oil. It wasn't until the 1970s that curcumin became the subject of scientific investigation.

This is how I make my Jamu at home:

- Use two cups of turmeric root, scrubbed clean then blended with one cup of clean water, one cup of lemon juice and one teaspoon of peppercorns.

- Pour mixture into a soup pot with seven more cups of clean water. Simmer gently for ten minutes.
- Allow to cool a little, then strain this heavenly, golden elixir. Add raw honey or maple syrup to taste, if desired.

chapter forty

ANTIOXIDANTS

Antioxidant is a generic term that describes the 'mopping up' of free radicals (cancer-forming substances) in the body, by increasing oxygenation. Some vitamins, such as C and E, are antioxidants.

Carotenoids are a select group of foods known to have antioxidant activity and should be introduced into the diet in small, potent amounts. The most powerful carotenoid is astaxanthin, found in microalgae and the sea life which consumes them, such as wild salmon, shellfish and krill.

Other foods with high levels of antioxidants include cacao, turmeric, goji berries, dried gooseberries, garlic, spirulina, chlorella, barley grass and matcha tea. In addition, Brazil nuts, eggs, brown rice, dark-green leafy vegetables, pumpkins, carrots, and eggplants all contain antioxidants.

Also include oysters, organic red meat, sardines and miso in your diet for their zinc/antioxidant levels, as well as herbs and spices like clove, cinnamon, oregano, turmeric and ginger.

chapter forty-one
BUTYRATE

One of the new heroes of gut health is butyrate, a short-chain fatty acid (SCFA) created when microbes (gut bacteria) ferment dietary fibre in your gut. It's important for protecting the gut from inflammatory and autoimmune diseases, such as Crohn's disease, ulcerative colitis and Hashimoto's, and has been shown to destroy colon cancer cells. People with type 1 diabetes are deficient in butyrate-producing bacteria in their gut. Butyrate improves insulin sensitivity. *See Chapter 49, Prebiotics*

To increase butyrate levels take:

- *A supplement.* A recent study found that four grams a day for eight weeks improved symptoms of Crohn's disease, and in some cases put it onto remission.[*]
- *Wholefoods.* The highest concentrations of butyrate are found in butter and other dairy products, organic of course.
- *Resistant starch.* Butyrate also loves the RS found in seeds, legumes, whole grains, cold potatoes, unripe bananas, and just about any vegetable.

---

[*] Sabatino, A. Di, Morera, R., Ciccocioppo, R., Cazzola, P., Gotti, S., Tinozzi, F. P., Tinozzi, S., and Corazza, G. R. 'Oral Butyrate for Mildly to Moderately Active Crohn's Disease.' *Alimentary Pharmacology & Therapeutics*, vol 22, no. 9 (November 2005): 789–794.

chapter forty-two
ESSENTIAL OILS

Essential oils (EO) are one of the safest, most creative, affordable and empowering ways to self-heal. Aromatherapy is gentle on our body, because our body/mind knows what to do with plants and oil-based compounds, as opposed to synthetic medicines.

I still find it awe-inspiring that something as tiny as a plant molecule can find its way into the oldest part of our brain (the limbic system) via our nostrils, then get to work within seconds. Conveniently, absorption through our skin into our bloodstream is also rapid, especially via the soles of our feet where the oil can be detected in every cell of the body within 20 minutes, often less, after an essential oil has been applied.

Essential oils are 50–75% more powerful than what you'll find in the herb or plant they came from, as much more of the raw material is used to make the oil. With EO, you're getting very high levels of the healing compounds, and that's why you only need to use a little at a time.

There's much evidence-based research easily available which proves the efficacy of EO and their potential for healing, including killing cancer cells, MRSA (an antibiotic-resistant bacteria), fungal infections and more. Much of this information has existed for twenty years or more.[*]

---

[*] Sánchez-Vidaña, Dalinda Isabel, Ngai, Shirley Pui-Ching, He, Wanjia, Chow, Jason Ka-Wing, Lau, Benson Wui-Man, Tsang, Hector Wing-Hong, and Sánchez-Vidaña, Dalinda Isabel. 'The Effectiveness of Aromatherapy for Depressive Symptoms: A Systematic Review.' *Evidence-based complementary and alternative medicine : eCAM* 2017 (2017): 5869315–5869315

To get the best from your oils, research their source to ensure they've been sustainably and ethically produced, grown and harvested, without the use of toxic chemicals. That way you'll know exactly what you are putting on and in your body. Always look for high-quality, organic, therapeutic-grade essential oils.

The first time you use a new oil, do a quick patch test on a small area of skin before applying to larger areas. It's also best to dilute the oil in a carrier oil before applying (see below). In Australia, it's not generally recommended to take EO oils internally, although some practitioners feel confident enough in their craft to do so. If doing so, remember a little goes a long way; 1–2 drops should do. As a general rule, use EO internally for three weeks only, then have a week off. In some situations, certain oils should be avoided, as they may be harmful to pregnant and/or breastfeeding women, babies, children and pets. So err on the side of caution. If you're new to EO, then preferably work with a qualified and experienced practitioner.

HOW TO USE ESSENTIAL OILS

For those with sensitive skin, it is best to dilute EO with a carrier oil like coconut, rosehip, fractionated (stays in liquid form) coconut, olive, sweet almond, hemp, castor or jojoba, before topical application. All of these oils have their own unique benefits, so depending on their strength and thickness, add 3–5 drops of EO per teaspoon of carrier oil. As essential oils are volatile (easily destroyed), try to buy and keep them in dark glass bottles.

There are many ways you can use essential oils to heal and enhance your life. I've listed some of them here:

- Place a few drops in a 25ml glass rollerball bottle, top with a carrier oil, and roll over your skin.
- Apply a drop on an organic cotton ball or hanky, to sniff throughout the day.

- Add a few drops to simmering water on the stove (or to a nebuliser, if you own one) for a steam treatment for sinus or hayfever. The steam will also hydrate dry skin.
- Add 5–10 drops to an aromatherapy diffuser/vaporiser.
- Add 10 drops to your bath.
- Add 20 drops to three tablespoons of carrier oil. Rub all over your body, before getting into the bath or shower.
- For coughs and headaches, blend four drops of EO with one tablespoon of a carrier oil. Apply a small amount to the chest, back of neck and temples, massaging gently. Keep it away from your eyes.
- For gut, period and/or back pain, blend oils as above and gently massage into your abdomen or back.
- Add a few drops to a small spray bottle, fill with clean water and use as a spritz. It's beautiful to do this in warmer months, using lavender or rose oil.
- When cooking, add 1–2 drops per recipe for a safe way to use some of the stronger oils like cinnamon, clove, peppermint and thyme.
- Oil pulling is a safe way to use EOs to help treat oral thrush and any infection. Blend just one drop of clove oil or two drops of tea tree essential oil with one tablespoon of coconut oil and swish in the mouth for 5–20 minutes.
- Dilute 5 drops of tea tree essential oil in ½ cup clean, cool water to use topically on fungal skin problems like psoriasis, athlete's foot, fungus under your nails, bottom, or on your face or back. Or add 2 drops to a douche for vaginal thrush.

SPECIFIC USES FOR INDIVIDUAL OILS

For anxiety and depression

Lavender, vetiver, lemon balm, chamomile, bergamot, clary sage, ylang-ylang, rose, sandalwood, cedarwood, frankincense, neroli, turmeric

For inflammation
Thyme, clove, rose, eucalyptus, fennel, bergamot, Roman chamomile, ginger, helichrysum, patchouli, turmeric, chamomile, lavender, sweet marjoram, eucalyptus, peppermint, rosemary, thyme, clary sage

For arthritis
Ginger, turmeric, myrrh, orange, frankincense

For appetite balance
Bergamot, nigella, peppermint, cinnamon, grapefruit

For weight loss
Grapefruit, cinnamon, peppermint, lavender, orange, lemon, eucalyptus

For antibacterial use
Cinnamon, thyme, oregano, tea tree, eucalyptus, peppermint, lavender, bergamot, neroli, lemongrass

For antifungal use
Thyme, clove, geranium, peppermint, tea tree, lavender, oregano, black pepper, myrrh

For allergies
Eucalyptus, lemon, peppermint, basil, tea tree, oregano

For antiparasitic use
Clove, oregano, lavender, myrrh

For blood sugar balancing
Melissa, nigella, cinnamon, oregano, fennel, cumin

For cramps
Ylang-ylang, lavender, cypress, peppermint

For digestive problems
Rosemary, peppermint, ginger, chamomile, cardamom, fennel, thyme, oregano, caraway, lemon, turmeric with ginger

For detox
Turmeric, lemon myrtle, lemon, grapefruit, peppermint, oregano, wild orange, ginger, lemongrass, lemon tea tree, juniper, fennel

For energy
Pine, eucalyptus, rosemary, lavender, black spruce, peppermint, basil, juniper

For estrogen dominance
Tea tree, lavender, citrus, cinnamon, peppermint, clary sage, thyme, sandalwood

For headache
Lavender, peppermint, eucalyptus, rosemary

For hormone balance
Clary sage, thyme, sandalwood, rose, lavender, frankincense, neroli, lavender

For heart issues
Lemon, lemongrass, frankincense, helichrysum and ginger, rose

For immunity
Clove, oregano, eucalyptus, cinnamon, grapefruit, lemon, pine, turmeric

For improved mood
Bergamot, rose, palmarosa, Roman chamomile, ylang-ylang, geranium, rosewood, lemon, mandarin, jasmin, lemongrass

For the liver
Peppermint, clove, oregano, thyme, oregano

For the lungs
Eucalyptus, peppermint, lemon, rosemary, thyme, bergamot, ginger, juniper

For memory, concentration and focus
Frankincense, basil, ginger, vetiver, sandalwood, lime, peppermint, cypress, turmeric

For pain (joint and muscle)
Sandalwood, chamomile, lavender, sweet marjoram, lemongrass, black pepper, helichrysum, eucalyptus, peppermint, rosemary, thyme, juniper, ginger, frankincense

For premenstrual syndrome
Lavender, eucalyptus, rose, chamomile, neroli, clary sage, ylang-ylang

For reproductive health
Clary sage, sweet fennel, yarrow, geranium, calendula, German chamomile, sage

For sleep
Lavender, bergamot, cedarwood, eucalyptus, peppermint, rosemary, vetiver, Roman chamomile, ylang-ylang, sandalwood, neroli

For sore throat
Tea tree, myrrh, thyme, juniper, oregano oil, lemon, lavender, peppermint, eucalyptus, oregano, hyssop, thyme, clove, turmeric

For thyroid
For an underactive thyroid use spearmint, lemongrass, peppermint, clove, frankincense, myrrh, cedarwood and rose geranium; for an overactive thyroid use wintergreen, lemongrass, sandalwood, frankincense, myrrh and black spruce

CARRIER OILS

Sweet almond oil

A light oil, easily absorbed by all skin types. It contains lots of vitamins including A, B and E, making it a highly nutritious oil. It is especially recommended for use on the face, but it's wonderful anywhere.

Coconut oil

Antifungal, anti-inflammatory, analgesic (pain relief) and can help to reduce pain, fungus and inflammation of the skin. It also helps the healing properties of the EO you're using to penetrate deeper into the skin. As previously advised, use 'fractionated' coconut oil, so it doesn't solidify during cooler months.

Jojoba oil

Has an indefinite shelf life, so can be stored for longer than other carrier oils. It's very similar to our own sebum (the oily substance produced by our skin to protect it), making it useful for anything from massage to cosmetics. It will reduce inflammation and keep your skin luscious by mimicking collagen. Especially good for use on sensitive skin, eczema, psoriasis and acne.

Apricot oil

Has a wonderful effect on older skin. It's beneficial for dry, inflamed and sensitive skin, due to its oleic and linoleic acid, as well as vitamins A and E. This carrier oil is light with a faint sweet scent, and is absorbed by the skin without leaving a greasy or oily feeling. But beware, it can leave stains on your clothes and sheets if not fully absorbed by your skin.

Olive oil

May be used as an emergency oil, if you don't have any other carrier oil. It helps reduce pain and inflammation, and relieve ear and joint pain. It has a sweet, strong scent, so if you're not a big fan of its smell, mix a small amount with another carrier oil, so you still get the benefits that only olive oil can bring.

Rosehip oil
Rich in Vitamin C and essential fatty acids, it protects the skin by making new skin cells and helping them regenerate. Some suggest that this is what gives rosehip oil its anti-ageing benefits. Also known as rosehip seed oil.

Grapeseed oil
Has a light, thin consistency, well suited to massage. A very moisturising oil due to its high content of linoleic acid, so it leaves a light, glossy film over the skin. Grapeseed oil has a relatively short shelf life.

Black seed oil
Contains 70–80% essential fatty acids, is anti-inflammatory, pain relieving, antibacterial and antioxidant. It has a woody, strong scent. Its deep and earthy fragrance lends itself perfectly for use with juniper, cedar, cypress and sandalwood essential oils.

Castor oil
There was a time when you'd be hard-pressed to find a home without castor oil. Has the ability to regrow hair, even eyebrows and eyelashes, to treat warts, skin tags, dry skin, acne, moles and cellulite. It deeply cleanses and detoxifies the skin, killing the bacteria that cause acne. Rich in ricinoleic acid, castor oil is antibacterial, anti-inflammatory and antiviral. Use it as you would any other carrier oil: blend with your choice of EO and rub it on.

chapter forty-three
PREPARING YOUR GRAINS

We've known for some time that if you have digestive problems or suffer from classic autoimmune reactions like allergies and achy joints, there's a big chance that eating gluten may be a problem for you. However, *all* grains have now been linked to many more health conditions, including Alzheimer's disease, MS, epilepsy and autistic spectrum disorders (ASD).

So what do we now know that's made us reconsider how we feel about grains? Substances in grains, including gluten, lectin, phytic acid, saponins and gliadin, may increase intestinal permeability—leaky gut syndrome. Leaky gut can cause digestive symptoms such as bloating, gas and abdominal cramps, as well as cause or contribute to many others symptoms such as type 1 and 2 diabetes, autoimmune and thyroid issues, fatigue, skin rashes, joint pain, allergies, psychological symptoms, weight gain and more.

The confusion for many of us, however, is the issue of fibre. We know we need a high-fibre diet, and traditionally have turned to grains like oats, wheat cereals, bread, pasta and rice to provide our intake. While they certainly all contain fibre, for some people they may raise insulin and leptin levels, which is a **major** driver of most chronic diseases, including diabetes and polycystic ovarian syndrome. To make matters worse, most grain products have been highly refined, massively reducing their nutritional value. So instead of increasing grains to get your RDI of fibre, think instead of including more vegetables, and in lesser amounts nuts, and seeds—**not** muffins and muesli.

Grains are not something we need to, or should completely eliminate from our diet, however. Research and time has proven to us that the Mediterranean diet is the healthiest of them all, and it includes whole grains. The secret is to eat them in moderation, and prepare them properly. And make them organic.

When it comes to grains, try to keep them to about three servings a week, during the day is better so you can use their energy, and be sure to prepare them properly to keep your gut, blood sugar, arteries and weight healthy. To do this, the toxins or 'antinutrients' in the grains need to be deactivated. Soak them in acidic water, preferably in a warm place like on top of your stove or coffee machine. (This will stimulate germination.) This process makes them much easier to digest, so their nutrients will be far more available to you. To do this, add one tablespoon of apple cider vinegar or lemon juice (to 'acidulate' the water) to every two cups of grain, leaving them to soak for at least a few hours (or up to 24 hours), then cook them in this water. Bring to the boil then drop to a simmer for 30 minutes. (Shorter for small grains like quinoa and millet.) After removing the pot from the heat, leave them to keep steaming for 10–15 minutes, covered. You'll find grains prepared and cooked in this way are softer, fluffier and sweeter, as well as more nutritious and less troublesome on digestion and overall health.

------- ------- ------- -------

Indigenous grains like kangaroo grass and native millet will soon be widely available in Australia, and look like providing our diet with much-needed variety and wholesome nutrition. They're highly nutritious, have a superior aroma and flavour to wheat flour, promote good digestion, and most don't have any gluten.

------- ------- ------- -------

By the way, another big issue with the wheat grain in Australia (and New Zealand, the UK and the US) is since the 1990's we have been adding the synthetic and toxic form of folate (folic acid) to our wheat, and to many other 'fortified' foods such as breads, cereals, and some packaged foods, and many supplements. The rest of the world, including Europe, consider their wheat grain sacred and won't allow it to be messed with too much, which is why we can eat baguettes in France, or Italian pasta without having the same reactions. So why are we doing this crazy stuff? Good question, (and the farmers are asking the same question, especially as they aren't at all subsidised for the huge expense of this process, yet it's mandatory), and it looks like another case of medicating the masses, in the hope this will prevent the entire population from having a baby with Spina Bifida. If you're planning on getting pregnant, it's especially important you're getting enough folate three months before conceiving, and during the first trimester of pregnancy. But it's folate (Vitamin B6) not the toxic version called folic acid that pregnant women need. Many of my clients tell me taking their prenatal supplement (that almost always contain folate acid) makes them feel like they've eaten gluten. How interesting, as it turns out it's the same thing causing the issue here, and that's synthetic folic acid. If you eat organic durum wheat, or spelt products, then there'll be no folic acid added, (yet). Even better, if the organic products you choose have been properly prepared into a sourdough for example, then chances are you'll have little or no issue digesting them, (unless you're a coeliac of course).When choosing any supplement containing folic acid, are sure it's the bioavailable form of folate called l-methylfolate (5-MTHFR). It must state either 'L form', 6(S) forms, L-5 forms—as in L-5-MTHF, 6(S)-L-MTHF = 6(S)-L-Methyltetrahydrofolate. You'll also see it called Folinic. Also look at the ingredients on all packaged foods. If it includes folate, leave it on the shelf.

chapter forty-four
IS DAIRY GOOD FOR YOU?

When discussing dairy, I'm referring to the organic, full-fat, unprocessed, grass-fed varieties. (Grass is a cow's natural food. Corn and other grains are not, especially not GM corn and soy.)

Widely available processed milk—in hormone-disrupting containers made from bisphenol A (BPA) comes from concentrated animal feeding operations (CAFOs), more commonly known as 'factory farms'. The animals are fed antibiotics, which alters their gut flora and the nutritional quality of the milk, not to mention the cruel conditions they are forced to endure.

Organic, whole milk naturally contains loads of healthy 'good' bacteria, including *Lactobacillus acidophilus*, which promotes the growth of healthy bacteria in your gut. As we know, this has a positive effect on our immune system, mood and overall health. Raw (or at least organic) dairy should cause little or no problems for most people; however, some of us just can't digest cow products, no matter how natural the milk is. For some people, it's even more inflammatory than gluten.

More often fermented/cultured (foods that have been fermented with lactic acid bacteria) cow products like kefir, yogurt, paneer and buttermilk are easier to digest. The fermentation process also increases the shelf life of the product, while improving the digestibility for most of us. The only way to know is to try a small amount and see how you feel. Don't keep eating them if they don't agree with you.

Sensitivity to a protein in milk called A1 casein can contribute to inflammatory gut conditions like leaky gut, ulcerative colitis, IBS and Crohn's disease. It's also been associated with acne, autoimmune disease and skin issues like eczema. However, milk that contains mostly or exclusively A2 casein produces none of these inflammatory effects, so is preferable. Jersey and Guernsey cows don't produce A1 casein, but the majority of bovines including buffaloes do.

If you have digestive difficulties, your gut may not have all the enzymes necessary to digest the proteins in milk (caseins). While we usually call it a lactose (milk sugar) intolerance, or a dairy allergy, these symptoms are more likely caused by difficulty digesting the protein casein. Avoiding casein altogether is as simple as avoiding most dairy foods. Although, as sheep and goat's milk products contain very little if no casein, they're usually much easier to tolerate. Look for manchego, lubneh, pecorino, rocquefort, haloumi and feta, but check the label that they have in fact used goat or sheep's milk in the product you're buying.

chapter forty-five
BUT LEGUMES GIVE ME GAS!

If these foods are prepared correctly (by removing the anti-nutrients), they become very healthy foods, delivering us plant protein, non-heme (vegetarian) iron, loads of fibre and good fats. We tend to see the terms legumes, beans, pulses, beans and peas used interchangeably, but there is a difference.

Legumes include all beans and peas from the Fabaceae (or Leguminosae) botanical family, and there are thousands of different species, including pulses, which are the dried seed of legumes. Pulses include chickpeas, beans (butter beans, borlotti beans, navy beans, cannellini beans, red kidney beans, adzuki beans and soybeans), peas (yellow split peas, black-eyed peas, blue peas for canning), lentils (yellow, red, green/brown, puy/French), and lupins (Australian Sweet Lupin and the Albus Lupin). Legumes can be eaten in a near endless variety of ways including whole, split, canned, frozen, or ground into flour.

Legumes have been a part of traditional diets for as long as we have been farming the Earth. But if they aren't prepared in a way that allows us to digest them properly, we may experience all sorts of digestive issues like gas, bloating and a rolling gut pain.

The anti-nutrients I'm talking about here are phytic acid, oligosaccharides and lectins, and they don't suit all of us. To remove these,

199

simply cover your legumes with three times the amount of clean water and one teaspoon unrefined salt per cup of dried ingredient, then soak for 2–24 hours, depending on which one you're using. Leave them in a warm place, such as the top of your stove or coffee machine. Don't use an acid in the water as you would to 'sour' your grains, as this will only cause them to constrict, preventing them from ever softening properly.

Next day, drain and wash your legumes well in clean water, then place them in a heavy-based pan (for even cooking). Add enough clean water to just cover them, then bring to the boil. Drop to a low simmer until very soft, skimming off any foam (releasing oligosaccharides) that forms on the surface along the way. These smell like gas.

Cooking time, like their soaking time, it will depend on which legume you're using, anywhere from 20 minutes to 4 hours. Strain the soft legumes once they cooked, making them even more digestible. Use immediately or store in the fridge for up to a week, or freeze for up to three months. You'll be really glad they're around to add to almost any meal, dip or snack, at a moment's notice. If you feel you can digest properly prepared legumes, then be confident about adding them to your meals, three or four times a week.

Legumes are gentle on the soil, so farming them is far less damaging to the environment than agriculture (animal protein). If you prefer to use canned legumes, then be sure they are organic, and the lining is BPA, and preferably also phthalate-free.

chapter forty-six
SEAWEED—WEIRD BUT WORTH IT

Packed with iodine, iron, omega-3 oils, protein, calcium and magnesium, sea vegetables have the impressive ability to remove toxic heavy metals such as mercury, lead and cadmium from our bodies. They have around 100–500 times more iodine than shellfish and contain ten times more calcium than cow's milk. Plus seaweeds are now being used, with exciting results, to clean up human sources of pollution in our oceans, as well as being investigated for novel ways to deal with the 5.25 trillion pieces of plastic in our ocean.[*]

Sea vegetables can be eaten pickled. Alternatively, flakes or powder can be added when cooking quinoa, brown rice, steamed veggies, soups, stir-fry or slow-cooked meals and roasts. Sea vegetables support new hair growth, stronger teeth and bones and improve iron levels. Because they are high in iodine, sea vegetables are an effective option for treating thyroid imbalance.

The most nutritious, and easily available sea vegetable varieties are arame, dulse, wakame, nori and agar. I use bladderwrack in my clinic as a liquid tonic to stimulate a sluggish thyroid, with the pleasant bonus of weight loss. (But it's not a easy herb to take due to it's taste and texture.) To use them in your diet, use toasted nori seeds to make

---

[*] Eriksen, Marcus et al. 'Plastic Pollution in the World's Oceans: More Than 5 Trillion Plastic Pieces Weighing over 250,000 Tons Afloat at Sea: E111913.' *PLoS ONE* 9.12 (2014): e111913.

quick nori rolls, and wherever you would flat bread. Yes, really. I also keep a jar of dulse or nori flakes near the stove, so I remember to add a teaspoon or so when I'm making soup, dahl or a stir fry, or cooking grains. You can't taste it, so don't be scared to try using it.

Not everyone can digest these treasures from the sea at first, so go slowly. Over time, seaweed will potentially deliver us the bacteria we need to digest it.

chapter forty-seven
HOLY HEMP

Hemp and marijuana are both varieties of cannabis. 'Industrial hemp' contains very little (0.03 or less) tetrahydrocannabinol (THC), the part that gets us high, while marijuana contains around 30%. Hemp has a unique protein called edestin, that is easy to digest and absorb. It increases our body's own natural defence system. Like soy beans this is a complete protein, meaning it contains all 22 amino acids. In addition, hemp contains many antioxidants.

Hemp seeds naturally contain 30% protein, with no carbohydrates; this can realistically be increased to 50% in the form of hemp protein powder. Hulled hemp seeds taste a bit like pine nuts and sunflower seeds, with the texture of cashew seeds, so they're pretty easy to incorporate into our daily diet. They don't need to be soaked or activated to make their nutrients available to us.

Hemp has been grown since ancient times and documented as far back as ancient China. Hemp has been hailed as a cure for cancer and improves many common conditions such as panic and anxiety, insomnia, pain, infertility, gut issues, spectrum disorders, and immune issues including auto immunity, to name just a few. Science bodies around the world are abuzz with excitement about new research showing the health benefits of hemp, and rightly so. This precious plant has over two hundred terpenes (organic compounds), some of which work synergistically with different cannabinoids (chemical compounds) to boost our body's metabolism. 'Cannabis and Cannabinoid Research' is the premier peer-reviewed journal dedicated to the scientific, medical, and psychosocial exploration of clinical cannabis, cannabinoids, and the endocannabinoid system.

According to traditional Chinese medicine, hemp has a 'cool' energetic quality, so it's wonderful for treating 'hot' conditions such as eczema (literally means 'boiling over'), acne, psoriasis, headaches and candida, from the inside out. The 'cooling' power of hemp calms and soothes the skin and restores balance to the body. (By the way, flaxseeds are 'warm'.)

Hemp has close to the perfect balance (2:1:1) of omegas-3, 6 and 9. This is unique in the oil world. It is the same ratio found naturally in human cells, so the body can metabolise these omegas more readily and reap the benefits. The essential fatty acids (EFA) that build omega oils are also necessary for healthy cell membranes, so will help heal a leaky gut.

Hemp seeds contain high amounts of both soluble and insoluble fibre, and the protein powder contains even more. Fibre helps to eliminate toxins from the body via our bowel, lowering our chances of colon, breast, prostate and rectum cancers as well as heart disease. It also helps keep blood sugar stable. These good EFAs can help reduce your weight, improve your skin, make for a healthier cardiovascular system, positively affect your immune and inflammatory response, and clean your bowel. They also help the kidneys, respiratory tract and cardiovascular systems.

The seeds and oil can be used to garnish almost any meal, or can be added to smoothies, salads or steamed veggies. Hemp flour and protein are both great to use in smoothies and baking. Keep hemp in the fridge to ensure the delicate omega oils are not damaged. Look for certified organic hemp products in airtight and dark packaging, and avoid buying hemp products stored in clear packaging, and plastic bulk bins, as the precious omega oils will be rancid and stale.

To make hemp flour, grind the seeds using your 'dry' blender or coffee/seed grinder, or buy it ready-made. The more it's refined, the higher the percentage of protein, commonly labelled as hemp protein powder. The less refined, the coarser the flour will be. Add it to your baking, either on its own or combined with other flours. Be sure to knead it well if you're making bread. It has a short shelf life of about three months, so only make small amounts and store in the fridge.

The mention of hemp brings about a certain fear in some people, as many are still unsure about the difference between hemp and marijuana. They're different. At present, hemp is legal and marijuana is not in some countries, including here in Australia, unless prescribed by an authorised medical practitioner. But, it's very expensive and there's a ton of red tape to get through before you get anywhere near the stage of getting a prescription. Hopefully the law will change sooner rather than later regarding the legal use of this incredibly healing, no-fuss plant, as it recently has in other countries.

chapter forty-eight
DIGESTIVE TONICS

Humans have evolved over thousands of years eating wild, bitter foods. There are a lot less of them in today's diets however, another reason digestive issues are increasing. Bitter foods like rocket, dill, kale, sesame seeds, turmeric, dandelion leaves and Jerusalem artichokes contain enzymes that help break down food, so we can better absorb our meal. When taken as herbal medicine, bitter plants like gentian, bitter melon, andrographis and rue will improve your digestion and reduce inflammation. Bitters can also be used to reduce sugar cravings and reset the appetite.

A bitter herb is essentially **any** herb with a bitter taste. Historically, people used these plants for ceremony, healing and cooking. Ranging from mild to strong, bitter herbs can be as light as chamomile or as biting as rue.

Until recently, the thinking was that a bitter herb needed to be tasted on the tongue, so that the bitter taste receptors (known as T2Rs) were stimulated, releasing digestive enzymes from the pancreas in preparation for digesting food. We now know that T2Rs are distributed throughout the stomach, intestine and pancreas. So this humble bitter herb or food keeps working all the way down the gut, producing digestive enzymes and your own personal combination of probiotics;

it also triggers a hormone that stimulates the digestion of fat and protein and limits the absorption of dietary toxins.

It is common for people to take bitters before meals, to get the gut ready to do its work. According to master herbalists, taking bitters **after** a meal can also be a helpful way to stimulate bile production, reducing any bloating and gas.

A diet high in processed food, emotional stress, ill health and/ or ageing can all cause the natural digestive enzymes in the body to decline, making digestion more difficult and uncomfortable. Digestive enzymes are essential to help break down our food, as well as support digestion and the process of nutrient absorption.

In Germany, 20 million doses of bitters are taken every day. The Italians and Swiss are also famous bitter takers, and they don't have anywhere near our level of digestive problems. Considering how toxic our environment is, it seems like bitter foods should be back on the menu!

chapter forty-nine
PREBIOTICS

Prebiotic means 'before life'. Taking prebiotics is one of the best ways to establish and support a healthy gut microbiome.

Prebiotics are carbohydrates that reach the colon intact, then selectively feed many strains of beneficial bacteria. You'll find them in Jerusalem artichoke, chicory root, onions, whole grains, bananas and garlic. Prebiotic fibre can favourably change the mix of bacteria in the lower gut (colon). Sources include an Indian lassi, traditionally enjoyed pre-dinner; fermented milk products such as kefir, quark, yoghurt and lubne; and natto miso which is a fermented soy product from Japan, high in vitamin K2.

Prebiotics are generally classified into the three categories listed below, each feeding different species of gut bacteria. Among these, resistant starch (RS) is emerging as uniquely beneficial.

1. *Non-Starch Polysaccharides (NSP)*. Large-sized carbohydrates that aren't digested, but some are fermented once they reach the large intestine (colon). They are found in everyday food or as supplements. Examples are inulin, lignin, pectin, oligosaccharides.
2. *Soluble Fibres*. Found in fruit and vegetables, legumes, oats, nuts, flaxseeds and psyllium. Beneficial prebiotics, so include them in your diet when you can.

3. *Resistant Starches (RS)*. These are a group of fibres that slowly ferment in the large intestine, selectively feeding the beneficial bacteria. After 'resisting' digestion in the small intestine, rather than being absorbed as glucose (like most starches), RS reaches the large intestine, where bacteria attach to, and digest or ferment the starch. Proving to be useful in treating various digestive disorders including inflammatory bowel diseases like ulcerative colitis, Crohn's disease, constipation, diverticulitis and diarrhoea.

––––––– ––––––– ––––––– –––––––

Most foods we eat feed only 10% of our cells; resistant starches and fermentable fibres feed the other 90%.

––––––– ––––––– ––––––– –––––––

Resistant starches travel through the small intestine to the colon, where they are turned into three beneficial, energy-boosting, inflammation-squashing, short-chain fatty acids (SCFA) by intestinal bacteria, feeding the friendly bacteria in your colon, increasing the bulk of your stools and helping you maintain regular and satisfying bowel movements. They also contribute to the overall health of the gut wall, as well as stimulating metabolism, decreasing inflammation and improving our response to stress. Because RS are fermented very slowly, they won't make you gassy, allowing you to eat far more of them without discomfort.

Since they're not digested, RS do not result in blood sugar spikes, as they help improve insulin and leptin regulation. They are also believed to help manage metabolic syndrome and possibly help you eat less. RS is extremely helpful in cases of autoimmunity, diabetes, IBS, ulcerative colitis and allergies. Foods high in resistant starch include under-ripe bananas, green banana flour, rolled oats, white legumes (like cannellini and navy beans), lentils, seeds, potato and tapioca starch, as well as brown rice flour and pasta.

--------- --------- --------- ---------

The bacteria in the gut outnumber the body's cells 10
to 1. So you could say we are only 10% human!

--------- --------- --------- ---------

You may have heard that white rice and spuds are now back on the health-conscious menu? Well, it seems that cooking normally digestible starches (such as potato, white rice or pasta) then cooling them in the refrigerator alters the chemistry of the foods, transforming them into more of a resistant-type starch. It's also the case if they're cooled after cooking, then reheated. Bonus! Think of adding organic pasta, potato salad, nori rolls and fried rice back into your menu, guilt free.

--------- --------- --------- ---------

I find it pretty exciting that white rice, potato and pasta
may actually be considered healthy and beneficial. Good
news for those of us who struggle with our weight!

--------- --------- --------- ---------

If you're monitoring your intake of carbs, you can still add RS to your diet without adding **digestible** carbohydrates, meaning they don't count as carbs. Remember also that our gut likes diversity, so try alternating the sources. (By the way, potato starch seems to be tolerated even by those who react adversely to nightshades.)

When you first start including resistant starches in your diet, expect some bloating and gas as your microbiome starts to adapt. This shouldn't cause any real discomfort though. If it continues, decrease the amount you're including in your diet until your symptoms disappear, then start increasing slowly. 15–30g a day is beneficial. Some people may not be able to handle this much, which could be an indication of SIBO or another gut issue. In such cases, it may be necessary to balance the microbiome first, using herbal antibiotics and probiotics, with the aid of an experienced natural healthcare practitioner.

chapter fifty
PROBIOTICS

Probiotic means 'pro-life'. Probiotics are live microbial organisms that populate the gut and have a positive effect on our digestive and immune systems and on our overall health. Good and not so good bacteria are continually competing for dominance in the gut, and long-term bowel health and wellbeing are supported by maintaining a *just right* Goldilocks balance of friendly and not-so-friendly bacteria in the colon.

If this balance is disrupted too much, then we end up with dysbiosis, an imbalance in our gut flora. To address this we need to re-establish the beneficial bacteria in our gut, by either eating probiotic foods or by taking a supplement. *See Chapter 51, Fermented Foods.*

BUT WHICH SUPPLEMENT?

For a supplement to be of benefit, the probiotic activity must be guaranteed throughout the **entire** production process, storage period and shelf life of the product. They need to survive the long journey through the digestive system to reach the large intestine—alive and well, in adequate numbers. Some strains are not robust enough for this, as the bile and stomach acids dissolve them along the way. However, the probiotic bacteria found in common fermented foods (such as yoghurt) can reach the gut in high numbers. It may be that the vitamin K that probiotics form after fermentation contributes to this effect.

Ideally we want to eat a **variety of fermented foods,** to maximise the types of bacteria we're consuming. One of the reasons why fermented foods are so beneficial is because they contain lactobacillus (as well as many other beneficial bacteria) that convert sugars lactic acid to healthy bacteria. If fermented with a probiotic starter culture, the healthy bacteria in a serving of fermented vegetables can easily exceed the amount you'll find in a probiotic supplement.

No single probiotic supplement will work for everyone. Until we know more about the actual bacteria that live in each of our guts at any one time, we're really just guessing. *Lactobacillus sporogenes* is a good place to start, as more people respond favourably to lactobacillus. The best probiotic supplements contain a blend of health-promoting strains, sometimes with around 20 of the best probiotic strains available, to cover all needs. Or you can do a stool sample to determine exactly which bacteria you're deficient in, then take those particular strains as a supplement.

Probiotics have a better chance of surviving the transit through the gut down to the colon if they're taken with food, as it happens naturally. So ideally, take your supplement with food or half an hour **before** you eat, or include some fermented foods with your meal.

chapter fifty-one
FERMENTED FOODS

Before we started canning food, our foremothers were fermenting fruits and veggies in salt water and spices, then leaving them to see out the winter in the cellar or a dark cupboard. By doing this, the sugars contained in these foods (things like glucose, fructose and sucrose) are converted into energy and lactic acid that destroy harmful organisms. The lactic acid produced feeds the veggies throughout winter and keeps them perfectly preserved. Often all that's needed for this process to happen is good salt, clean water and lovely organic veggies or (preferably raw) dairy. Fermentation also increases vitamin levels and contains antibiotic and carcinogenic (anti-cancer) substances.

Historically, people used cultured or fermented foods to support their intestinal and overall health, way before the invention of the probiotic supplement. What better way to ensure none of the abundance from spring and summer was wasted? It's a frugal, sensible and an extremely healthy way to use produce.

Yoghurt, quark, lubne, sauerkraut, kim chi, kombucha and miso paste are good sources of natural, healthy bacteria. In many countries, pickles and other fermented foods are eaten with most meals. Pickles help break down animal fat, so not surprisingly we see them served with ham, cheese and other rich, fatty foods. These are salty foods, so you only need a small amount.

Our digestive tracts have taken a battering during the past few decades from antibiotics, medication, stress, refined sugars, chemicals added to our food and tap water, chemicals used to grow our food, and from overeating. Some of the good flora simply must be replaced, if we want to have any chance at all of achieving good health. Thankfully, fermented foods have made a bit of a comeback in recent times. Macrobiotic (Japanese diet) followers never stopped including them; and it's the same situation in Europe, where foods like sauerkraut, quark and dill pickles continue to be a staple and important part of many traditional diets.

Because these foods are 'pre-digested', a lot of the work has been done before they even get into your mouth. This makes them easy for our digestive systems to handle, which is why they are easily tolerated by most people with a damaged digestive tract.

The process of fermentation creates good bacteria that lead to a healthy intestinal tract, which in turn creates good digestion, immunity and (we now know) mood. Microorganisms such as *lactobacillus* perform this work, and the science is known as 'zymology'. Considering around 80% of our immune system is in your digestive tract, it's pretty important we keep it healthy.

INTRODUCING FERMENTED FOODS

When you first start including fermented foods, start slowly. Begin with a teaspoon (of the liquid if there is any) daily, then work up to a tablespoon a few times a week. At first, some people experience symptoms like gut pain, bloating and belching. This is the bad bacteria dying off, and usually lasts only 5–7 days. It may also be due to a histamine intolerance, or the fact that you don't yet have the digestive enzymes needed to digest these foods. (The bacteria we need to digest different types of food comes on the back of that food.) If the symptoms are too severe to tolerate, then just have a teaspoon of liquid once a week for a month, then try again for a few times a week.

Fermented foods aren't a one-off deal. You have to maintain an ongoing relationship with them to sustain the colonisation, so you can enjoy their full benefits in the long term. It's more accurate to consider them as necessary food as medicine we need to eat regularly, rather than think of them as a supplement or short term medicine.

Popular fermented foods include:

- *Dairy*—yoghurt, kefir, quark, lubne, cultured butter, buttermilk, lasse
- *Soy*—tamari, miso, natto miso, tempeh
- *Pickled veggies*—cucumber, daikon, beets, dill pickles, sauerkraut, kim chi
- *Sourdough*—bread
- *Kombucha*—Japanese tea

chapter fifty-two
FATS AND OILS

When it comes to fats and oils, there's the good, the bad and the ugly. But how can we tell the difference?

LET'S START WITH THE GOOD

Monounsaturated fatty acids (MUFA) are found in avocado, olives, olive oil, coconut oil, nuts like cashews, almonds and pecans, nut butters and dark chocolate. Eating a diet rich in MUFAs actually decreases belly fat. MUFAs may also help improve heart health and insulin sensitivity, which is important for good blood sugar control and the prevention and management of diabetes. Good daily portions to stick to are a quarter of an avocado, ten olives, two tablespoons olive oil, two tablespoons nuts, two tablespoons nut butter, and a quarter cup of dark cacao nibs.

Before we relied so heavily on processed foods, we consumed omega-3 and omega-6 fatty acids in roughly equal amounts. Today most of us get far too much omega-6 and not enough omega-3. This imbalance may contribute to the rise in asthma, heart disease, many forms of cancer, autoimmunity and diseases of the brain, all of which are believed to stem from inflammation in the body. Omega-3 oils

(DHA and EPA) are found in seafood, particularly oily fish like wild salmon, mackerel, sardines and anchovies.

The three most important categories of omega-3 fatty acids are DHA, ALA and EPA. DHA is stored in the body, while EPA is not (in significant quantities). ALA is an essential fatty acid mostly found in plants; it acts as a building block for omega-3 fatty acids. As we cannot produce our own, omegas must be obtained through our diet. Plant foods that contain ALA include chia, hemp, walnuts, pecans, hazelnuts, tahini, seaweed, organic soy and flaxseeds. While these sources aren't as potent as what we get from the omega-3 oil in seafood, they are a good vegan alternative and a sustainable plant source.

ALAs do convert to EPA and DHA (omega-3) in our gut, but the process is slow and not always efficient, partly determined by our age, sex, genes and diet. Reducing our intake of linoleic acid (omega-6) found in corn, cottonseed, soybean, safflower and sunflower oils, as well as grains and processed foods, will help our body's ability to convert ALA into DHA and EPA. (Saturated fat doesn't seem to do this.)

Microalgae like spirulina has emerged in recent years as a popular source of ALA essential fatty acid for vegetarians or anyone else with a reduced conversion rate in the gut. Flaxseed oil consists of approximately 55% ALA, which makes it six times richer than most fish oils. Hemp has the perfect balance of omega-3, 6 and 9, mimicking the ratio they exist in our cells. Green-lipped mussels from New Zealand are another great source of omega-3 fatty acids.

Our modern diet overloads us with omega-6 oils in the form of linoleic acid (LA). This is found mainly in vegetable oils extracted from seeds and nuts, and from the meat and milk of animals fed with grain. These oils (such as soy and canola) are used in fast foods, most snack foods, biscuits, crackers and sweets. Our body also makes hormones from omega-6 fatty acids. In excess, they tend to increase inflammation, blood clotting and cancer, while hormones from omega-3 fatty acids have the opposite effect. Both types of hormones must be in balance to maintain optimum health.

However, not all omega-6 fatty acids behave in the same way. GLA (gammalinolenic acid) is an effective anti-inflammatory agent, recommended for arthritis, autoimmune disorders, premenstrual syndrome and for the healthy growth of skin, hair and nails. Borage, black currant and evening primrose oils are all natural sources of GLA. The dose of evening primrose oil or black currant oil is 500 mg twice a day. (I usually do not recommend borage oil, because it may contain compounds that damage the liver.)

Omega-7 (palmitoleic acid) helps increase our metabolism, and also helps to stimulate the production of 'brown fat' found in the leaner of us, perhaps due to its ability to burn more calories. Omega-7 oils are found in borage, blackcurrant and evening primrose oil, and we only need a small amount to positively affect the way our body uses energy (calories) and stores fat. Omega-7 also kindly reduces the amount of new fat molecules, especially those that damage our tissues and increase our risk of heart disease. In fact, the beneficial effects of omega-7 resemble those of many cholesterol drugs, such as Lipitor®, Actos®, Lopid® and others commonly used by Western medicine to lower high cholesterol and/or blood sugar. It's important you use an omega-7 supplement that has been purified to reduce the damaging effect of palmitic acid to less than 1% and also concentrated to increase the omega-7 content to around 50%.

NOW TO THE BAD ONES

Trans fatty acid (TFA), also seen as 'partially hydrogenated oil', is found naturally in small amounts in foods like butter, meat and cheese. However, most trans fat is formed through an industrial process that adds hydrogen to vegetable oils like GM soybean, canola and cottonseed oils, which creates a solid oil at room temperature. Liquid vegetable oils are 'hardened' during this process, to create spreads such as margarine, cooking fats for deep-frying and shortening for baking. TFA extends the shelf life of whatever food it's added to, thus its appeal in food manufacturing.

Trans fat is very possibly the worst type of fat you can eat and really needs to be avoided altogether. Trans fats are made from GM oils for a start, and they both raise your LDL (bad) cholesterol and lower your HDL (good) cholesterol, increasing your risk of heart disease, the leading killer, and mess up our hormones and immunity. Some TFAs are also formed during high temperature cooking, like frying. Processed trans fats can be found in many packaged foods: cake mixes and icings; biscuits and crackers; potato, corn and tortilla chips; pizza and pie crusts; microwave popcorn; anything battered or fried like French fries/hot chips, crumbed seafood, doughnuts and fried chicken; margarine and other butter alternatives; frozen dinners; packaged puddings; Asian crunchy noodles; frozen burgers; ground beef, sausages and hot dogs.

Check food labels for trans fat and partially hydrogenated vegetable oil, which indicates that the food contains some trans fat. However if a 'food' item has less than 0.5 grams of trans fat in a serving, there's no law in Australia or New Zealand requiring the manufacturer to declare TFAs on the label. In such cases, the food label can read 0 grams trans fat.

In June 2015, the US Food and Drug Administration (USFDA) announced that partially hydrogenated oils are no longer 'generally recognised as safe' (GRAS).* This is a positive move that is expected to reduce heart disease and prevent thousands of fatal heart attacks each year. The USFDA had given food manufacturers three years to reformulate products. This is good news, especially if Australia follows suit. (The deadline has now been extended to 2020, as food manufacturer weren't happy with this decision, so the USFDA has recently yielded to this powerful industry).

---

* http://www.lexvivo.com/2015/06/where-gras-is-leaner.html.

But what will the food industry replace trans fats with? Ideally, not more environment-wrecking palm oil, a trans fat-free vegetable oil already found in snack foods such as biscuits, crackers and microwave popcorn. But that's likely to be the case. It's typical now for many processed foods to contain some palm oil, as well as GM soybean, canola or cottonseed oil. Potentially (and frighteningly), there could soon be a lot more of both, just not in the form of a trans fat, which I guess is something.

Please check your labels to avoid trans fats, palm oil **and** GM oils. Better still buy organic products, so you know you're getting none of those nasty toxic oils.

By now, most of us are aware that the food we eat contributes enormously to our health. What we don't necessarily know is that what we **crave** is mostly what our microbiome wants us to eat. Processed oil, (among other things) can change the composition and function of our gut flora, leading to poor food and life choices. So try to make your food as organic and unprocessed as possible, free of GMOs, pesticides, chemical additives and antibiotics. Eating high-quality, nutrient-dense food is critical when you're considering a way towards regaining or maintaining your health. Additives in our food are addictive, so be prepared for cravings and withdrawals once you start to decrease your intake. They won't last long, so stay focused on your health goals.

chapter fifty-three
CARBOHYDRATES

Until recently, most of us thought that starchy stuff like bread, pasta, cereals and grains were the only carbohydrates, and that the majority of our diet should come from this food group. Now we know better. Carbs include non-starchy vegetables like asparagus, cabbage, broccoli and zucchini, along with starchy vegetables like white potatoes, carrots and squash.

In the past there was no differentiation between good and bad carbs. We now know how wrong this is. There is much debate about the optimal amount of carbs to eat daily and what **kind** of carbs they should be, adding to the confusion.

Breastmilk is considered to be the perfect food for infants. It is 40% carbohydrate, as babies need more glucose for their rapid brain development. We all **need** carbs, just not as much as a rapidly growing baby. And definitely not refined carbs, such as white bread, cakes, pastries, donuts, burgers, and refined sugars.

Complex carbohydrates are made up of at least three sugar molecules, and are healthy in moderation. Fibre and starches are both examples of complex carbohydrates. Refined grains, such as white flour and sugar, need be avoided. It seems that consuming too many whole grains and starchy veggies isn't that great long-term either. However cutting out **all** grains and starchy veggies may increase your 'bad' cholesterol (LDL) levels. Your energy levels also decrease and you become glucose deficient, which can interfere with other bodily functions, and may worsen kidney function. Although a ketogenic (very low-carb) diet may work better for men than women, we also know that a low-carb diet can raise cortisol levels, so your adrenal and thyroid function may get worse. Going grain-free when you're suffering with a chronic and complex condition such as Adrenal Fatigue, Chronic Fatigue or a combo' of, is not only *not* recommended, but a really hard thing to maintain.

Bacteria like carbohydrates, so it makes sense to decrease carbohydrate intake, to reduce bacteria by limiting their food supply. Ideally, we want to feed **us** and starve the bacteria. The only carbohydrate that bacteria do not eat much of is insoluble fibre. *See Chapter 38, Understanding Fibre.*

_____ _____ _____ _____

High caloric foods do stimulate serotonin, our happy hormone, which is why we refer to them as comfort-foods. This effect lasts but moments, then we're on the seesaw of low and high blood sugar plus all the addictive, sneaky behaviour that comes with being an addict. This is when we need a reset

_____ _____ _____ _____

Carbs include whole grains, fruit, veggies and legumes. Carb management isn't just about weight loss, but regaining and maintaining good health. For you, this might mean weight loss; to someone else, it might mean a healthy gut, a stronger immune system, clearer skin, better mental health, a healthier heart or better sleep.

AVOID REFINED CARBS

For the majority of us, simply cutting out refined carbs will massively improve our health and happiness. Plus once you cut the nasty, refined grains and sugar out of your diet, you will inadvertently be cutting out a lot of other horrible stuff found in processed foods: trans fats, stabilisers, preservatives, refined salt, palm oil, MSG, antibiotics, colourings, GMO foods, bromines, sulphur dioxide, and so many more chemicals.

_____ _____ _____ _____

The optimal carb range varies quite a lot between individuals over the course of their lives, depending on activity levels, current state of health, age, cultural background, and a few other factors.

_____ _____ _____ _____

If your carb intake is below 25% of your daily intake (the Paleo Diet is about 23% carbs for example), your body will have to adapt to less glucose, which can cause hormonal changes that may negatively impact on your health, especially in women.

But not all carbs are created equally. For example, a bowl of spaghetti bolognese has around 45g carbs, and not the good kind; stir-fry veggies have around 9g and adding in a cup of white rice puts an extra 40g on the total; granola has 60g per serve; Vegemite on toast has approximately 16g; potato salad has 25g; a Big Mac has 35g; Tim Tams about 12g each; and a cup of cooked quinoa equals 30g.

Happily, white rice, organic pasta and potato are back on the menu, if they've been cooked then cooled, thanks to their prebiotic properties. *See Chapter 49, Prebiotics.*

Brown rice generally contains more toxins (heavy metals) than white. Gluten is still something to avoid, so there goes wheat, barley and rye as your staples. Oats don't contain gluten, but look for oats labelled GF, especially if you're coeliac, to be sure they haven't been grown in the same field as grains containing gluten, or mixed in the same bulk bin in the store. Plus oats are usually grown with a truckload of Roundup, so buy them organically grown, or not at all.

Quinoa, millet, buckwheat, amaranth and teff are all gluten-free, and not grains, but still high in anti-nutrients and inflammatory properties unless prepared properly. Keep an eye on your carb intake, as these high-energy quasi-grains are better to eat during the day so you can use their glucose as energy, instead of storing it as fat overnight. See *Chapter 43, Preparing Your Grains*

DON'T JUDGE A FOOD BY ITS CARB CONTENT

By the way, remember that every food has its own unique qualities, besides its carb content. For example, cooled white rice and potatoes are prebiotics; quinoa is full of protein, iron, fibre and calcium; and sweet potatoes are loaded with antioxidants. So be careful not to judge a food by its carb content. Eat a varied diet, **including** complex carbohydrates like whole grains, just not too many. And be mindful that the 'sweet spot' for your carb intake does vary from person to person. Besides, many foods have been modified to be sweeter. For example, sweet potato now has 20g carbohydrate per 100g, so they're like half-veggie/half-fruit now. Apples used to have 3–5g, but now have 14g.

CARB STATISTICS

Low carb: < 5g
Moderate carb: > 5g–10g
High carb: > 10g

Carbs per 100g food

Almonds	22g
Apple	14g
Banana	23g
Brown rice	30–40g
Chickpeas	61g
Grapes	11g
Lentils, raw	60g
Pepitas	54g

Quinoa, cooked	17g
Sweet potato	20g
White potatoes	17 g
White sugar	100g
Yams	28g

Low-carb vegetables at 5g or less
Asparagus, avocado, broad beans, green beans, broccoli, brussels sprouts, cabbage, capsicum, carrot, celery, chicory, cucumber, eggplant, fennel, lettuce, mushroom, onion, pumpkin, radish, silverbeet, tomato, zucchini

Moderate-carb vegetables at 10g or less
Beetroot, broccolini, carrot, potato, pumpkin (butternut)

High-carb vegetables at 10g or more
Peas, Jerusalem artichoke, potatoes (desiree, sebago), orange sweet potato, sweetcorn on cob, taro

chapter fifty-four
AVOID HEAVY METALS

Heavy metal toxicity is not uncommon in the 21st century. To help reduce your levels of toxicity, it's helpful to be aware of the sources so you can avoid them.

Mercury in fungicides and pesticides has decreased in recent years due to environmental concerns; but it's still a worry, as mercury hangs around a long time in the environment. It's also used in the paper industry, and significant sources of mercury pollution arise from coal-fired power plants as well as hospital and local incinerators. This metal makes its way into our soil and water, and eventually to the ocean. Therefore freshwater and ocean sediments contain a good deal of poisonous mercury, and it accumulates in sea animals and fish. It becomes more concentrated as it goes up the food chain, reaching dangerous levels in large fish. So avoid larger species of fish, like swordfish, marlin, shark, king mackerel, yellowfin tuna and bluefin tuna. (Skipjack tuna is a better choice; it's smaller, so will have less of a build-up.) Pregnant and breastfeeding women and advised to keep seafood serves to once or twice a week, and avoid the larger species listed above.

Farmed fish (currently Atlantic salmon, bluefin tuna and barramundi in Australia) are also full of mercury, as are most dental fillings. Some vaccines and medications use it as a preservative.

Arsenic toxicity can occur through water, soil and food contaminated with pesticides, herbicides, insecticides and copper, and may also be absorbed through our lungs and skin. Brown rice products, including brown rice syrup, will mostly have high levels. Shockingly, arsenic continues to be added to animal food (mainly US-based industrial poultry and swine production) as a way to stimulate growth and prevent disease. And it may come as a surprise to learn that around 70% of the world's arsenic production is used to preserve timber for outdoor products, such as decks, play structures, fence enclosures and picnic tables. If you see a greenish tinge to the wood and the structure was built before 2004, it's likely it was treated with arsenic to prevent decay and insect damage.

You'll find **aluminium** mostly in cookware, including your coffee pot. It's a great heat conductor, distributing heat evenly without a high price tag. But this is where its virtues end. Aluminium has been linked to bone and brain damage (like Alzheimer's) and has been found to interfere with the central nervous system. It has been shown to cause cancer in estrogen receptors in human breast tissue. In cookware, it reacts with highly acidic or salty foods. Aluminium is also found in bicarb, unless the label specifies organic or aluminium-free, antiperspirants, cosmetics, pharmaceutical drugs, as an adjuvant for vaccination, and in desensitisation procedures. For more on this topic, you may wish to have a look at *Aluminium and Alzheimer's Disease*, edited by Christopher Exley.

Cadmium is dispersed into the environment from cigarette smoke, e-cigarettes, contaminated soil, the smoke from smelting, and the manufacture of rechargeable batteries. The kidneys and livers of animals and shellfish can contain higher levels of cadmium than other foods.

Lead is still used in the mining industry, in pigments and paints, photographic and engraving processes, nuts and bolts, batteries, plastics and synthetic rubber. Other sources of lead to be aware of are old paint, batteries, the joints in some municipal water systems, some toys and products from China, glazes on (foreign) ceramics, leaded fuel, fishing sinkers, and artist paints with lead pigments. Most lead toxicity occurs via contaminated food or water. A deficiency of zinc, calcium or iron may also increase how much lead you're ingesting, as does an empty stomach.

chapter fifty-five
CHICKEN

While red meat has traditionally been a favourite, chicken is now top of the list as the world's favourite meat. So, what do we need to look for when buying and eating chicken?

Animals raised for food don't have the same legal protections that we give to dogs and cats. There's nothing to prevent farmers from performing surgical procedures like beak trimming or tail cutting without anaesthetics, or raising chickens in extremely cramped conditions, which increases the incidence of sickness, skin diseases and an increased need for antibiotics. Many of the antibiotics fed to mass-produced chickens are identical to the ones given to humans. Buying **certified** organic poultry is the only way to be sure the animals you're eating haven't been given GM feed or antibiotics, or been subjected to cruelty.

By the way, 'free-range' doesn't mean chickens haven't been fed GM food and antibiotics. It only means they have access to the outdoors. And while free-range chickens *technically* have access to the outdoors, this doesn't mean they actually go outside. Typically, meat chickens don't go outside until they are fully feathered, perhaps not at all, as the life they know is indoors. Being labelled 'free-range' doesn't mean the birds are actually ranging free.

Organic chicken products all come from free-range animals that have access to clean pastures and pesticide-free food for their entire lives, as well as eight hours of continuous darkness so they can get adequate rest. Thriving in a stress-free environment makes all the difference in terms of health, nutritional value and taste. Organic chicken farming has a strict focus on environmental sustainability, animal welfare and protecting the habitats of native animals. So be sure to purchase **certified organic poultry** only.

chapter fifty-six
RED MEAT

I t's looking likely that the association between eating meat (lamb, beef, veal, pork) and cancer may be in part due to our own individual microbiome. This means that if we have an unhealthy gut flora, we may be at increased risk of developing cancer if we consume high amounts of either fresh or processed red meat. However, a normal, healthy microbiome may not be.

But what are considered 'high amounts'? It's difficult to find consistency around recommendations. They vary widely, between 60g twice a week to no more than seven serves a week, no bigger than 100g each, and beyond and below this. Results from the 2009 EPIC-Oxford study suggest that if moderate meat eaters (less than 100g daily) consume enough fruits and vegetables, their death rates may be similar to vegetarians.*

I wonder just how accurate these studies are, and what type of meat is being used in the research (organic, pasture-fed or conventional), as there is a world of difference between them. Animals grown for food today are typically fed GM feed, when their natural diet is simply grass and air, and not genetically modified. Plus they're given antibiotics to prevent disease. This difference in the animal's diet

---

* Key, Timothy J, Appleby, Paul N, Spencer, Elizabeth A, Travis, Ruth C, Roddam, Andrew W, Allen, Naomi E. 'Cancer incidence in vegetarians: results from the European Prospective Investigation into Cancer and Nutrition (EPIC-Oxford).' *The American Journal of Clinical Nutrition*, vol 89, no. 5, (May 2009): 1620S–1626S

creates an enormously different type of meat. This meat is toxic, hormone-disrupting and disease-causing.

––––––– ––––––– ––––––– –––––––

The World Health Organization (WHO) report 'Global Strategy for Containment of Antimicrobial Resistance' states that farmers' use of antibiotics in livestock enables microbes to build up defences against the drugs, leap up the food chain and attack human immune systems. They're one of many major health organisations calling for an end to antibiotics in poultry and livestock. Public Health Rep. 2012 Jan-Feb; 127(1): 4–22

––––––– ––––––– ––––––– –––––––

Apart from the addition of antibiotics and GM feed that come with a serve of meat, there is a little-known pathway in our body called *mTOR* (mammalian target of rapamycin). Yet it's important, as it plays a key role in cancer and also the ageing process. Eating too much protein (not only from red meat) is one way to stimulate this pathway in your body. Another issue is that too much protein also affects your insulin and leptin (leptin being the hormone that tells you when you've had enough to eat). So if you're doing your best to eat a high-protein, low-carb diet and are **still** struggling to lose weight, especially with insulin resistance or diabetes, then this way of eating is probably not for you.

Livestock have been fed GM crops since this technology was first introduced in 1996; each of the top six GM crops are heavily utilised by the global animal feed market. Some of the most common ingredients in animal feed are soy, cotton, corn, canola, sugar beet and alfalfa—the top six GM crops. The countries that produce the most animal feed (US, Brazil and China) are also the leaders in GM production, so it's no surprise to learn that their animal feed products are made up of significant amounts of GMOs. In the US, the commercial animal feed industry is the largest purchaser of GM corn and soybean meal. Of the two largest GM crops in the US, 98% soy and 79.5% of corn go directly into feeding animals. (By the way, they are also used for fuelling cars in the US.)

chapter fifty-seven
GM FOODS

Genetically modified (GM) food is a source of great controversy, yet most of us are eating it every day. If you cook with canola oil (also labeled 'vegetable oil'), eat margarine or other butter alternatives, animal products, buy any packaged or takeaway food, eat any Asian food in a restaurant otherwise, snack on biscuits or chocolates, drink soy milk or eat tofu or tempeh, then you're probably tucking into 'frankenfood' at every meal. Many fear GM foods may be linked to gut issues, allergies, antibiotic resistance or cancer. Others suggest these concerns are unfounded.

GMO stands for 'genetically modified organisms' and refers to genetic material that has been removed then artificially altered through genetic engineering, to change a food's characteristics. The new genetic material doesn't have to come from a plant; it can include bacteria and viruses.

Scientists genetically engineer (GE) seeds to give GM foods stronger colours, increase their shelf life, or eliminate seeds. That's why we have seedless watermelons and grapes now. This also makes the 'Big 6' pesticide and GMO corporations extremely wealthy.

Contrary to what the Big 6 like to tell us, there is a huge difference between **crossbreeding** and GMOs. Humans have been manipulating the genetic make-up of plants and animals for thousands of years.

Very few of the animals and plants we eat today have any resemblance to their wild relatives, but the major difference is that crossbreeding is done through sexual reproduction—not artificial manipulation, as in genetic engineering. Plus GMOs have the ability to add new characteristics, or turn other characteristics off.

According to *GMO Myths and Truths* by Claire Robinson, editor of *GM Watch*: *It's not like Lego; you can't just take out one bit, put in another bit, and expect there to be no knock-on effects.* Another problem is that the new proteins created in this weird process could be toxic or allergenic, not to mention less nutritious.

Genetically modified products are in an estimated 60% of processed foods, and that's being conservative. They're also used to make vaccines and medicines. Soybean is one of the biggest crops that uses genetic engineering globally. As much as 90% of soy is GM; it is also used to make lecithin and oil, which go into *many* different foods. GM soy is used to make some bioidentical hormones, contraceptive pills and intra-uterine devices (IUD's) that contain estrogen.

Corn is made into high-fructose corn syrup (HFCS) and is in a lot of sweetened products, such as soft drinks, ice cream and sauces. By the way, 90% of corn grown in the US is genetically modified. Chips, tacos, fried foods and confectionery are likely to contain GM corn or potato from the US, American maize/corn is mostly GM, as is beet sugar that's often used as a sweetener. Another way we may be consuming GM 'food' is through the animal products we eat, from GM soy, corn and sugar beet imported as a stock feed ending up in our milk, butter, eggs, fish and meat.

Canola and cotton are major GM crops in Australia. While you may think you don't eat cotton, oils derived from it are present in most vegetable oils, unless organic; GM cotton is used to make tampons, pads, clothing and bedding too. And medical cannabis, wheat and bananas are now being trialled!

Currently, no fresh fruits or vegetables grown in Australia are genetically modified. However, all GM foods grown overseas and imported into Australia don't require labelling. The European Commission (EU) requires GM food products in Europe to be labelled as such, but elsewhere, no federal law exists for labelling GM foods. Imported food is even more likely to be genetically engineered, as the laws change from country to country. More than three dozen countries, that's more than half of the countries within the European Union have as of 2019 a complete ban, or severe restrictions on GMOs, as well as the pesticides that go with them. These countries include Germany, France, Italy, Austria, Greece, Poland, and Belgium. Russia has said 'not yet' to GMOs stating their focus is on establishing themselves as the world's largest exporter of organic food.

Many are calling for a freeze on GM products until thorough, long-term studies are completed. But with the US pressing ahead and expanding their list of GE crops, that may be wishful thinking.

A lack of long-term studies on the effects of GM foods is a huge concern for many people, and rightly so. There are clinical and peer-reviewed scientific papers showing the hazards of GM crops. Short-term studies have found that liver and kidney toxicity and immune reactions tend to be the most prevalent, but inflammation, digestive and fertility issues have also been seen.[*]

Another issue of concern is that the most common genetically engineered products are used in conjunction with toxic herbicides inccluding Roundup. (Commercial formulations such as Roundup, which are complex formulations of chemicals, are up to 1,000 times more toxic than glyphosate in isolation. Roundup gets incorporated into the entire plant and cannot be washed off.) Many GM crops are engineered to tolerate ten times the normal level of this and other herbicides. And in March 2016, the World Health Organization (WHO) classified glyphosate-based herbicides as 'probably carci-nogenic'. Glyphosate, the active ingredient in Monsanto's herbicide Roundup (or Roundup Ready), first patented as an antibiotic, that

---

[*] Dona, Artemis, and Arvanitoyannis, Ioannis S. 'Health Risks of Genetically Modified Foods.' *Critical Reviews in Food Science and Nutrition* 49.2 (2009): 164–175.

can devastate human gut bacteria. It's in the foods we eat, the air we breathe and the water we drink. Glyphosate, like all antibiotics, kills beneficial bacteria in the soil and in the human gut. Not surprisingly, crops heavily sprayed with glyphosate have lower nutrient density. They're now also using glyphosate on non-GM crops to 'ripen off' the crop just before harvest.

In May 2019, a Californian jury ordered Monsanto to pay $US2 billion ($2.8b) to a couple who say they contracted cancer after using the commonly used weedkiller, Roundup. This is third case they have lost. Lawyers say there will be thousands more cases against Monsanto.

So if you're concerned about your health or the future of our planet, stick to fresh, locally grown foods and look for products **certified organic**. Avoid the four major GM foods—cotton, canola, soy and corn, unless organic—and look for products that are labelled 'GM-free'. Basically, avoid processed foods and oils, and all animal products from unknown sources.

chapter fifty-eight
BROMINES

The damaging effects and widespread use of a class of chemicals called halogens is relatively unknown, let alone bromine itself. Halogens include fluoride, chlorine, iodine and bromine. Halogens with a higher weight displace those with a lower weight, which means that heavier halogens like fluorine, chlorine and bromine can bully a lighter one, iodine, out of the way.

So if you are ingesting or absorbing fluoride, chlorine or bromine, chances are that you'll be iodine deficient. Your thyroid won't able to hold onto the iodine it needs because when you ingest or absorb bromine, it displaces iodine and you could end up with an iodine deficiency. This is bad news as iodine affects every tissue in your body, not just your thyroid.

Too much of any halogen results in toxicity. In the case of bromine, it's known as the Bromide Dominance Theory, and it has many detrimental consequences for our health.

Bromide-containing pesticides (methyl bromide) are also widely used to treat our soil, so residues in non-organic food are the most common way we are exposed to bromines. They tend to accumulate through the food chain too, so we face the real risk of these chemicals slowly building up in our bodies. They're also in fire retardants, as well as in our computers, pillows, cushions, fabrics, carpets, TV, mattress and car upholstery. They can also be found in bakery goods and some flours, as a dough conditioner for impatient bakers (potassium bromate). In soft drinks (including Mountain Dew and until recently Fanta and Gatorade) and other citrus-flavoured sodas, in the form of brominated vegetable oils (BVOs) to help suspend the flavour and colour evenly in the liquid. Also in medications such as some inhalers and nasal sprays, drugs to treat ulcers, and anaesthetics.

Bromine-based hot tubs and swimming pool treatments are common ways to get bromine toxicity. A better option than bromine and chlorine is an ozone purification system. That way it's possible to keep the water clean with minimal chemicals. Bromine toxicity can also come from the materials used to make computers and your car's dashboard. Toothpastes and mouthwashes containing potassium bromate can cause bleeding and inflammation of the gums.

-------- -------- -------- --------

We hear a lot about the importance of iodine, but not much about how the absorption of it is inhibited by a class of chemicals called halogens. This a group in the periodic table consisting of five related elements: fluorine, chlorine, bromine, astatine and iodine. Any of these chemicals can displace iodine in your thyroid gland. These chemicals need to be removed before iodine can be absorbed and do its work.

-------- -------- -------- --------

LIMIT YOUR EXPOSURE

It's not easy to eliminate bromines, but you can limit your exposure. Open the windows to your building, home and car to let fresh air in. Environmental toxins are much higher inside buildings and cars than outside, due to the higher temperatures inside. Use fans to circulate the air, and open your car windows before turning on your air conditioner. Look for organic wholegrain breads and flour or 'no bromine' or 'bromine-free' labels on baked goods. Eat organic as often as possible to ensure its absence. Use glass and ceramic storage containers; avoid eating, drinking or storing food and fluid in plastic. If you own a hot tub, look into ways of keeping the water clean with minimal chemical treatments.

Today, bromine is extracted on an industrial scale from salt lakes that are especially rich in the element, like the Dead Sea. It's huge business.

In 1990, the United Kingdom banned bromate in bread. In 1994, Canada did the same, followed by Japan in 2010. Brazil recently outlawed bromide in flour products. Unfortunately, the US and Australia have no laws around its use.

chapter fifty-nine
SOY

With all the controversy out there about soy, it's hard to know whether to include it in your diet or not. One minute it's great for increasing bone strength and decreasing menopausal hot flushes; the next it's likely to give you cancer and thyroid disease. Yes, soy can act like estrogens in the body, which may or may not be a good thing.

We're now eating soy in forms it was never eaten before, genetically modified, highly processed and just weird. Plus our Western diet includes more soy than was ever eaten in the East. In Asia, traditionally the beans have been soaked for around 15 hours, then undergo a long, slow cooking time before they are ready to eat. Like most of our food these days, there's the **wholefood** version that nature created, then there's the genetically modified type. Soy is one of the crops grown using this dangerous new science, along with canola, corn and cotton, with wheat, cannabis, and many others soon to be added to this list. Guess what foods we eat the most of? You got it—corn, soy, wheat and rice!

GM soy is changed into strange things, such as soy protein isoflavones, soy protein isolates and soy lecithin. And the food industry is allowed to stuff this carcinogenic 'food' into as many packaged products as they can! So avoid processed soy at all costs. This means any soy product that doesn't specify that it's **not** genetically modified. Or better still, **certified organically grown.**

So this cuts out lots of soy: edamame, soy sauce at Asian restaurants and take away, any tofu dish including vegetarian pad thai or agedashi tofu from your local takeaway place. Also avoid textured vegetable protein (TVP), used to make soy burgers, vegetarian sausages and other meat substitutes. Then there's soy cheese made from GM soybeans (and toxic chemicals); also soy milk that isn't made with Australian organic whole soy beans. Basically, most of what is in your supermarket and coffee shop: soy protein powder, soy milk powder and soy crisps. Most other snack and packaged food needs to be avoided also. GM soy is not just in the food we eat directly; animals are fed most of the soy (and corn and canola) grown on the planet today. Unless organically raised, this kind of meat, fish and eggs need to be avoided also.

Fermented, organic soy products like tempeh, natto miso, tamari, soy sauce and miso paste are much easier on our digestive tract than unfermented soy products such as milk and tofu. Miso paste is a wonderful food, especially for your gut (and these days, it's also made using other ingredients apart from soy). Tempeh is high in protein; being a fermented food, it's very good for gut health also. Like miso paste, tempeh is now available made from other ingredients like red lentils, brown rice and fava (broad) beans. Natto miso, another lovely fermented soy product, contains vitamin B12 and is the best source of vitamin K2 that we have (K2 is the latest celebrity vitamin that we'll be hearing a lot more about in the future). For cases of both hypo and hyperthyroidism, choose organic, fermented soy over processed soy.

It's never a good idea to throw the baby out with the bathwater though. Remember that organic, fermented soy has been considered a healthy food in the past. But if you're uncomfortable including organic, fermented soy in your diet, then just leave it out.

We now know that soy may not be dangerous for women with breast cancer; of course, that refers to organic or at least GMO-free soybeans. Women with breast cancer who have consumed more soy do not have a higher risk of dying over nine years than women who have eaten less. And among women with a certain type of breast cancer, soy actually lowered their risk of dying from any cause during that time.*

Similarly, researchers done by the University of Southern California in January 2008, found that women who included an average of one cup of soy milk or about one-half cup of tofu daily have about 30 percent less risk of developing breast cancer, compared with women who have little or no soy products in their diets. But it looks like the soy consumption may have to occur during adolescence when breast tissue is forming.† The Women's Healthy Eating and Living Study showed that women diagnosed with breast cancer gain a major advantage by incorporating soy products into their diets. Those who consumed the most soy products cut their risk of cancer recurrence or mortality in half.‡

We should not recommend that women with breast cancer avoid organic soy, because there's been no evidence to support that it's harmful.

---

* Zhang Fang Fang MD, PhD, Haslam Danielle E., MS, Terry, Mary Beth, PhD, Knight, Julia A., PhD, Andrulis, Irene L., PhD, Daly, Mary B., MD, PhD, Buys, Saundra S. MD, John, Esther M. PhD. 'Dietary isoflavone intake and all-cause mortality in breast cancer survivors: The Breast Cancer Family Registry.' *American Cancer Society*, vol 123, no. 11 (1 June, 2017): 2070–2079

† Wu, A, Yu, M, Tseng, C-C, and Pike, M. 'Epidemiology of Soy Exposures and Breast Cancer Risk.' *The British Journal of Cancer*, vol 98, no. 1 (January 15, 2008): 9–14.

‡ Dieli-Conwright, Christina M., Lee, Kyuwan, and Kiwata, Jacqueline L. 'Reducing the Risk of Breast Cancer Recurrence: An Evaluation of the Effects and Mechanisms of Diet and Exercise.' *Current Breast Cancer Reports*, vol 8, no. 3 (2016): 139–150.

chapter sixty
WATER

Filtering the water we drink and bathe in is more of a necessity than an option these days. Most of us just aren't aware that bathing in contaminated water may be even more harmful to our health than drinking it, as the chemicals absorbed through our skin go directly into the bloodstream, skipping our digestive and filtration systems. Chlorine intensifies once heated, so having a shower or bath may not be getting us as clean as we think. We really do need to avoid tap water, due to the fluoride, chlorine and antibiotics it contains. (No, we don't need this kind of fluoride.) Then there's the heavy metals in tap water, including lead, chromium and arsenic, all sources of xenoestrogens.

Drink fluoride and chlorine-free filtered water at room temperature. To go a step further, use a chlorine filter on shower heads if you're not on tank water, especially if you're suffering from a skin condition like eczema or psoriasis. If you are on tank water you still need to filter your water, but in this case you'll need a carbon filter to remove parasites, not heavy metals and xenoestrogens.

Mountain spring water is some of the healthiest water on the planet, because it is still alive and has the optimal pH of around 7. We aim to eat living food in its raw natural state, so why not include the water we drink? If you can't access crystal-clear pure mountain water, and let's be real, not many of us can anymore, then buy a filter that gives you the ideal pH of water (6.5–7.5) which is neutral. A pH of 8–10 may be too alkaline and could create problems in your body; distilled water is too acidic. Clean water is the best liquid to drink, but we also get plenty of water from fruits, vegetables and their juices. Coconuts are another lovely source of fresh pure water and electrolytes.

Currently, water treatment plants are not designed or required to remove hormonal pollutants from water, and agricultural and pharmaceutical run-off has created a serious epidemic among fish and frogs in many waterways in the developed world. Our aquatic friends are actually switching gender now, due to the high levels of estrogen in effluent.

Dehydration is a serious issue. This occurs when our body has lost a significant amount of water due to illness, excessive exercise or sweating, or an inability to get or keep fluids down. So how much is water is enough? The amount we require depends on what we're eating, where we live, our age and weight, and our level of physical activity. We need to be drinking enough water so our urine is a light-coloured yellow, without a strong odour. Our thirst mechanism decreases as we age, so it's important for older people to be especially mindful of the colour and smell of their urine.

By the way, avoid drinking from plastic bottles as they leach toxic bisphenol A (BPA) that ends up in our body, (and waterways). Use glass, or metal or a container that states it is BPA-free.

part four
40-DAY RESET PROGRAM AND RECIPES

chapter sixty-one
INTERMITTENT FASTING

Over the next 40 days, you're going to be eating really easy-to-digest foods for two days a week. Foods like blended soups, smoothies, medicinal mylks and soft desserts. You can choose to do these two days of **intermittent fasting** either consecutively or separately throughout the week. On those two days, you'll be giving your gut a break. As an added bonus, microbes in your gut make serotonin when you're fasting, so be prepared for 'the faster's high' (usually after Day 3).

Not eating for 12–18 hours a day is another way to practise intermittent fasting. It is really effective, but let's be realistic. Restricting eating to only six hours a day is difficult and not so practical to begin with, especially if you're new to the world of cleansing. Plus, this kind of fasting will never suit everyone, especially those who are frail, underweight, weak or unwell.

For the other five days a week you'll enjoy delicious, healing foods, that are also easy to digest but are not in pureed form. These are the days when you could plan your social nights; just be sure to order mostly vegetables with some fish, organic chicken or tofu, or legumes (if you can digest them), and be careful not to overeat, or drink.

I've included easy recipes for all three meals, plus healing teas, mylks and desserts. By cutting down (not eliminating) the harder-to-digest foods like grains and legumes, and preparing them properly when they are included; and by avoiding processed dairy, red meat, sugar, alcohol, coffee, all refined and processed foods, and all the toxic chemicals you can manage, you'll allow your digestive organs to relax. Our gut is a big muscle after all, and it probably hasn't had a break in a while, so this is giving it some time out. At the same time, you'll be adding in clean, easy-to-digest foods to strengthen and heal your whole body.

If I've used an ingredient or food group that you're allergic or currently intolerant to, just leave it out or replace with something you can digest. For example, I like to use onions and garlic in my recipes. Of course leave them out if you want, and consider substituting with one teaspoon of asafoetida powder. If you can't tolerate mangoes, use berries. If you prefer to use ghee as your main healthy fat, then go ahead, just make sure it's organic. If you know eggs aren't a problem, then include up to six organic eggs a week any way you prefer, like in an omelette, fried, poached, scrambled or in a frittata or fritters.

Regarding coffee, it's up to you whether you remove it or just reduce the amount you're currently having. The reason for this is that we all process coffee differently; for some of us it can actually be beneficial, rather than detrimental. Benefits range from helping to prevent diabetes and liver disease, protection against Parkinson's disease, and keeping your heart healthy. However, if you know that coffee causes a negative reaction like headaches, insomnia, an irritable tummy or nervous system, then it's best to leave it out during your Reset, at least. If you keep it in, make sure it's fair trade and organic. In no way is instant coffee acceptable, unless of course you can find an organic one.

During your Reset, it's best avoid red meat altogether. After the 40 days, introduce it back in if you like, but restrict it to 60g serves of organic meat, two to three times a week.

Regarding dairy, you may just be having problems with the processing of it. Either completely remove it from your diet during your Reset or, if you can handle some dairy, include organic goat or sheep products, preferably cultured/fermented products like yoghurt, kefir and curd, with some feta and haloumi. After the Reset, if your gut is handling these foods, then keep them in your diet. After your gut heals, there's a strong possibility you'll be able to tolerate quality, organic, grass-fed cow's dairy.

After the 40-Day Reset, try to keep the ritual of intermittent fasting (IF) up, perhaps for two days a week. The ultimate aim is to eat around 800 calories a day, and preferably within 6–12 hours of the day on these 2 IF days. To do this, have a late breakfast and lunch, and miss (or eat a very light) dinner, and no alcohol. The crankiness does pass. Promise. Use any of your favourite recipes I have provided in the Reset for these IF days going forward.

If you feel adrenally exhausted, have been diagnosed or suspect you are living with adrenal fatigue, chronic fatigue, low thyroid function or fibromyalgia, or you have trouble keeping weight on, it may be necessary to include grains more than a few times a week, as having any less may cause further fatigue and other unpleasant symptoms. Other early side effects of the 40-Day Reset Program could be head-aches, nausea, fatigue, pimples, grumpiness, different kinds of bowel movements and anger. This is pretty normal and is sometimes referred to as a 'healing crisis'. It's due to toxins (both physical and emotional) being released faster than we can eliminate them. If you do start to experience these symptoms, then drink more water to help flush the toxins out faster. It won't last long, maybe a day or two at most. By the way, Day 3 or Day 5 is when this usually happens, if it's going to.

If you have an unexpected blowout, instead of spending the next day in regret and self-loathing, just get back onto your Reset program. This is a not a punishment, a diet, nor a self-imposed prison sentence for 40 days, but a chance to give our mind/body a break, with all the benefits that come along with that. The reason I'm stressing that this program is not a diet is because when we feel deprived, we tend to binge the moment we can. Plus this is **not** a diet; it's simply a healthy change in the way you eat. The main thing here is to keep eating organic food, mostly plants. This alone will ensure better health.

I'm sure you'll find the 40-Day Reset Program tasty, inexpensive and really enjoyable. It's a good idea to plan your meals seven days ahead, at the beginning of each week. I've included a meal planner for four weeks to help with this. The soups freeze well, as do many of the other dishes, so feel free to double or triple up on the recipes you like, so you have a stash of them ready for your meals. Simply pull the next day's meals out of the freezer on the night before.

chapter sixty-two
RECIPES FOR TWO DAYS A WEEK

Your meals for the two days of intermittent fasting will be either pureed, mashed, pounded, blended, whizzed or ground. Whichever way you choose, they will be smooth, a bit like baby food, but tastier.

SMOOTHIES
(ALL RECIPES ARE FOR 1 SERVE)

To create your ideal smoothie …
- Choose your mylk (non-dairy), fruit and nut butter, unless I've specified one to use.
- If you like, add a few drops of honey or ½ banana (not too ripe) to sweeten your smoothies. Use stevia, if you know you can't handle any sweeteners right now.
- Feel okay about leaving an ingredient out (or replacing it), if you don't have it on hand, don't like it or can't digest it.
- Add as much clean water (or more or less mylk or coconut water) as you need, to reach your preferred smoothie consistency.

1. IGNITE IMMUNITY

Reishi has been proven to be greatly beneficial for our immune system. Combining it with these other wonderful ingredients with similar actions, makes this a great smoothie for fighting any dis-ease.

½ cup	paw paw
½ tsp	reishi powder
½ tsp	acai powder
½ tsp	turmeric, ground
½ tsp	cinnamon, ground
½ tsp	cacao powder
⅓ cup	aloe juice
1 cup	coconut water

Method Add all ingredients to a blender and whiz until smooth.

2. HORMONE HAPPINESS

Flax seeds contain hormone-balancing lignans and plant estrogens that help regulate our moon cycle and reduce menopausal hot flushes. They are also anti-inflammatory, assist with weight loss and act as an antidepressant.

½ cup	raspberries
1	cacao bean or 1 tsp cacao powder
1 tbsp	flax meal
1 tsp	maca powder
½ tsp	vanilla bean powder or essence
½ tbsp	coconut oil
1 tsp	evening primrose oil
1½ cups	mylk

Method Add all ingredients to a blender and whiz until smooth.

3. LIVER LOVING

Chlorella is nature's best cleanser and detoxifier, helping to flush out stored waste and pollutants from our temple via our liver and gut.

¼ cup	pineapple
1	small banana
1 tsp	microalgae (chlorella, spirulina, wheatgrass or barley grass)
2 drops	peppermint essential oil (food grade) or 3 mint leaves
1½ cups	coconut water

Method Add all ingredients to a blender and whiz until smooth.

4. PROTEIN POWER

Hemp has an unique, easy-to-digest protein called edestin that increases our body's own natural defence system that helps fight off dis-ease.

½ cup	berries
1 tbsp	hemp seeds or an organic vegan protein powder
1 tbsp	almond butter
1 tsp	spirulina
½ tsp	vanilla essence or powder, or seeds from ½ pod
1½ cups	almond mylk

Method Add all ingredients to a blender and whiz until smooth.

5. CURB THE CRAVINGS

Cinnamon helps to control our need to overeat, by balancing our blood sugar levels. At the same time, it dramatically reduces gut problems associated with irritable bowel syndrome (IBS). If you have stomach issues, a cup of cinnamon tea 2–3 times per day will really help reduce the pain and bloating.

½ cup	pineapple
1 tsp	slippery elm powder
1 tsp	maca
1 tbsp	chia seeds, any colour
1 tsp	chlorella
½ tsp	cinnamon, ground
½ tbsp	coconut oil
1½ cups	coconut mylk

Method Add all ingredients to a blender and whiz until smooth. Drink immediately, otherwise the chia seeds and slippery elm will set the smoothie like a pudding. Be sure to drink lots of water after you have these foods, otherwise they may slow down the elimination of waste from your body.

6. BALANCE YOUR BLOOD SUGAR

Soluble fibres such as psyllium husks are prebiotics that help encourage a healthy bacteria in our gut and have a positive effect on our immune system and mood as well.

½ cup	paw paw or rockmelon
1 tsp	raw cacao nibs or powder or 1 cacao bean
½ tsp	fresh ginger
½ tsp	cinnamon, ground

1 tbsp	chia seeds
1 tsp	psyllium husks
½ cup	baby spinach or kale
1½ cups	mylk

Method Add all ingredients to a blender and whiz until smooth. Drink immediately, otherwise the psyllium husks and chia seeds will set the smoothie like a pudding. Be sure to drink lots of water after this smoothie, otherwise it may cause a sluggish gut.

7. GET YOUR GUT GOING

Chlorella's detoxification power comes from its incredibly high content of chlorophyll. Its 'cracked cell' walls have the ability to grab onto unwanted materials and pollutants, and remove them from our body.

½ cup	rockmelon
1 tsp	licorice powder
1 tsp	slippery elm powder
⅓ cup	berry aloe vera juice, or 1 tbsp fresh gel
1 tsp	chlorella
1⅓ cups	mylk or coconut water

Method Add all ingredients to a blender and whiz until smooth.

8. THE GUT SWEEPER

Like other foods high in antioxidants and fibre, slippery elm bark is wonderful to help relieve symptoms of IBS, ulcers and too much acidity in our body.

| ¼ | avocado |
| ½ cup | spinach leaves |

⅓ cup	lemon (or any) aloe vera juice, or 1 tbsp fresh gel
1 tsp	slippery elm powder
½ tbsp	coconut oil
2 drops	peppermint essential oil or a few mint leaves
1⅓ cups	coconut water

Method Add all ingredients to a blender and whiz until smooth.

9. MOJO RISING

Maca powder is the superfood of the Incas, where it was revered for its hormone-balancing qualities. It's a high-fibre root vegetable, also used to improve stamina and libido.

½ cup	berries
½ cup	baby spinach
1 tsp	microalgae, like spirulina, wheatgrass or barley grass
1 tsp	maca powder
1 tsp	matcha powder
4	fresh mint leaves, or 2 drops peppermint essential oil
1½ cups	coconut water

Method Add all ingredients to a blender and whiz until smooth.

10. OPTIMUM OMEGA-3

Chia seeds are packed with alpha-linolenic acid (ALA), a short-chain omega-3 fatty acid, making them the highest plant source of these anti-inflammatory oils. If you don't have a high-speed blender, use flax meal instead of the flax seeds, as these hard little seeds are too difficult to digest unless ground into a meal, an oil or rehydrated.

½	banana
1 tsp	hemp seeds
1 tsp	chia seeds
1 tsp	flax seeds
1 tbsp	walnuts
½ tsp	dulse or nori flakes (you won't taste these)
1½ cups	organic soy mylk

Method Add all ingredients to a blender and whiz until smooth.

11. HEAVY METAL DETOX

Toxicity occurs when we're exposed to 'heavy metals' for too long. It can lead to mental health issues and damage our organs. Good fats and coriander help draw out these metals; chlorella attaches to and removes them via the liver and bowel. I've included spinach as a probiotic, to improve gut detoxification and boost immunity. Add in half a cup of fruit if you'd prefer it sweeter.

¼ cup	coriander
½ cup	spinach leaves
½ tsp	seaweed, like powdered dulse or nori
1 tsp	oil (olive, hemp, pumpkin seed, flax, avocado, coconut) or tahini
1 tsp	chlorella
¼ tsp	vitamin C powder (or 250mg)
1 drop	peppermint oil
1 cup	coconut water or filtered water

Method Add all ingredients to a blender and whiz until smooth.

12. GOLDEN GLOW

All of these ingredients help us lose weight and keep it off. They'll keep your blood sugar from dipping, so you'll feel full and focussed for longer. Other benefits include a boost to healthy gut flora, reduced inflammation and an increase in mojo (vitality plus libido). It'll also help balance wayward hormones.

½ cup	berries
½ cup	spinach leaves
¼	avocado
1 tsp	chia seeds
1 tsp	hemp seeds
1 tsp	psyllium husks
½ tsp	ground turmeric, or 1 tbsp grated fresh
½ tsp	ground cinnamon
1 tsp	maca powder
1½ cups	coconut water or mylk

Method Add all ingredients to a blender and whiz until smooth.

SOUPS
(ALL RECIPES ARE FOR 4 SERVINGS)

Follow these basic rules for great soups, every time:
- Choose the stock you'd like to use as your base, be it vegetable, mushroom, meat, chicken, turkey or seafood. To get the consistency you like, use more stock or clean water.
- If you're avoiding garlic, onions and leeks, replace these with one teaspoon of ground asafoetida powder. This is a (smelly) spice

frequently used in India cooking that gives a similar flavour and helps digest whatever you add it to. Its also said to help open your crown chakra. Available from Asian grocery stores, health food stores and well-stocked supermarkets.

- Use whatever vegetables you can tolerate. In most cases, my recipes will allow for a neat swap.

- For deeper flavours, roast your spices in the pot in a little oil (or dry) over a low heat at first, then add the veggies and protein, then herbs and stock. For a lighter, milder soup, you can start your soup with a pot of water or stock, then add the other ingredients, leaving out the oil.

- Add lots of different fresh and dried herbs for maximum flavour and antioxidants.

- Season with sea salt, tamari, miso paste, fish sauce, coconut aminos or Bragg's seasoning.

- Most soups freeze well for about three months, so double the quantities, then freeze your soup in portions of one or two servings for when your hungry self walks into the kitchen.

- In most cases, you can decide on the protein you choose to add. Organic chicken or turkey, locally-caught seafood, organic tofu or tempeh, properly prepared legumes, or goat's haloumi. Garnish with goat's feta, or use hemp seeds or oil. (Remember hemp doesn't like to be heated.)

- Leave an ingredient out (or replace it), if you don't have it on hand. In most cases, this will be fine.

- During the 40-Day Reset Program, puree your soups to a liquid for two days a week; on the remaining five days, keep them chunky. After 40 days, serve them as you (and your gut) prefer.

1. KOHLRABI AND COCONUT

Fenugreek helps reduce internal and external inflammation. It is also known to promote mother's milk, decrease menopausal hot flushes, increase your sex drive, balance blood sugar and lower cholesterol. Fenugreek also improves reproductive function, as well as digestive problems from nausea and constipation to ulcerative colitis.

2 tbsp	olive oil
1	brown onion, roughly chopped
2	garlic cloves, crushed
1 tbsp	fenugreek seeds ground, or 2 tsp powder
1	medium-sized cauliflower, cut into florets
2 cups	small kohlrabi bulbs, peeled and roughly chopped
1 × 400g	BPA-free tin coconut milk and 600ml water, or use stock
1 tsp	unrefined salt, or to taste
6	basil leaves, fresh
	Cracked pepper and extra olive oil to serve

Method In a soup pot, warm oil over a medium heat. Gently sauté onions until translucent, about 2 minutes. Add garlic and fenugreek, then sauté for another minute or so, until fragrant. Next add in the veggies and stir until they're covered with the spices. Now pour in 1 litre of liquid (coconut milk and/or stock). Add the salt. Bring to a boil then drop to a simmer until veggies are soft, about 20 minutes. Add basil leaves. Cover and remove from heat to allow to cool a little. Using a stick blender, puree the soup in the pot, or pour into a blender and puree until smooth. Garnish with a crack of pepper and a swirl of olive oil.

2. CREAMY THAI

Kohlrabi is a German veggie that translates in English to 'turnip cabbage'. It belongs to the Brassica family that includes cabbage, turnips, broccoli, collard greens, cauliflower, kale and brussels sprouts. It has a similar taste and texture to a broccoli stem or cabbage, but milder and sweeter, like a cross between a turnip and cauliflower. Kohlrabi leaves or tops are also full of nutrients, including vitamin C (it provides 62 mg per 100g, meeting your daily needs), so you can blanch these, slice finely then serve as a garnish. Try to get smaller kohlrabis, as the bigger ones tend to be stringy.

3 cups	kohlrabi, peeled and roughly chopped
1 litre	stock, bone broth or filtered water
4	spring onions, trimmed and roughly chopped
1–2	garlic cloves, crushed
1 tbsp	fresh ginger, grated
1 tbsp	fresh turmeric, grated
6	kaffir lime leaves
Small handful	Thai basil, Vietnamese mint or coriander leaves
2 tsp	unrefined salt, or coconut aminos to taste
200ml	coconut milk or stock
	Olive or pumpkin seed oil to garnish

Method Place everything in a soup pot, except the coconut milk. Bring to the boil, then drop to a simmer until veggies are cooked. Remove kaffir lime leaves and add coconut milk or more stock. Blend with a stick blender until smooth, then drizzle with an unrefined oil like olive, pumpkin or avocado, or garnish with a tablespoon of the Nut Paste from my Spiced Indian Soup.

3. ORIENTAL CHICKEN

Use a whole chicken, to save money and waste. It will also provide you with the base and extra flavour for your soup. The bones will make bone broth to use in another soup, or drink separately. When you're making the stock, you could use aromatics like smashed, fresh lemongrass, a few kaffir lime leaves and the skins from the onion, garlic, ginger and turmeric.

	Flesh from 1.8kg organic chicken, shredded
2 tbsp	olive oil
1	onion or 1 large eschalot, roughly chopped
2	garlic cloves, chopped
1 tbsp	fresh ginger, grated
1 tbsp	fresh turmeric, grated or 1tbsp ground
1 tsp	dulse or nori flakes
1	small bunch coriander, leaves and stems chopped separately
1	large potato, diced
1½ litres	chicken stock or broth (made from the whole chicken)
1 tbsp	apple cider vinegar
6	shiitake mushrooms, fresh and sliced (or whole dried)
½–1 tbsp	tamari

Method In a soup pot, warm the oil over a medium heat, then gently sauté the onions until translucent, about 2 minutes. Add the garlic, ginger, turmeric, seaweed and coriander stems. Stir and allow to sauté until fragrant, another minute or so. Add in the chicken and potato. Stir, so they're covered with the spices. Now pour in 1½ litres of chicken stock or broth, along with the vinegar, mushrooms, coriander leaves and tamari. Bring to the boil, then drop to a simmer until the veggies are soft—about 15 minutes. Remove from heat and allow to cool a little. Using a stick blender, puree the soup in the pot, otherwise pour into a blender and puree until smooth. Or keep chunky for your five non-puree days.

4. ASPARAGUS, JERUSALEM ARTICHOKE AND GARLIC

Asparagus and Jerusalem artichokes (not the artichokes you get marinated, but the knobbly ones related to sunflowers that look a bit like fresh ginger) store most of their energy in the form of inulin (instead of glucose). Inulin is a long chain of fructose (sugar) molecules that

RECIPES FOR TWO DAYS A WEEK

human digestive enzymes cannot break apart and use for energy, making it a fibre instead of a starch. Other vegetables that contain significant amounts of inulin include garlic and chicory root. Avoid these veggies if you're on a low FODMAP diet, or if you know these foods hurt your gut.

1 tbsp	olive oil
1	brown onion, chopped
2–4	garlic cloves, crushed (or none)
1 cup	Jerusalem artichokes, scrubbed clean then chopped quite small
1 tbsp	fresh thyme leaves, or 1 tsp dried
1	bunch asparagus, ends trimmed and cut into 6 pieces
1 litre	stock or bone broth
1	lemon, juiced and zest grated
2 cups	spinach
1 tsp	unrefined salt, or to taste
1 cup	hazelnuts, soaked overnight then drained, optional
½ tsp	white pepper, ground or cracked, or cayenne or smoked paprika
	Drizzle truffle or hemp oil to serve, optional

Method In a soup pot over a medium heat, gently sauté the onions in olive oil until translucent, about 2 minutes. Add garlic, artichokes and thyme and stir to coat. Add stock and bring to the boil, before reducing heat to a simmer, until the artichokes are tender. This will depend on how small you cut them, but about 20 minutes. Now add asparagus, zest, spinach and salt to the pot, and simmer until the asparagus is tender. Remove from heat and allow to cool slightly. Using a stick blender, food processor or blender, puree until the mixture is smooth. To add some protein, fibre and more good oils to this soup, and a lovely nutty flavour, add the hazelnuts when you add the

263

asparagus, and garnish each bowl with a drizzle of truffle or hemp oil, and a sprinkling of pepper, cayenne or smoked paprika.

5. CREAM OF MUSHROOM

It's easy to make rich and creamy dishes without using cream. Use nuts, especially cashews. They're full of tryptophan, fibre, magnesium and fatty acids, nutrients proven to help improve our mental health and wellbeing. Lubne, tahini, coconut milk/cream, feta, cottage cheese and ricotta will all add richness and a thickness to your bowl too. As a bonus, these foods are wonderful for healing the gut. Using soaked porcini and/or shiitake mushrooms as well as or instead of the fresh mushrooms, will add a magnificent depth of flavour and even more medicinal properties. Be sure to also add the soaking liquid to your soup.

1 cup	cashews, soaked for a few hours (then drain onto your plants)
2 cups	kohlrabi, peeled and roughly chopped
2 cups	button or Swiss mushrooms, halved
1 litre	stock or bone broth
1 tsp	unrefined salt or to taste
½ tsp	white pepper, ground or cracked
½ cup	fresh basil leaves, loosely packed
1 tbsp	apple cider vinegar
1 tbsp	hemp seeds or oil, optional
	Sprinkle cayenne pepper to garnish

Method Place all ingredients in a soup pot over high heat and bring to the boil. Drop to a simmer until the veggies are soft, about 20 minutes. Cool slightly then puree, using a blender, food processor or stick blender. To add more anti-inflammatory properties to this soup, serve with hemp seeds or oil.

6. SEAFOOD CHOWDER

Seafood is an easy and tasty way to meet our protein and omega-3 fatty acid requirements. However, we need to be mindful of the type of seafood we're eating, as it can be full of horrible additives and caught unethically. In the case of prawns, it's the sodium metabisulphite they've been washed in which can cause wheezing, nausea, pain, a skin rash or itch, or all of the above. Look for sulphur-free prawns, or ask your fishmonger to source them for you. By the way, ethically sourced seafood does not mean wild-caught. It means farmed, and that means chemicals and antibiotics come with your seafood.

200 g	smoked cod or smoked haddock (undyed)
200 g	chemical-free green prawns peeled, deveined, roughly chopped
1	bay leaf
500ml	filtered water
2 tbsp	olive oil, ghee or butter
1	large leek, halved lengthways, white parts thinly sliced
½ cup	celery sticks, thinly sliced
2	garlic cloves, chopped.
2 cups	kale or baby spinach, loosely packed
1	sweet corn, kernels removed
2 tbsp	fresh thyme chopped, or 2 tsp dried thyme
1 cup	almond, soy or coconut mylk
1 cup	stock
	Sea salt (taste first before adding)
¼ cup	chopped parsley

Method Place seafood in a deep, wide pan with the bay leaf and 500ml water. Cover and simmer for 2 minutes. Turn off the heat and leave to stand covered for a further 5 minutes. Drain, keeping the liquid for later. When cooled, roughly flake up the fish fillet using your fingers, keeping it fairly chunky. In the same pot, heat the oil, ghee or butter. Add the leek, celery, corn and garlic then gently fry over a medium heat until softened, about 10 minutes. Add your thyme and the reserved cooking liquid, then bring to the boil. Reduce heat and simmer for 10 minutes, until the vegetables have softened. Add in the seafood, stir, then allow to heat through. On your two days of liquid meals, using a food processor, blender, or stick blender, process your chowder until smooth. (On the other five days, process only half, then return this to the pot.) Finally, add enough mylk and/or stock to reach the creamy consistency you like, then simmer for 3 minutes before tasting and adjusting the seasoning. To serve, sprinkle with finely chopped parsley.

7. ROASTED RAINBOW VEGETABLE

For this soup, use any combo of low starch veggies you like—asparagus, cauliflower, brussels sprouts, kohlrabi and mushrooms. Use starchier veggies like potatoes, pumpkin and sweet potatoes, if they don't cause you any problems.

1	medium red onion, peeled and roughly chopped
0–8	garlic cloves, skin left on
1	whole leek, trimmed and roughly chopped
2	medium carrots, trimmed and roughly chopped
1	red capsicum, deseeded and roughly chopped
1	parsnip or turnip, peeled and roughly chopped
4	juicy tomatoes, roughly chopped
4	celery stalks, roughly chopped
2	medium zucchini, trimmed and roughly chopped
1 tsp	fresh rosemary or thyme leaves, or 1 tsp dried rosemary or thyme
2 tsp	unrefined salt
1 tsp	cracked black or white pepper

2 tbsp   olive oil
    Big handful of spinach
    Stock or water to thin the soup

Method Preheat oven to 200°C. Put all your veggies in a large bowl and toss well to coat veggies with the oil and seasoning. Now spread the leek, carrot, capsicum and turnip on a large oven tray (or two) and bake until golden and tender, turning once if needed. After about 20 minutes, put tomatoes, celery and zucchini in the oven too. The whole process will take about 45 minutes, depending on your oven. Allow to cool a little, then find the garlic and remove the skins. Place everything in a soup pot, add spinach then puree the veggies, using a stick blender or your food processor. (Leave this step out on you non-puree days.) Adjust seasoning. If you like a thinner soup, use stock or water to reach the consistency you like.

8. MY FAVOURITE FISH SOUP

If you don't have some of the ingredients (turmeric or seaweed for example), still go ahead and make this soup as it'll be wonderful anyway. You can use organic chicken instead of fish. For vegetarians and vegans, add one cup of diced, firm tofu, and/or a teaspoon of protein-heavy hemp seeds or oil as a garnish. If you don't like coriander, you can replace it with basil, Thai basil or Vietnamese mint, adding it in with your stock. I sometimes serve this soup with a scoop of cooked quinoa, instant bean thread vermicelli noodles, kelp noodles, konjac or instant brown rice noodles.

2 tbsp   olive or coconut oil
   1   **onion or large eschalot, or white part of a leek, chopped**
  1–4   **garlic cloves, crushed**
1 tbsp   **fresh ginger, grated**

1 tbsp	fresh turmeric, grated
½	bunch coriander, stems and leaves chopped separately, or 1 cup basil leaves
1	large celery stalk, diced
1	large carrot, diced
1	zucchini, diced
1 cup	broccoli florets
1 cup	kale or spinach, chopped
1 cup	cabbage, chopped
200 g	piece of white fish like flathead, snapper, kingfish, mahi-mahi
1 litre	stock or bone broth
6	shiitake mushrooms, fresh, sliced (or whole dried)
1 tbsp	nori or dulse flakes
1 tbsp	tamari, miso paste, fish sauce or sea salt to season (none if your stock is already salty enough)
	A few drops sesame oil (toasted or not) to garnish, optional
2	spring onions, sliced on the diagonal

Method Heat oil in a soup pot over a medium heat. Slowly sauté your onion or leek until translucent, about 2–3 minutes. Add garlic, ginger, turmeric and coriander stems. Sauté until smelling gorgeous, about 1 minute. Add in veggies and stir well to coat them, then add fish pieces, fresh herbs (reserving some for garnish) and stock to the pot, along with mushrooms and seaweed. Bring to the boil then drop to a simmer until veggies are soft, about 15–20 minutes. Season. If you've used dried shiitakes, then take them out of the pot, remove stems and slice finely before putting back into the soup. Blend the soup, if it's one of your two intermittent fasting days. Serve garnished with sesame oil, spring onions and reserved, chopped herbs.

9. SPICED INDIAN

To shorten the prep time of this soup, you can use an organic store-bought curry paste or dried curry blend. Make sure it has no added sugar, GMO ingredients, palm oil, sugar or toxic additives (like MSG or sulphur).

SOUP

2 tbsp	coconut oil
1	brown onion or large eschalot, peeled and chopped
1–4	garlic cloves, chopped
1 tbsp	fresh ginger, grated or 1 tsp ground
1 tbsp	fresh turmeric, grated or 1 tsp ground
½	bunch coriander, stems and leaves chopped separately
2 tsp	fenugreek seeds or ground
2 tsp	cumin seeds or ground
2 tsp	mustard seeds, any colour
1 cup	green beans, roughly chopped
1 cup	Jap or butternut pumpkin, skin on and chopped into 3cm chunks
2 cups	cauliflower florets, roughly chopped
1	small eggplant, roughly chopped
1	medium potato, roughly chopped
1	litre stock or bone broth
2 tsp	seasoning like tamari, coconut aminos, miso paste or sea salt
½ tsp	cayenne pepper (optional)

NUT PASTE

½ cup	Brazil (or any) nuts, soaked overnight then drained
½ cup	coconut flakes or shredded, additive-free
	Zest of one lime or lemon, grated
½ tsp	unrefined salt

Method Heat the oil in a soup pot, over medium heat. Sauté the onion until translucent, about 2–3 minutes. Then add garlic, ginger, turmeric and coriander stems, and gently sauté for another minute. Next add the fenugreek, cumin and mustard seeds. Sauté until they start sticking to the base of the pot and smell lovely, about 1 minute. Now add in the veggies and stir well to coat them in the fragrant spices. (You may need to add a little water here, to stop the spices from sticking.) Next, add the stock to the pot and bring it to the boil, then drop to a simmer until veggies are soft, about 15–20 minutes. Season to your liking, using salt. Make the nut paste while your soup is simmering. Place the nuts, coconut, zest and salt in a processor and blitz until fairly smooth and looking like nut butter. You may need to add a little oil (coconut, olive, sunflower) to form a paste. Serve your pureed soup topped with a heaped teaspoon of Nut Paste; sprinkle with a pinch of cayenne (optional). Keep it chunky on your non puree days.

MEDICINAL MYLKS
(ALL RECIPES ARE FOR 1 SERVE)

If you like your mylks sweet (and haven't got a severe case of candida or SIBO), then use a little maple, rice or coconut syrup, or raw agave, raw honey or yacon. If you're not sure, or you just can't handle any sweeteners at all without a sugar crash, then use stevia during the 40-Day Reset Program. After that, you might like to add organic dates back into your diet, if that's your preference.

Warm mylks are good anytime but especially in the evening, as they contain medicinal ingredients such as tryptophan, an amino acid that makes us sleepy. It's up to you which type of mylk to use, either coconut, almond, soy, cashew or rice.

1. GOLDEN MYLK

This type of mylk has become increasingly popular here in the West over the past few years. In the East, it's been favoured for many centuries for its healing properties and comforting taste. Feel free to use just the turmeric, vanilla and pepper for a simpler Golden Mylk.

½ tsp	ground turmeric
Pinch	vanilla powder
Pinch	freshly cracked black pepper
Pinch	cardamom, ground
Pinch	cinnamon, ground
Pinch	freshly grated ginger
1 cup	mylk
	Sweetener, optional

Method Heat mylk in a small pot over a medium flame. Meanwhile, place the spices in your mug. Pour a little mylk in your mug then using a small whisk or spoon, make a paste out of your spices. Then fill the rest of your mug with the mylk.

2. MOCK MOCHA

There's no caffeine in this recipe, but you're likely to feel quite energised after you drink it. Cacao stimulates the secretion of feel-good endorphins, helping us to experience a nice buzz, plus the theobromine it contains is a mild, natural stimulant that helps us burn fat. It also increases our pleasure sensations by boosting serotonin (a happy hormone). Maca can be overstimulating in the evening for some of us, so if you're new to it, have it in the morning at first, to see how your own body reacts.

1 tsp   cacao powder

½ tsp   maca powder

Pinch   ground cinnamon

1 cup   almond mylk

        Sweetener, optional

Method Gently heat almond mylk in a small pot over a medium flame. Meanwhile, place the powders in your mug. Pour a little mylk in your mug, then use a small whisk or spoon to make a paste. Fill the rest of your mug with the mylk.

3. LATTE SPICED DANDELION

During my twenties, in the 90s, it was considered a bit cool to order an LSD, a latte made with ground dandelion root instead of caffeine, plus soy rather than cow's milk. Like many other 'weird' foods, it quickly found its place on any self-respecting hipster cafe menu. I've tweaked it a little, to include spices known to improve our wellbeing and connection to each other. The bitter flavour of dandelion root stimulates our digestive system, absorbs and transports toxins from the bowels out of the body, balances intestinal flora, and soothes the gut in the process. The vanilla flower is named Xanat, after the daughter of a fertility goddess bringing pleasure and happiness.

30ml   shot dandelion root

1 cup   coconut mylk

½ tsp   cinnamon

½ tsp   nutmeg

½ tsp   vanilla

        Sweetener, optional

Method Make your dandelion shot as you would coffee, simply using ground dandelion root instead of coffee. Heat your mylk in a small pot over a medium flame, then add your spices and dandelion shot. Whisk well to combine.

4. PUMPKIN PIE

The combination of these spices tricks you into thinking you're having pumpkin pie, which is a good thing, in my mind. Make lots of this spice mix and store it in an airtight jar for continued and regular use, because you'll want it. For medicinal purposes only, of course!

½ tsp	cinnamon, ground
¼ tsp	ginger, ground
¼ tsp	nutmeg, ground
Pinch	allspice, ground
Pinch	cloves, ground
Pinch	vanilla powder
1 cup	almond mylk
	Sweetener, optional

Method Heat almond mylk in a small pot over a medium flame. Meanwhile, place the powders in your mug. Pour a little mylk in your mug to make a paste, then fill the rest of your mug with the mylk.

5. CARROT CAKE MILKSHAKE

This is a great smoothie for wayward reproductive and appetite hormones. Carrots are wonderful for balancing hormones, plus they have a positive effect on our immune system and skin, thanks to the beta carotene they contain. Walnuts and chia seeds are a nice source of omega-3 oils, also known to be of benefit in balancing hormones. If you'd like it sweet, and can tolerate bananas (not too ripe) or dates, then add half of one in. Or use a complex sweetener.

       1   small carrot, steamed then cooled
 1 tsp   chia seeds
 1 tsp   of shredded coconut
 1 tsp   cinnamon, ground
       2   pecans or walnut halves
 1 tsp   maca powder
1½ cups   almond milk, chilled
          Sweetener, optional

Method Place everything in a blender and puree. Serve with a sprinkling of cinnamon.

Variation—If you increase the chia seeds to 4 tbsp then pop it in the fridge after blitzing, in a few hours you'll have a chia pudding instead of a milkshake.

6. CREAMY GREEN CALMNESS

Matcha green tea has long been used by Daoists and Zen Buddhist monks to relax and meditate while remaining alert. This is potentially due to L-theanine, the amino acid in the leaves, which promotes alpha waves in the brain, inducing relaxation without drowsiness. L-theanine is also involved in the production of dopamine and serotonin—two chemicals that enhance mood, improve memory and promote concentration.

 1 tsp   matcha
2 tbsp   hot water
 ¼ tsp   zest of lemon or lime, grated
 ¾ cup   cashew mylk
        Sweetener, optional

Method In a mug, dissolve the matcha in hot water, then add the citrus zest. Top with warm mylk. (Quality matcha often comes with a cute, little wooden whisk, specially designed for this purpose—to reduce the chance of a lumpy matcha tea.)

7. SLEEPY TIME

Almonds contain both tryptophan, an amino acid that acts as a sedative, and magnesium which acts as a muscle relaxant. Tryptophan is a substance found in many foods known to help us sleep, and pumpkin seeds (pepitas) are one of the highest sources. To grind pepitas, put them in your high-speed blender, coffee/spice grinder or food processor, or you can use a mortar and pestle if you're feeling strong.

1 tsp	pepitas, ground
½ tsp	cinnamon
2 drops	vanilla powder or essence
1 heaped tsp	almond butter
1 cup	almond mylk
	Sweetener, optional

Method In a small pot, combine the ground pepitas with the cinnamon and vanilla. Move onto a medium heat, then mix in the butter and top with the mylk. Or place warm mylk and the rest of the ingredients in a blender and whiz until smooth.

DESSERTS

After you've completed the 40-Day Reset Program, you'll more than likely be able to occasionally include any unrefined sweetener you like, without side effects. However, during your Reset, it's better if you can stick to just one teaspoon per day, or less. In these recipes, feel free to add zero to two teaspoons of the sweetener of your choice, as they all make two serves. If you can't tolerate any healthy sweetness at all, and that's just too much to bear for 40 days, then use powdered stevia.

Choose whatever mylk you prefer for these recipes, as long as it's sugar, additive and GMO-free, in a non-toxic container, or preferably organic, of course. It's a good idea to vary your mylks a little, but not too much. Our gut likes variety, but in a 'just right' Goldilocks kind of way.

1. MATCHA AND AVOCADO ICE CREAM

Avocados are a wonderful source of healthy monounsaturated fats (MUFAs), folate and fibre. Recommended daily serving size is around one-third of a medium avocado, or 50 grams.

1	avocado
1 tsp	matcha powder
½ cup	cashew mylk
1 tsp	lemon rind or 2 drops lemon essential oil
¼ tsp	vanilla extract
	Sweetener, optional

Method Place all of the ingredients in a blender or food processor until smooth. Either use an ice cream machine to churn the mixture, or pour it into a freezer-proof container and freeze uncovered for a couple of hours, until it's just starting to set. Empty the semi-set mixture into a bowl and beat well with a wooden spoon or spatula, then return to the container, freeze and repeat procedure. Put it back into the container, cover and freeze until firm. You could leave out the matcha powder, if you don't have any. I use it for an extra hit of anti-oxidants, calmness and fibre, and because it has a gorgeous, vibrant green colour. Make two or four times this recipe, as it will keep for a few months in the freezer.

2. JAFFA MOUSSE

Recently, a study found that eating a diet rich in MUFAs actually decreased belly fat and improved insulin sensitivity. Foods containing MUFAs are olives, olive oil, coconut oil, cashews, almonds, pecans, nut butters, avocado and dark chocolate. Hooray!

1	medium avocado
2 tbsp	coconut milk or cream
¼ cup	cacao powder
½ tsp	vanilla extract or powder
2 tsp	grated orange zest or 2 drops of orange essential oil
	Sweetener, optional
2 tbsp	coconut milk or cream, extra, optional

Method Put all ingredients in the blender, then whiz until it is a lovely, smooth texture. Adjust consistency with a little more coconut milk, if it's too thick. You want it to be the consistency of mayonnaise, not hummus. Pour into 2 wide-mouth glasses and serve chilled, with a drizzle of coconut milk or cream if you like.

3. GINGER, LEMON AND MINT ALOE JELLY
(MAKES 2 ICE CUBE TRAYS)

Aloe vera produces at least six natural antiseptic agents, killing mould, bacteria, fungi and viruses. This magical plant is so powerful that researchers and scientists are looking at its potential to fight AIDS and cancer. If you use commercially prepared aloe vera, get certified organic juice. If using it fresh, split a large leaf down the middle and scrape out the flesh, avoiding the mildly toxic, yellow part closest to the leaf. These jellies are useful for when you're feeling nauseous, or feeling like you're coming down with a cold or 'flu, suffering with any gut pain at all, or reflux.

400ml	aloe vera juice, unflavoured
2 tsp	agar flakes
2 tbsp	fresh ginger, grated
2 tsp	grated lemon zest, or 2 drops lemon essential oil
1 tbsp	fresh mint, finely chopped or 1 drop peppermint essential oil
	Sweetener, optional

Method Squeeze the grated ginger over a small bowl, so you get the juice, then set aside. (Use the ginger fibre in your cooking.) In a saucepan over medium heat, gently warm your aloe vera juice, then whisk in the agar flakes until dissolved. This should take a minute or two. Bring to the boil then remove from heat. Allow to cool slightly, then whisk in the ginger juice, zest and mint (or essential oil). Pour into ice cube trays and chill until set, about an hour.

4. STRAWBERRY, MACADAMIA AND ORANGE SORBET

Macadamias contain omega-9 monounsaturated fatty acids, the same fatty acid found in olive oil. They're great for lowering bad cholesterol

(LDL) and the MUFAs improve insulin and leptin resistance, reducing sugar and carb cravings, helping to keep our weight more stable.

2 cups	frozen strawberries
2 tbsp	macadamia butter
2 tsp	orange zest, grated, or 2 drops orange essential oil
about 2 tbsp	coconut water or clean water to help it blend, if needed
	Sweetener, optional

Method Place all ingredients in a processor or blender and whiz until almost smooth. Eat immediately.

5. WALNUT BROWNIE PUD

Available hulled, unhulled or black, tahini is 20% complete protein, making it a higher protein source than most nuts. Quality tahini will have a lovely layer of very healthy unsaturated oil on the top, so give it a good stir before using it. It's easy for our body to digest because of its highly alkaline mineral content, which is great for weight loss and reducing inflammation.

1½ cups	almond milk
2 tbsp	walnuts, plus 2 halves for garnish
½ cup	avocado
4 tbsp	chia seeds
1 tbsp	raw cacao powder, plus a little extra for dusting
1 tbsp	tahini, hulled
¼ tsp	cinnamon, ground
¼ tsp	vanilla extract
Pinch	salt
	Sweetener, optional

Method Place all ingredients in your processor or blender and puree until smooth, or you can mix it by hand. (Chop the nuts finely if you do it this way, or smash in a mortar and pestle.) Pour the mixture into a dish or two medium-sized ramekins, and chill until set. This will take a couple of hours. Finish each with a dusting of cacao (or cinnamon) powder, and a teaspoon of crushed walnuts.

6. COCONUT AND LIME SORBET

Canned coconut milk is best here. It has a higher fat content, which helps the sorbet become extra creamy. Buying it off the shelf in a tetra pack will work also, just not as well.

1 × 400g	BPA-free tin of unsweetened coconut milk
1	lime, zest grated, and flesh juiced
½ tsp	cinnamon, ground
½ cup	clean water
	Sweetener, optional

Method Place all ingredients into a blender and whiz until smooth, or mix by hand. Pour the mixture into a bowl and leave in the fridge to completely cool. Add it to your ice cream maker to complete, or pop it into the freezer until firm. Then put it back into your blender and whiz again. Serve immediately.

7. CHOCOLATE PUDDINGS

Gut-loving green banana flour is made from green Cavendish bananas, grown on the Atherton Tablelands. This grain-free flour is gluten-free and readily replaces any other flour in cooking. When converting recipes, be sure to reduce this flour by at least 25% though, as it absorbs more liquid.

2 tbsp	green banana flour
3 tbsp	raw cacao powder, plus a little extra for garnish
1½ cups	mylk
½ tsp	vanilla extract
1 tsp	agar agar flakes
2 tsp	grated orange zest with a little extra for garnish, or
	2 drops orange essential oil
	Sweetener, optional

Method Sift the banana flour and cacao powder into a pan, then whisk in the mylk. Add the vanilla. Bring to a simmer, stirring constantly for a few minutes, then remove from the heat. Meanwhile, in a separate pan add a cup of water, sweetener (if using) orange zest and the agar, and simmer gently until dissolved, about 2 minutes. Add this liquid to the pan with the flour and milk and whisk together over a low heat. Cool slightly, then pour into two medium bowls and put in the fridge. They're ready to serve when the mousse is completely chilled and firm. Serve with a sprinkling of orange zest and cacao powder.

chapter sixty-three
EASY-TO-DIGEST RECIPES FOR
FIVE DAYS A WEEK

For five days a week, your meals will be mostly whole, although still cooked to increase their digestibility. Remember, your evening meal ought to be the lightest of the day, and it's much better if you can avoid eating anything at all at least three hours before bedtime.

BREAKFASTS
(ALL RECIPES 2 SERVES, UNLESS OTHERWISE INDICATED)

If you're rushing in the morning, or haven't yet got yourself organised for the week ahead, you can always have two eggs for breakfast, any way you like. Or simply fruit and yoghurt, topped with maca powder and hemp seeds, if you have them. Or a smoothie from the intermittent fasting recipes. Your meals can have as few or as many ingredients as you like or can manage; it doesn't have to be complicated, fancy or hard. If you can, avoid eating as soon as you get up, as this will give your gut more time to rest. Remember to have a big glass of warm water first thing, before any food or drinks.

1. GOLDEN MUSHROOMS

Mushrooms absorb and concentrate whatever they grow in, good or bad, so it's really important to eat only organically grown mushies. Interestingly, humans share the same bacteria and viruses as fungi. They have developed strong antibiotic properties as a defence against bacterial invasion, which also happen to be effective for us. Like us, mushrooms produce vitamin D when exposed to sunlight, which we absorb when we eat them. Make double or more of these mushies, and keep for another meal. Try them topped with one poached, boiled or fried egg.

1 tbsp	olive or coconut oil, ghee or butter
1	garlic clove, optional or double
1 tsp	fresh ginger, grated or finely sliced
1 tsp	fresh turmeric grated, or 1 tbsp ground
3 cups	Portobello, button or Swiss mushrooms
2	big handfuls of baby or English spinach, or chopped silverbeet
¼ cup	cashew pieces, soaked for a few hours then drained (and then toasted, if you like)
½ tsp	unrefined salt or coconut aminos
1 tbsp	hemp seeds, and/or toasted pepitas (optional)

Method In a frying pan, heat oil over a medium heat. Add garlic, ginger and turmeric. If using powdered turmeric, add it in with the mushrooms. Gently fry until fragrant, about 1 minute. Add mushrooms and toss for a few seconds, so they're covered with the spices. Add about ⅓ cup clean water to the pan, to help the mushrooms cook better. Now add in the cashews, spinach and salt, and toss to combine. Take mushrooms off the heat, cover and allow the spinach to wilt. Serve topped with hemp and/or pepitas.

2. SPROUTED BUCKWHEAT CREPES
(MAKES 12 CREPES)

Buckwheat is a seed high in protein and fibre. It's great for heart health, including its balancing effects on cholesterol and blood pressure, and can also help prevent diabetes. Recently it's been proven to help heal digestive disorders by relieving constipation. This recipe makes 12 crepes, so freeze what you don't use for up to 3 months, then pull them out of the freezer a few hours before you want to use them; or simply freeze the batter. A serving size is 2 medium-sized crepes with filling.

To make sweet crepes, use 1teaspoon of ground cinnamon instead of rosemary or oregano in the crepe mixture. Fill each crepe with a half a tablespoon of any nut butter plus paw paw, banana or berries. Drizzle with a little honey, if you like. To make this recipe even better gut food, you can add a tablespoon of lubne, quark or cottage cheese per crepe to the filling, in either the sweet or savoury version.

CREPES

2 cups	buckwheat kernels
2 tsp	unrefined salt
	Coconut or olive oil, butter or ghee for frying
1 tsp	dried rosemary, and/or oregano

Method In a bowl, cover your buckwheat with double the amount of filtered water. Leave the bowl out on the kitchen bench overnight, covered. In warmer weather put it in the fridge overnight, after it's been left out for a few hours. This will prevent the kernels fermenting. Next day, drain the kernels, rinse, then cover again with 2 cups of filtered water. Place the kernels, salt and herbs in your food processor, and whiz until smooth. Check the consistency. Add more water if it looks too thick for crepes. Heat a frying pan (preferably a crepe or cast iron pan) over medium heat. Add 1 tsp oil for each crepe, then spoon or pour about 2 tbsp batter into the pan. Gently tilt the pan to evenly coat the base with the batter, until you get a round, smooth pancake. Allow the batter to form bubbles, then flip. Repeat on the other side until golden. The heat of your pan is really important. Adjust if they're cooking too fast or too slowly. (The first crepe isn't usually the best one!) Stack your crepes onto a plate and keep under a tea towel until you've used all the batter and you're ready to serve.

FILLING

200 g	tin of wild caught salmon
2 cups	broccoli florets, steamed until almost falling apart
1 cup	baby spinach
1 tbsp	fresh herbs like basil, oregano, parsley and chives, chopped
	Squeeze of lemon juice, and 1 tsp grated zest
	Cracked pepper

Method In a bowl, add the salmon and broccoli to a bowl and mash until they both break up into smaller pieces, leaving it a bit chunky. Now fold through the spinach and herbs, finishing off with the lemon, zest and pepper. To serve, place quarter of the salmon mixture on one side of four crepes, then gently fold the other side over.

3. BREAKFAST CHIA BOWL

Matcha is premium green tea powder, unique to Japan. It's mostly drunk as tea, and to achieve a vibrant green colour in recipes. One cup of matcha contains ten times the antioxidants of one cup of brewed green tea. It has a third of the amount of caffeine in coffee, so if you can't tolerate caffeine at all, leave matcha out and try maca or acai powder instead. This is a good recipe to put in 2 × 250ml mason jars or small ramekins, to have on hand for breakfast throughout the week, as it will last at least five days in the fridge.

⅓ cup	chia seeds
300ml	water
1½ cups	paw paw or banana, roughly mashed
1	lime, zest grated and flesh juiced
¾ cup	coconut cream or milk
1 tsp	cinnamon, ground
1 tsp	fresh ginger, grated
1 tsp	matcha powder
2 tbsp	any nut, unsalted and toasted

Method Place chia seeds in a bowl. Using the back of a spoon, break them up, making sure there aren't any lumps. Pour the seeds into the water and stir to combine, then leave on the bench at room temperature for about 20 minutes, so the seeds soak up all the water and are nicely plump. Now add in all other ingredients and stir well. Allow the mixture to chill in the fridge for about 1 hour, then it's ready to eat.

4. ACAI HEALING BOWL

Purple acai berries get their colour from high concentrations of the antioxidant anthocyanin, which gives them their anti-inflammatory and anti-ageing properties. Acai contains 10–30 times the amount of anthocyanin contained in red wine! The acai berry has loads of fibre, which is extremely important for good gut health. It's capable of speeding up bowel transit time, preventing foods from fermenting in the intestines causing SIBO, candida, constipation, bloating, gas and pain. Buy fair-trade powder or pulp, avoiding supplements that can sometimes be more than just acai.

2 tbsp	acai powder
1 cup	berries, pear, banana or paw paw
½ tbsp	maca powder

1 tbsp   cacao powder
1 tsp   cinnamon, ground
1 tsp   vanilla extract or powder
2 tbsp   coconut, flakes, chips or shredded
1 tbsp   coconut oil
1 cup   coconut water
2 tbsp   chia seeds

Method Put everything into a bowl, blender or food processor and mix well. Divide between two bowls. Eat immediately or pour into 2 × 250ml mason jars and leave to set in the fridge overnight.

5. BLUEBERRY, BRAZIL AND QUINOA BREAKFAST BOWL

Selenium is an important antioxidant for strong immunity and optimum thyroid function. Selenium also helps reduce the negative effects of some heavy metals, including cadmium, mercury and arsenic, and it helps keep blood vessels healthy. Don't forget to activate/sour your quinoa overnight, or at least for a few hours. (See Chapter 43, Preparing Your Grains.)

4   Brazil nuts, roughly chopped
1 cup   quinoa flakes, soured
2 tbsp   coconut shredded, flakes or desiccated, additive-free
1 cup   blueberries
1 tbsp   chia seeds
1 tbsp   hemp seeds, optional
½ tsp   cinnamon, ground
1 tsp   lemon rind, grated
2 cups   coconut water or any mylk

Method In a processor, grind the nuts, quinoa flakes and coconut until you have the consistency of chunky breadcrumbs. Now add the berries, chia and cinnamon to the processor and give it a quick whiz, until just combined and the berries are broken up a little. Lastly, add your liquid and mix again. Gently heat on the stove for a few minutes to cook the quinoa flakes. To make it even easier on digestion, leave overnight in the fridge, then serve hot or at room temperature for breakfast. It's a bit like Bircher muesli or porridge.

6. CINNAMON LOAF WITH VANILLA CASHEW BUTTER

Other nuts and seeds will work also for this delicious Cashew Butter recipe. Or try it also with ¾ cashews, then add in some Brazil nuts, pecans and pepitas to make up the cup. You can easily make it with only sunflower seeds, but avoid using sesame seeds, as you'll end up with tahini.

CINNAMON LOAF

¾ cup	green banana flour
1 cup	almond meal, or any ground nut
½ cup	coconut flour
2 tbsp	chia seeds
2 tbsp	melted coconut oil
½ cup	coconut milk
1 tsp	ginger, ground
2 tsp	cinnamon, ground
1 tsp	vanilla extract or powder
1 tsp	baking powder, aluminium-free
1 tsp	baking soda
1 tsp	stevia powder, or ⅓ cup raw honey

Method Preheat your oven to 180°C, and line a loaf tin. In a mixing bowl combine all dry ingredients and spices. In a separate bowl, mix together eggs, melted coconut oil, coconut milk and sweetener. Add the wet ingredients to the dry and stir well to combine. Pour this mixture into your loaf tin and bake in the oven for 30–40 minutes or until golden. Place a skewer in the centre of the bread and when the skewer comes out clean, it is ready. Allow it to cool in the tin, before turning out onto a wired rack.

VANILLA CASHEW BUTTER

4 cups	cashew pieces, raw
¼ cup	almond, hazelnut, sunflower or safflower oil
1 tsp	unrefined salt
2 tsp	vanilla powder, or 1 tsp extract

Method Preheat oven to 180°C. Place your nuts (or seeds) on an oven tray and mix with the oil and salt. Bake for about 10 minutes until they start to turn golden brown, then let them cool on the bench. Once cool, place in a food processor with the vanilla powder and blend for about 10 minutes, until the butter is smooth and creamy, like hummus. It may look like this will never happen and it will never be anything but a crumbly mess. But it will get there, in time. Keep scraping down the sides along the way. You will need a strong food processor or blender to do this.

7. BUCKWHEAT PORRIDGE

Pawpaw is one of my favourite fruits, but I know its not everyone's idea of yummy. If this is you, then substitute it for a fruit you do love. We've known of paw paw's cancer-fighting benefits for some time; now we know one of its chemicals (acetogenin) is effective at suppressing cancer. The seeds are antiparasitic, so I add these to smoothies too. (You won't notice they're there, if you have a high-speed blender.)

1 cup	buckwheat kernels, soured
3 cups	filtered water
¼ tsp	unrefined salt

    1 cup   almond or soy mylk
    ½ tsp   cinnamon, ground
    ½ cup   paw paw or berries
    1 tbsp   macadamias, lightly toasted and chopped

Method Soak buckwheat overnight in double the amount of clean water and ½ tbsp lemon juice or apple cider vinegar. In warmer weather, leave the kernels out for a couple of hours only, then place in the fridge overnight to prevent them fermenting. In the morning, add another cup of clean water and a pinch of salt to the soaked kernels and stir. Bring to the boil, then drop to a low simmer until the kernels are tender, about 20 minutes. Stir regularly and add more water when it gets too thick. Now stir in the almond mylk and cinnamon and keep cooking for a further few minutes over a low heat, until your porridge is looking luscious and soft. To serve, top with the fresh fruit and nuts. Sweeten with a banana, honey or stevia, if you like.

8. BREAKFAST BREAD

(MAKES 1 × 900G LOAF)

You'll be surprised how simple and satisfying this loaf is. After it cools, you might like to slice the whole thing up and freeze most of it, so you have it ready to pop into the sandwich press for those mornings when time is elusive. Spread with a nut butter, cottage cheese or avocado. And for a sweet, divine version, spread with organic butter or Vanilla Cashew Butter, or enjoy just as it is. For the sweet version, add ⅓ cup raw honey in with the eggs and leave out the rosemary.

       3   eggs
    ½ cup   extra virgin olive oil
    2 cups   almond or hazelnut meal
    ½ cup   buckwheat flour
    1 tsp   ground cinnamon

1 tsp	vanilla extract
1 tsp	bicarb, aluminium-free
Pinch	unrefined salt
	Juice and zest of a small lemon, lime or orange
3 tbsp	chia seeds
½ cup	walnuts, pecans or almonds, roughly chopped
1 tbsp	fresh rosemary, finely chopped, or 1 tbsp dried
1½ cups	sweet potato or banana, cooked and mashed to a puree

Method Preheat the oven to 160°C. Place the eggs, olive oil, almond meal, flour, cinnamon, vanilla, bicarb, salt, citrus zest and juice in a blender or processor, until the ingredients are combined and you have a thick paste. Pour the mixture into a bowl, then fold in the chia seeds, walnuts, rosemary and sweet potato until **just** combined. Oil a loaf tin (20 or 30 × 10cm) well with olive oil, then spoon the batter into the tin, tapping the tin on the bench to even out the mixture. Bake for 50 minutes, or until a skewer comes out clean. Allow to cool in the tin a little, then place on a wire rack to cool further. Store in an airtight container in the fridge for up to a week. Or slice and freeze for about three months.

LUNCHES
(ALL RECIPES 2 SERVES, UNLESS OTHERWISE INDICATED)

As in many European countries, lunch should be your main meal, then take a nap if you can. Take time to enjoy your lunch, eating slowly and mindfully. It's much better for you to take a nap, or meditate after a leisurely lunch than woofing it down at your desk in front of a screen, then straight back to work. True!

1. ROAST VEGGIE, NUTS AND QUINOA SALAD WITH AVOCADO MAYONNAISE

I have used mainly non-starchy veggies in these recipes, to help reset your blood sugar levels and appetite. But if you're not struggling with your insulin or leptin levels (PCOS, diabetes, excess weight, sleep issues, metabolic syndrome) some pumpkin, potato, corn, peas and sweet potatoes are going to be fine 2–3 times a week. I've used hemp seeds as a source of protein, omega-3 oil as an anti-inflammatory, their fibre will increase beneficial bacteria. It's up to you if you use the Avocado Mayo' or not, as either way it'll be a beautiful, tasty and gut-loving dish. Use any fresh herbs, nuts and seeds you like.

SALAD

1	parsnip, scrubbed and quartered
2	large Portobello mushrooms
1	zucchini, cut in quarters, lengthways
4	asparagus spears
1	small fennel bulb, trimmed and halved
1 cup	Jap pumpkin, cut into 4cm (1½-in) chunks with skin on (optional)
1	small red onion, peeled and halved
1	whole, large garlic knob, cut in half horizontally, skin on
2 tbsp	olive oil
2 tbsp	fresh thyme or oregano sprigs or rosemary leaves
1 tsp	unrefined salt
	Cracked black pepper, 5 turns of the mill
1	handful flat-leaf parsley leaves, to serve
1 cup	quinoa, soaked overnight in the cooking pot with 2½ cups of water and ½ tbsp lemon juice or ACV
4 cups	filtered water

2 tbsp	hemp seeds
½ cup	mixed nuts, lightly toasted
¼ cup	mixed seeds (sesame, sunflower, ground pepitas, nigella), lightly toasted

DRESSING

1 tsp	lemon juice or apple cider vinegar
1 tbsp	extra virgin olive oil
1 tsp	Dijon or seeded mustard
	Season with salt and pepper
1	small garlic clove, crushed (optional)

MAYONNAISE

1	medium avocado, ripe
1 tbsp	basil leaves, chopped
1½ tbsp	cold-pressed olive or sunflower oil
1 tbsp	lemon or lime juice
1 tbsp	clean water
½ tsp	unrefined salt

Method Scoop the flesh out of the avocado and place in your blender or food processor with all the other ingredients and whiz to a puree.

Method Preheat oven to 190°C. Place all your veggies, along with the garlic, oil, thyme, rosemary and seasoning in a large mixing bowl; using your hands, rub the seasoning all over the veggies. Spread them out over one or two large oven trays, with the garlic cut side down. Transfer to the oven, then roast for 20 minutes. I don't generally turn my veggies but if you need to, go ahead and turn them. Roast for another 10–20 minutes, until cooked and golden. Meanwhile, place the activated quinoa and its soaking liquid over a high heat and bring to the boil. Drop to a simmer, put the lid half on and cook until you can't see any water left, but little 'volcano holes' appear in the quinoa.

This will take 10–15 minutes. Taste the quinoa. It should be tender and almost cooked. If not, add a splash more water, then put the lid on and turn the heat off. Allow the quinoa to cook in its own steam for at least another 10 minutes, then allow it to cool before fluffing up with a fork.

For the dressing, whisk all ingredients together in a small bowl or combine in a small jar and shake vigorously. To make the salad, spread the quinoa out on a large shallow bowl with your fresh herbs, seeds and nuts on top then gently toss them together. Next, carefully fold through your veggies, pour the dressing over and toss again. Or you can serve the veggies on top of the quinoa, then dress.

For the mayo', scoop the flesh out of the avocado and place in your blender or food processor with all the other ingredients and whiz to a puree.

2. FLAX CRACKERS WITH CASHEW CHEESE
(MAKES 16 CRACKERS)

If you want to keep these crackers raw, use a dehydrator (method below) or set your oven at 48°C and bake for much, much longer. I bake them for about 6 hours in the oven at this low temperature, then turn and bake for another 2 hours. I only add in hemp seeds when I keep the temperature below 48oC, either in the oven or dehydrator, as anything over this will start to destroy the anti-inflammatory omega-3 oils they contain. Otherwise a quicker, cooked method is below. Experiment with other flavours like caraway seeds, cumin seeds, mixed herbs, dried onion or garlic, or sweet or smoked paprika.

CRACKERS

⅓ cup   of either chia seeds or flax meal, or a combo
⅔ cup   mixed seeds (sesame, sunflower, pepitas, nigella, poppy)
1 cup   water

1 tsp	unrefined salt
1 tbsp	turmeric, grated, ground or paste
1 tsp	dulse or nori flakes, (optional)
2 tsp	rosemary, dried or 1 tbsp fresh leaves, finely chopped

Method Preheat oven to 150°C. Line a 30cm × 40cm baking tray with greaseproof paper. Place everything in a bowl, then mix well to form a wet dough. Let the dough sit for about 15 minutes, to allow the chia/flax to swell up and become thick and gooey. Using wet hands or a spatula, spread the dough out until about 5mm thick on the prepared tray. Score into 16 rectangles with a sharp knife. Bake for one hour, then turn crackers over and cook for another 30 minutes or until crunchy. Turn off the oven, leaving crackers in the oven for a further hour to dry out. If using a dehydrator, evenly spread the mixture onto three or four Teflex sheets on the sliding drawers. Score, then set at 175°C for 9 hours. After this time turn crackers over, then return the trays to the dehydrator for another three hours. Allow crackers to cool slightly, before storing in an airtight container for up to a month or more. They'll stay fresh for much longer in the fridge.

CASHEW CHEESE (MAKES ABOUT 1 CUP)

1 cup	raw cashews, soaked in 1½ cups water for an hour
1 tsp	lemon zest, grated
1 tbsp	lemon juice
1 tsp	apple cider vinegar
1	garlic clove (optional)
½ tbsp	Dijon mustard
1 tsp	unrefined salt
½ tsp	white pepper, ground

Method Drain the cashews then place in a high-speed blender or food processor with the other ingredients, and whiz until they are thick and creamy. Adjust seasoning to your liking. It will form a paste once chilled, making it more like spreadable cheese. If you'd like to use it as a sauce for lasagne, pasta, or as a side to your protein, then leave it out of the fridge for a while before using it. It will stay fresh in the fridge for about a week.

3. MILLET PATTIES WITH KALE AND HEMP PESTO

Ancient pharmacologists discovered that hemp seeds were an ideal source of food. Hemp has the perfect balance of omegas 3, 6 and 9 (2:1:1), the same ratio found naturally in human cells. As these oils are from one perfect source, the body can metabolise the omegas in hemp more readily, and easily reap the benefits. If you prefer to bake your patties rather than shallow fry, preheat oven to 180°C and place the balls on a greased tray for 20 minutes until golden.

PATTIES
[MAKES ABOUT 8 SMALL PATTIES]

½ cup	millet, washed well, covered with 1 cup water and ½ tbsp lemon juice or ACV, left covered overnight
3 tbsp	olive or coconut oil, or ghee
½	onion or leek (white part), finely diced
1	large celery stalk, finely diced
1	small carrot, finely diced
1	small zucchini, grated and squeezed dry
2 tbsp	chia seeds, any colour
2 tbsp	hulled tahini, mixed with 1 tbsp water until combined
½ cup	fresh herbs like mint, basil, oregano, chives, coriander, finely chopped
1 tbsp	sesame seeds
1 tbsp	almond or hazelnut meal
1 tsp	unrefined salt

Method Place the millet over a high heat in the same pot as the soaking liquid, then bring to the boil. Drop to a gentle simmer for 10 minutes, until the millet is tender. Remove from heat and cover. Let it sit and continue cooking in its own heat, while making the patties and the pesto. Heat 1 tbsp of the oil in a cast iron pan over medium heat. Add onions or leek and sauté until translucent. Stir in the veggies and sauté for another minute or two, until the veggies are just soft. Add the rest of the ingredients, besides the tahini sauce and stir well. Place the cooked millet into a bowl and press out any lumps with a fork or spoon. Add the veggie mixture and tahini to the bowl and mix well. Check for seasoning. Pop the mixture into the fridge to chill for around 30 minutes. Squeeze about two tablespoons of the mixture into a ball, then shape into patties before flattening slightly. The mixture should easily hold together. Wipe out the cast iron pan with a paper towel and heat the rest of the oil. Fry patties over a medium heat for about 2 minutes on each side until golden. (Or put on the barbie or a griddle pan and chargrill.) Serve with the pesto.

PESTO

2 cups	kale leaves, washed well and roughly chopped
½ cup	hemp seeds
1–2	cloves garlic
1	lemon, juiced
1 tsp	unrefined salt
½ cup	olive or flax oil, or a combo'

Method Bring a pot of salted water to the boil then quickly blanch the kale until it changes colour. Pour the contents of the pot into a colander in the sink and allow the kale to drain. Cool a little, then squeeze it dry. Now put your kale into your food processor with the other ingredients (apart from the oil) and whiz until smooth. Drizzle the oil in from the top to create the pesto. Taste and adjust seasoning.

4. BUCKWHEAT RISOTTO WITH FENNEL, MINT AND PEAS

I really love making risotto; adding one ladle of stock at a time and watching the rice (or in this case buckwheat) drink it up. I appreciate that not everyone shares my sentiment or has the time. So, to speed up this process, you can cook your buckwheat first, until al dente, then add it to the onions. The fennel may be cooked on the barbie for a smoky-flavoured risotto. This is a fairly heavy dish, so better to eat for lunch than dinner.

FENNEL

1 tbsp	olive oil
1	medium-sized fennel bulb, trimmed and quartered
½ tsp	each of unrefined salt and white pepper
2 cups	baby spinach
2 tbsp	fresh mint, chopped or 1 tsp dried
1 tbsp	Dijon mustard

Method Reserve the fennel fronds and set aside for the garnish. To cook the fennel, either bake it for about 30 minutes at 180°C turning once, or cook in a heavy-based pan. Heat the oil, then place the fennel cut side down. Cook over a medium heat with the seasoning until tender, about 3 minutes depending on the size of the bulb. Flip then cook for another 5 minutes, or until tender all the way through when pierced with a sharp knife. Allow to cool a little, then put the fennel in a blender or food processor (or just chop finely) with the spinach, mint and Dijon mustard until fairly smooth. Set aside.

RISOTTO

2 tbsp	olive oil
½	onion, diced
1–2	garlic cloves, roughly chopped

        1   celery stick, diced
    ½ cup   peas, frozen or shelled
    1 tsp   unrefined salt and white pepper
    ½ cup   buckwheat kernels, soaked for a few hours with 1 tsp
            acid (like vinegar or lemon juice), then drained and
            allowed to dry
    1 tsp   dulse or nori flakes (optional)
    500ml   stock
        1   bay leaf
    2 tsp   lemon zest

Method Have your stock simmering in a pot next to the risotto pan that you cooked the fennel in. Heat oil then gently fry the onion, celery and garlic until soft, but not brown. Add the peas and seasoning and roughly mash together using a fork, while sautéing for another minute over a low heat. Add in the raw (or al dente for a faster cooking time) buckwheat and seaweed. Stir well to coat with the onion and pea mixture. Add a ladle of stock, and the bay leaf. Stir over a medium heat until the liquid has been absorbed. Continue adding your stock, one ladle at a time, until buckwheat is soft. If you run out of stock, you can use water, (but remember the pureed fennel will add more liquid to your risotto.) When it's almost ready, pour in your fennel puree and lemon zest, then stir well, the spinach to cook a little. Taste for seasoning, remove the bay leaf, then serve with the finely chopped fennel fronds.

5. GADO GADO

Originating in Indonesia, gado gado typically contains more components than I have here. This is my modern, earth-friendly, gut-loving version. If you know you can digest boiled eggs, go ahead and serve your gado gado with half an egg for each serving. Or serve this dish, as is the tradition, with ½ cup each of panfried or deep fried tempeh pieces. (Use peanut, safflower or sunflower oil to deep fry.) For a change, you can also serve the peanut sauce with barbecued fish or chicken skewers and veggies. Make loads of the peanut sauce and freeze it in sizes to suit you.

GADO GADO

1 cup	broccoli or cauliflower florets
1 cup	string/snake beans, trimmed
1 cup	any Asian greens (bok choy, choy sum), trimmed and halved
1	carrot, julienned
1	zucchini, cut into half moons
1 cup	bean sprouts
2 tbsp	toasted peanuts, dry toasted then lightly crushed
½ cup	shredded coconut, lightly dry toasted
Handful	Thai basil or coriander leaves
1	lime, quartered

PEANUT SAUCE

1 tbsp	coconut oil
2	cloves garlic, crushed
1	medium eschalot (pink onion), finely sliced
1	large red chilli, halved seeded and sliced
1 tbsp	fresh turmeric, grated or 1 tsp ground
2	kaffir lime leaves, finely sliced
¼ cup	organic peanut butter, crunchy
1 tbsp	tamarind pulp, optional
	Season with tamari, fish sauce or coconut aminos
2 tbsp	dry roasted peanuts, slightly crushed
2	lime cheeks to serve

Method Steam or quickly blanch your veggies separately, until just tender. Rinse under cold water to stop them cooking, then drain and set aside. For the sauce, heat the oil in a heavy-based pan. Add the garlic, eshalots, chilies and turmeric and gently fry until fragrant. Add the peanut butter and lime leaves, then gradually add the tamarind pulp and enough warm water (about half a cup) to make into a thick, pourable paste. Add seasoning to taste. To serve, gently toss veggies together in a large bowl, then divide between two plates. Add enough sauce to cover but not drown the vegetables. Finish with a few peanuts, shredded coconut, your fresh herbs and a wedge of lime on each plate.

6. POTATO SALAD WITH SALSA VERDI

There are four different types of resistant starch. One is formed when certain starchy foods, including potatoes, pasta and rice, are cooked and then cooled; it remains even if you reheat it. The cooling process turns some of the digestible starch into resistant starch (RS), via a process called 'retrogradation'. RS feeds the friendly bacteria and also reduces the pH level in the colon. Serve the salad with a boiled egg per person if you feel like it.

POTATO SALAD

400 g	new potatoes, washed
½ cup	dry roasted almonds, roughly chopped

SALSA VERDI (GREEN SAUCE)

½	bunch asparagus, trimmed and steamed slightly
1 cup	mixed, fresh herbs such as mint, parsley, thyme, basil, coriander, oregano, tarragon and a little rosemary
2	organic dill pickles, roughly chopped
2 tbsp	capers
1 tbsp	green olives, pips out
2	garlic cloves
1 heaped tsp	Dijon or seeded mustard

½	small red onion, roughly chopped
1 tbsp	any citrus zest, grated
2	spring onions, roughly chopped
1 tsp	apple cider vinegar
½ cup	extra virgin olive oil
1 tsp	unrefined salt
2–4	anchovies (optional)

Method For the sauce, place all the ingredients in a blender or food processor and pulse (or roughly chop by hand), keeping a lot of texture. Taste and adjust flavours to your liking, and set aside. Boil the whole potatoes until soft but not squashy. Drain in a colander and shake any excess water off. Tip them into a large mixing bowl and while still hot, pour on ½ cup of the sauce. Mix gently, crushing the spuds a little as you mix. Carefully spoon/pour the dressed spuds onto a platter. Garnish with the almonds and drizzle with another tablespoon or so of the sauce. Leftover sauce will keep in the fridge for over a week in a sealed jar. Use it on steamed veggies, chicken or fish, or with eggs for breakfast.

DINNERS

Make this meal light but nutritious, and try to eat before 7pm, or three hours before bedtime. It's difficult to skip dinner altogether when you're living with others, so at least try to avoid any grains. Definitely avoid overeating in the evening, as this will only lead to more gut and sleep issues.

1. CHICKEN WITH EGGPLANT, SAFFRON AND CAPERS
(SERVES 6)

The reward you'll gain from this dish far outweighs the little effort it'll take to prepare. It's very tasty, and freezes well too. Free-range chicken means 'free to range'; it doesn't mean the girls are roaming carefree through the rolling hills, grazing on their natural diet. So buy organic chicken, or no chicken at all.

1 × 1.2 kg	organic whole chicken, cut into 6 pieces
2 tbsp	olive oil
1	onion, finely sliced
1–4	garlic cloves
½	large eggplant, cut into a big dice
½ cup	parsley, chopped finely
1 tbsp	apple cider vinegar
2 tbsp	white wine or 1 tbsp white wine vinegar
2 tbsp	capers
1 big tsp	saffron threads, soaked in one tbsp warm water
1–2 cups	stock or water
	Sea salt and cracked pepper, to taste

Method Heat oil in a large heavy-based pan over medium heat. (I use a wide cast iron pan with a lid for this dish.) Pat your chicken dry, using a tea towel or paper towel. Place the pieces skin side down evenly around the pan and cook for about 6 minutes on each side, or until golden. Take the chicken out of the pan and set aside. Add the onion and garlic to the same pan. Sauté over a medium heat until the onions are soft and just starting to brown. This will take about 5 minutes. Put the chicken back in the pan and add the rest of the ingredients. Pour in enough water (or stock) so that all the ingredients are covered. Stir gently to combine. Reduce to a low heat. Simmer until the eggplant is really soft, about 30 minutes. Add more water as it cooks, so your final dish is nice and saucy. Serve in the pan.

2. STEAMED VEG WITH BRAZIL NUT AND HEMP HUMMUS
(SERVES 2)

It's helpful to have hummus in your fridge. This makes meal prep so much faster, as you've got your protein needs covered in the nuts (and hemp). You can also bake your veggies instead of steaming for this recipe, or use leftover roasted veggies. Use kale instead of (or as well as) basil for extra antioxidants, iron, fibre, magnesium and calcium.

VEGGIES

2	small carrots, trimmed then cut in quarters
1 cup	pumpkin, sliced and skin off
1 cup	brussels sprouts, trimmed and halved
1	small zucchini, cut into half moons
2 cups	broccoli florets

BRAZIL NUT AND HEMP HUMMUS
(MAKES 2 CUPS)

1 cup	Brazil nuts, soaked overnight
1 cup	basil leaves and/or chopped kale
⅓ cup	hemp seeds
¼ cup	hulled tahini
1 tbsp	lime or lemon juice
2	garlic cloves
2 tsp	unrefined salt
1 tsp	hemp oil or seeds to garnish, optional

Method For your hummus, place the drained nuts in a food processor. Whiz until they resemble chunky breadcrumbs. Now add in the rest of the ingredients apart from the garnish. Whiz until fairly smooth. You may need to add a little clean water to thin your hummus out to reach the consistency of mayonnaise. Taste and adjust flavours. Set aside. To cook veggies, place the carrots, pumpkin and brussels sprouts in your steamer and allow to steam until tender, about 7 minutes. Add in the zucchini and broccoli and steam until tender, about 5 minutes. Serve veggies in a shallow bowl and dollop 3 tbsp of hummus on top, plus garnish if using. Keep the remaining hummus in a sealed container in the fridge, and use for up to 3 days.

3. ALMOND AND CHIA FRITTERS WITH GREEN TAHINI SAUCE
(MAKES 12 FRITTERS/3 SERVES)

If you're using supermarket soy sauce, then don't. It's made with GM soy beans and is high in refined table salt, and often has fructose added. Organic tamari (wheat-free soy sauce) is a much better choice. If you're avoiding soy altogether, use coconut aminos, which is sap from organic coconut trees and organic sea salt, that's all. Use whatever veggies you have in the fridge for these fritters. Veggies like broccoli, cauliflower, capsicum, beans and kohlrabi work well. You can bake these fritters, if preferred. Preheat oven to 180°C. Place fritters on a greased tray and bake for 20 minutes, or until golden.

FRITTERS

3 tbsp	coconut or olive oil
1	small onion or leek, pale part only, washed well, diced
1 tbsp	finely chopped coriander stems, optional
1–2	garlic cloves, crushed
1 tsp	each of fresh ginger and turmeric, grated
1 cup	button mushrooms, finely diced
1 cup	sweet potato, grated
1	medium zucchini, grated then squeezed dry
3 tbsp	chia seeds

1 cup	almond meal
½ cup	chopped mixed herbs such as flat-leaf parsley, thyme, mint, dill, basil or coriander
1 tsp	unrefined salt, tamari, Bragg's seasoning or coconut aminos, or to taste

Method In a heavy-based frying pan, heat 1 tablespoon of the oil over medium heat. Add onion or leek and coriander stems, if using. Sauté for 1 minute until translucent. Next add in the garlic, ginger and turmeric. Stir for a few seconds. Now add all the veggies, stirring well to mix everything together. Cook over a medium heat for a minute or two, until the veggies start to soften. Place the mixture in a clean bowl. Add the chia seeds, ½ cup almond meal, herbs and seasoning, mixing well. If you'd like a finer texture to your fritters (or you're trying to hide the veggies), place the mixture in a food processor and blitz for a few seconds. (You can also do this step by hand, using a masher or fork.) Place the mixture in the fridge for about 30 minutes. With wet hands, divide the mixture into 12 and roll into balls about the size of a large walnut. Flatten into a patty and press into the remaining half a cup of almond meal. Wipe the frying pan with paper towel, reheat to a medium heat, then add the remaining oil. Fry the fritters in batches until golden, about 3 minutes each side, being careful not to overcrowd the pan. Drain on paper towel if needed.

GREEN TAHINI SAUCE
[MAKES ABOUT ¾ CUP]

⅓ cup	tahini
½ cup	coriander, rocket or basil leaves
1 tsp	cumin, ground
1	lemon, juiced and zest grated
1	garlic clove, crushed
1 tsp	unrefined salt
¼ tsp	cayenne pepper, optional

Method In a small bowl (or food processor), whisk (or process) all the ingredients together, adding in a little water to achieve the consistency of mayonnaise. Taste and adjust seasoning to your liking. Serve with a sprinkle of cayenne pepper. One serving is 4 fritters and 3 tbsp sauce, so these quantities will serve 3.

4. PUMPKIN MISO SOUP
(SERVES 4)

Look for organic unpasteurised miso paste in your health food store or farmer's market. Miso is exceptionally healing for our gut. Miso soup is my go-to meal when I'm feeling nauseous, achy, run-down, flat or all of the above. Use Bone Broth for the base if you like. Miso soup is yummy served with konjac or kelp noodles in the base of the bowl. You'll find them at your health food store or well-stocked supermarket. I have added diced daikon into this especially healing miso soup recipe as it has been shown to possess similar enzymes to those in the human digestive tract, facilitating better digestion of complex carbohydrates, proteins and fats, making them easier to absorb and use. This can reduce constipation and increase nutrient uptake in the gut. If you're avoiding onions, leeks and garlic, then just leave them out.

1 litre	veggie, chicken or beef stock
1 tbsp	each of fresh ginger and turmeric, grated
¼	bunch coriander, stems and leaves chopped separately
1 tbsp	dulse, or nori flakes, or 1 tsp wakame
1 cup	pumpkin, skin on thinly sliced
1 cup	button or shiitake mushroom, halved, or quartered if large
1 cup	firm tofu, cubed, or shredded cooked chicken
2 tbsp	miso paste, unpasteurised
1 tbsp	tamari
2 tsp	fish sauce (optional)

2 cups	Asian greens like bok choy or choy sum, or use kale or spinach
1 tsp	toasted sesame oil, for garnish
2	spring (green) onions, slice finely on the diagonal, for garnish
2 tbsp	toasted sesame seeds or pepitas, for garnish, (optional)

Method Into a soup pot add stock, ginger, turmeric, coriander stems, seaweed and veggies, and bring to a rolling simmer. When veggies are tender (about 5 minutes) add in your protein (tofu or chicken) then remove from the heat, then stir through the miso paste and tamari. Adjust seasoning by adding more tamari, miso or fish sauce, if using. Serve in 4 bowls topped with a few drops of sesame oil, coriander leaves, spring onions and toasted seeds.

5. ROAST CHICKEN WITH CRUSTED PUMPKIN WEDGES AND CAULIFLOWER MASH
(SERVES 2)

This dish will take 15–20 minutes of prep time and you'll be eating 30 minutes after that. Roast a whole chicken and have the leftovers for meals over the next couple of days. Make stock or bone broth with the leftover carcass, if you like. You could use 2 × 150g pieces of any wild-caught fish instead of the chicken. Vegetarians can use 100g diced tofu, baked with 1 tbsp tamari and a few drops of sesame oil, and/or sprinkle the veggies with hemp seeds and toasted pepitas.

ROAST CHICKEN

2	organic chicken thighs
1 tbsp	olive oil
1 tsp	each of unrefined salt and cracked pepper

PUMPKIN WEDGES

400 g	butternut or Jap pumpkin, skin on
2 tbsp	olive oil
2 tbsp	almond or hazelnut meal
Small handful	parsley, finely chopped
1 tbsp	fresh thyme or dill, (or 1 tsp dried) finely chopped
1	lemon or orange, zest grated
1	garlic clove, crushed
½ tsp	each unrefined salt and white pepper

CAULIFLOWER MASH

3 cups	cauliflower florets
1 tbsp	nut butter, like almond, peanut or cashew
1 tsp	unrefined salt
	Dash of mylk, maybe

Method Preheat oven to 180°C. Rub chicken with olive oil, salt and pepper. Put in an ovenproof dish and set aside. Line a separate oven dish with greaseproof paper. Cut pumpkin into fairly thin slices, around 3 cm thick. Toss in a bowl with half the olive oil before lying flat on the greaseproof paper. Next make the crust by mixing all the remaining ingredients in a small bowl, reserving one teaspoon of the zest. Gently press this mixture onto the wedges. Put the chicken and pumpkin trays into the oven. Bake for about 30 minutes. Using a knife to pierce, check the pumpkin is tender and the chicken is cooked through. Meanwhile, steam your cauliflower until very soft, then allow it to cool slightly. Drain, then place in a food processor with the nut butter and salt and pulse, keeping it a bit chunky, (or use a masher). You may need to thin it out a little with some mylk or water, so in this case pulse again to incorporate the mylk. Serve the chicken and pumpkin wedges with a generous dollop of the mash. Finish with the remaining zest sprinkled on top.

Tip: If the pumpkin skin starts to get too brown before the flesh is tender, loosely cover with a tray or foil.

6. HAZELNUT CRUMBED FLATHEAD WITH BROCCOLINI SALAD AND BLACK TAHINI SAUCE
(SERVES 2)

You can use any 'better choice' white fish you like here—wild barramundi, kingfish, wahoo, mackerel, whiting or flathead. (Cooking time will be halved if using whiting.) You may bake it instead of pan-frying, if preferred. In this case, place the fillets onto a few lemon slices, in an oven tray, cover and bake at 190°C for about 15–20 minutes. If you're using thicker fish, bake until fish is translucent and flakes when pierced with a knife. If preferred, swap the fish for two 150g organic chicken breasts or 100g firm tofu.

BROCCOLINI SALAD

1	bunch broccolini, trimmed
1	small handful green beans, tops removed
1	bunch asparagus, trimmed
½ cup	coriander, dill or basil leaves, chopped
2 tbsp	white or black sesame seeds, toasted
1 tsp	olive or hazelnut oil

BLACK TAHINI SAUCE

1 tbsp	black (or white) tahini
2 tbsp	water
1	small garlic clove, crushed
	Dash of tamari or coconut aminos
1 tsp	apple cider vinegar
1 tsp	mirin (optional)

FISH

1 tbsp	orange zest, grated
2 tbsp	fresh parsley or thyme, finely chopped
½ cup	hazelnut or almond meal
1 tsp	unrefined salt
½ tsp	white pepper, ground
2 × 150g	pieces of flathead, skin off
1 tbsp	olive oil

Method For the salad, try to get a similar thickness to all the veggies, so they will cook at the same time. If the broccolini or asparagus is thick, then slice it in half or quarters. Leave the beans whole or slice in half lengthways, if they are thick. Bring a large skillet of salted water to a rolling simmer and blanch your veggies until just tender, taking about a minute. Using tongs, lift the veggies out of the water and into a colander in the sink. Rinse under cold running water to stop them cooking any further. You want a bit of a crunch to them. Gently tip them onto a tea towel and allow to dry well. In a wide bowl, gently toss the veggies, fresh herbs, toasted seeds and oil until combined well. Set aside.

For the sauce, in a small bowl whisk or blend all the ingredients together, until smooth and thick. Adjust consistency with a little water if necessary. It should be thick but easy to spread, like the consistency of hummus. Set aside.

For the crumbs on the fish, combine all ingredients in a small bowl, apart from the fish and oil. If using a food processor to make your crumbs, you can use ¾ cup whole hazelnuts instead of the meal. Pat fish dry using a clean tea towel or paper towel. Press the crumbs all around your fish. Heat the oil in a cast iron pan over medium heat and gently lay your fish in and cook until golden brown, about 3 minutes on the first side and 2 minutes on the other, depending on the thickness of your fillets. Using a spatula, gently remove them from pan when the fish feels firm to the touch, then rest on unbleached paper towel.

To serve, place a piece of fish on each plate. Pile up the veggies on the other side, then dollop the sauce over the veggies, or serve in a small ramekin on the plate.

7. GREEN MILLET WITH ITALIAN MUSHROOMS AND SLIVERED ALMONDS
(SERVES 2)

Foods that naturally contain glutamate help us feel more satisfied after a meal. The natural flavour of glutamate is valued for making foods taste 'meatier' and more rewarding. Umami means 'delicious' in Japanese. Mushrooms, in particular shiitake and porcini, are rich in umami. They're also antiviral, immune-boosting and are currently being researched for their outstanding medicinal properties in treating cancer. If you don't like mushies, eggplant, kohlrabi, zucchini and/or capsicum will work well also in this recipe.

GREEN MILLET PUREE

½ cup	millet, soaked overnight in 1 cup water and 1 tsp lemon juice or ACV
1 tbsp	chia seeds
1	medium zucchini, grated
300ml	water or stock
1 tsp	unrefined salt
½ tsp	white pepper

Method Place the saucepan with the millet and soaking liquid on a high heat, then add in the chia seeds, zucchini, stock and salt. (You may not need the salt, if you're using store-bought stock.) Bring to the boil then reduce to a simmer for 20–25 minutes, or until the millet is tender. It should have the consistency of a wet porridge, so add more water if needed. Remove from the heat, cover to keep it warm. Start on your mushrooms whilst the millet is cooking.

MUSHROOMS

2 tbsp	olive oil
2 cups	fresh mixed mushrooms, sliced
1–2	garlic cloves
1 cup	chopped tomatoes, canned or fresh
2 tsp	tomato paste or puree
½–1 cup	water
1 tbsp	capers
1 tbsp	fresh oregano, parsley, basil and/or thyme, chopped, or 1 tsp dried
1 tsp	unrefined salt
½ tsp	cracked pepper
¼ cup	slivered or chopped whole almonds, slightly toasted

Method Heat oil in a pan over medium heat. Add mushrooms and cook gently. Add a little water and ½ tsp salt to help this process along. Put the lid on to help them cook. When the mushrooms are soft, add in the rest of the ingredients (apart from the almonds), and simmer gently for about 10 minutes. Taste for seasoning and consistency, as you don't want them to be too thick. (Add more water if they are.) Meanwhile, make your Green Millet Puree.

To serve, divide the millet between 2 shallow bowls, and make a dent in the middle with the back of a spoon, as you would polenta. Spoon your mushrooms on top of the millet, then sprinkle the almonds over the top.

8. EGGPLANT WITH ZA'ATAR, CASHEW HUMMUS AND SAUTÉED SPINACH
(SERVES 2)

Za'atar (or dukkah in Hebrew) is the Arabic name for a blend of dried oregano and sesame seeds, sometimes with thyme and sumac added. Mix za'atar with olive oil and salt and slather it on almost anything. Oregano has many healing properties. The Greeks used oregano oil as a powerful antiviral, antibacterial, antiseptic, and antifungal agent. Also as a remedy for pain and inflammation. Oregano was the main antibacterial tool used by Hippocrates. Its leaves were traditionally used to treat illnesses related to the respiratory and digestive systems. Oregano has eight times more antioxidants than apples, and three times as many as blueberries.

EGGPLANT

1	large eggplant
½ cup	olive oil
2 tsp	za'atar
1 tsp	unrefined salt
	Cracked pepper

Method Preheat oven to 200°C. Cut the eggplant lengthways through the middle, including through the calix (green stalk). Using a small sharp knife, make 4 parallel cuts in the open side of both halves. Cut about ¾ of the way down, avoiding cutting through the skin. Repeat at a 45° angle, so you get a diamond shape. Place on a baking tray, cut side up. In a small bowl, mix the oil, za'atar (reserving a little to serve) and salt together, then brush over the cut side of the eggplant. Keep brushing until the flesh has absorbed all the oil. Season with pepper then pop into the oven to roast for about 40 minutes. Your eggplants are ready when the flesh becomes quite soft and golden brown.

CASHEW HUMMUS

2 cups	cashew pieces, soaked overnight
¾ cup	hulled tahini
2 tbsp	lime or lemon juice
	Zest from a lemon or lime, grated
2	garlic cloves

Method Place your drained nuts in a food processor and whiz until they resemble chunky breadcrumbs. Add in the rest of the ingredients and process again until fairly smooth. You may need to add a little clean water to thin your hummus out. Taste and adjust flavours. Set aside. These quantities will make about 3 cups of hummus, so store the rest in a sealed container in the fridge for 5–7 days.

SAUTÉED SPINACH

1 tbsp	olive oil
1	garlic clove, thinly sliced or crushed
1	large bunch English spinach, ends trimmed
1 tsp	unrefined salt
½ tsp	white pepper, ground or cracked

Method Heat a flat pan over a low heat. Chop the bunch of spinach in half widthways, keeping the stalks on. Gently fry the garlic until a little soft, but don't let it go brown. Add spinach to the pan with the garlic. Gently sauté until the spinach is quite soft, using tongs to turn it over a few times. To serve, place an eggplant half on each plate, then spread about 3 tbsp hummus over the cut side of each eggplant, or on the side if you prefer. Sprinkle a little extra za'atar over the top of the eggplant. Using tongs, place half the spinach on each plate next to the eggplant.

9. STEAMED KINGFISH WITH MUSHROOM PÂTÉ AND OVEN-BAKED ROOT CHIPS

(SERVES 2)

This delicious pâté lasts up to a week in the fridge. You can also use basil instead of parsley, or 2 tbsp thyme leaves for a different flavour. If you don't have a food processor, it's okay to keep your pâté a bit chunky. It'll still be delicious. To make the veggie chips, a mandolin is the preferred kitchen tool, so you can get the veggies nice and thin. If you don't have one (or expert knife skills), simply chop the veggies into similar sizes and roast them for about 40 minutes at 190°C or until tender.

MUSHROOM PÂTÉ

2 tbsp	coconut oil
10	field mushrooms, chopped
1 tsp	unrefined salt, or to taste
½ tsp	white pepper, ground
1 cup	flat-leaf parsley
½ cup	walnuts, lightly toasted
2 tsp	hemp seeds to serve, optional

Method Line a small (15cm × 5cm approximately) dish with wax paper and set aside. Heat the oil over a medium heat in a heavy-based pan. Add the mushrooms and seasoning. Gently sauté until the mushrooms are juicy and soft. You may need to add in a splash of water to help this happen. Allow them to cool a little, then place in a blender or food processor with the parsley and walnuts. Blitz until very smooth, then pour into your lined dish. Put in the fridge overnight, or at least until the oil has solidified. Pull the pâté out of the dish, turn upside down on a plate, then remove the paper. In warmer months, serve your pâté immediately, before the oil melts too much.

OVEN-BAKED ROOT CHIPS

2 cups   root vegetables, scrubbed (such as red and yellow beetroots, purple and orange carrots, parsnip, turnip and kohlrabi)

1 tsp   sweet or smoked paprika

2 tsp   fresh rosemary, chopped finely or 1 tsp dried

1 tbsp   olive or coconut oil, melted

1 tsp   unrefined salt

Method   Preheat oven to 180°C. Scrub your veggies clean, leaving the skin on. Using a mandolin, carefully slice them into ½ cm thick rounds. In a large bowl, use clean hands to toss the vegetables well with the spice, herbs, oil and salt. Next, line a large baking tray (you may need 2) with parchment paper. Spread vegetables out in a single layer, making sure they don't overlap. They can be nearly touching though, as they will shrink as they cook. Roast in the oven for 25–30 minutes or until your chips are evenly cooked and a little crispy.

STEAMED KINGFISH

2 × 150g   pieces of kingfish, no skin

1 tsp   unrefined salt

½ tsp   white pepper, ground

½   lemon or small orange, zest grated then flesh sliced thinly

Method   Cut 2 × 40cm square pieces of parchment paper. Place half the lemon slices in the middle of each piece then lay the fish on top. Season each piece and finish with the grated zest. To secure your parcels, bring opposite sides of the paper together folding down until you reach the fish. Then fold the other ends in the same way. Place the parcels in an oven dish and bake with the chips for about 20 minutes. (Put fish in oven about 10 minutes after veggies.) The fish will keep cooking until you open the packet and let the steam out, so you may need less cooking time if you use a fish with a thinner fillet.

To serve, carefully lift the fish out of the packet onto your plate using a spatula, leaving behind the sliced citrus, then pour the juices from the packet over the top of the fish. (Or serve it in the parce.) Slice off a 5cm piece of pâté and place it on the plate next to your fish, then pile up the chips between the fish and the pâté. Store the rest of the pâté sealed in the fridge for up to a week. Have it with your eggs in the morning, or with 6 seed crackers and 100g fish, tofu or chicken for lunch.

10. THAI TOFU AND VEGETABLE CURRY
(SERVES 2)

Once thought to be fattening and detrimental to our heart and waist-line, most of us now recognise the goodness of coconut for reducing oxidative stress and strengthening our body's defences against illness and disease. Oxidative stress is associated with basically all dis-ease. Be sure to get coconut product that are organic, or at least additive (sulphur)—free. Swap out the tofu for the same amount of shredded chicken if you prefer.

1 cup	coconut milk, from a BPA-free tin
2 tsp	green (or yellow for a milder heat) curry paste, store bought and additive-free
1 cup	butternut pumpkin, de-seeded and cut into bite-sized pieces
½	eggplant, cut into 3cm dice
1	large carrot, thinly sliced diagonally
1 cup	green beans, trimmed
1 cup	cauliflower florets
1 cup	firm tofu, 3cm dice
500ml	stock

1 tbsp	fish sauce (optional)
10	Thai basil, coriander and/or Vietnamese mint leaves
2	kaffir lime leaves (optional)
1 tbsp	coconut palm sugar (optional)
1 tsp	unrefined salt, Braggs seasoning, or tamari, to taste (depending on how salty your stock is)
2 tbsp	toasted seeds or nuts like sesame, sunflower and pepitas, and almonds, cashews or macadamias (optional)

Method In a medium-sized pot or wok over medium heat, add half the (shaken well) coconut milk and all of the curry paste. Gently cook until the coconut milk reduces a little. This takes a couple of minutes and will start smelling great. Next, add your veggies, tofu, the rest of the coconut milk, stock, fish sauce, herbs and sugar, and seasoning of choice, then stir to combine. Bring to the boil, then drop to a simmer and cook for 10–15 minutes, until the veggies are tender. You may need to add more water if it's getting too thick. Adjust seasoning, and serve with a sprinkling of toasted seeds and/or nuts.

11. POACHED CHICKEN WITH EGGPLANT MASH
[SERVES 2]

Use a whole white fish approximately 2kg in weight instead of chicken if you like. Try basil leaves if you don't like coriander. Reserve the poaching liquid (now stock), strain it, then freeze it for use in another recipe. It will keep for about 3 months. Serve this dish with a side of sautéed spinach, if you feel inclined.

POACHED CHICKEN

2 × 150g	organic chicken breasts or thighs
750ml	water or stock
2	whole cloves

5cm   piece of ginger, roughly chopped

¼   bunch coriander, roughly chopped, stems and leaves separated

Method Place all of the ingredients (coriander stems only) in a pot or deep skillet. Bring to the boil, then drop to a gentle simmer for about 20 minutes, or until the chicken is cooked through (not pink). Lift the chicken out and set aside. While the chicken is poaching, get started on your mash.

Using a whole chicken is more economical, and makes for a better flavoured dish. In this case, use enough water to cover the chicken and triple the other ingredients. This will then make 6 serves.

EGGPLANT MASH

1   medium-sized eggplant

2–3   garlic cloves, halved

4–6   anchovies

1 tsp   turmeric, ground

2 tbsp   olive oil

1 tsp   cumin seeds

1   onion, finely chopped

1 tsp   fresh ginger, grated

1 tbsp   fresh turmeric, grated or 1 tsp dried

1   long green chili

1   large ripe tomato, chopped

1 tsp   unrefined salt

Method Preheat your oven to 220°C. Using a small knife, pierce your whole eggplant in 4–6 places. Insert a piece of garlic and an anchovy in each slit. Rub half the oil over the outside of eggplant and bake for 10–15 minutes, or until the skin is well blackened. Remove it from the oven and allow it to cool a little. Using a spoon, scrape the flesh away from the skin. Place in a bowl and mash well. Set aside. In a heavy-based pan, heat the remaining oil over medium heat. Add the cumin seeds and gently fry until fragrant, about one minute. Add the onions to the pan and sauté over a medium heat until translucent. Next add the ginger, turmeric and chili. Continue cooking for another minute or two, stirring a few times. Spoon this mixture over your mashed eggplant, then add in the tomato and salt then gently fold everything together.

To serve, spread half the mash over the base of each plate. If you're using chicken breasts, slice them into 1cm pieces on an angle, then arrange the chicken nicely on top of the mash. If you've used thighs, keep them whole and serve the mash to the side. For the fish, serve the fillets with a dollop of mash. Finish with the fresh herbs, either coriander leaves or chives.

DESSERTS

At first, it'll probably be a bit strange eating dessert without any sweetness, but it'll get easier after the first week. And you don't have to avoid healthy sweeteners altogether, if you know you don't usually have a problem digesting them. In this case, still use them sparingly during your Reset. If you don't mind the taste of stevia, then go ahead and use it, as it is unlikely to upset your tummy. Try to get stevia as unprocessed as possible. If you do decide you need to completely eliminate all sweeteners during the 40-Day Reset Program, you can start to introduce unprocessed sweeteners in again after the 40 days, and see how your body reacts. It'll tell you if it doesn't want it. All recipes make 2 serves, unless I've stated otherwise.

1. PISTACHIO, PEPPERMINT AND MATCHA HALVA
(MAKES 10 SLICES/5 SERVES)

Derived from the Arabic word 'halwa' (meaning sweet confection), we have been happily enjoying halva for centuries. Dating back to 3000 BC, it often contains rosewater, white sugar, honey, sesame oil, tahini, pistachios, pine nuts or almonds, coconuts and dates—depending on where in the world you're eating it. It eventually made its way into our lives sometime in the last century, via the Ashkenazi Jews.

1 cup	sesame seeds, toasted
2 tbsp	pistachio nuts
2 tbsp	raw honey or rice syrup, or 2–3 drops of liquid stevia
1 drop	peppermint essential oil, or 6 fresh mint leaves
2 tsp	matcha powder

Method In a spice grinder, dry blender or mortar and pestle, grind the sesame seeds to a fine powder. Transfer to a food processor. Add the rest of the ingredients and pulse until you get a stiff batter.

Spoon the mixture onto a piece of unbleached baking paper about 30cm long and firmly shape into a log, or press into a small lined loaf tin. Roll the log in the matcha powder, covering it evenly, or sprinkle on top if using a loaf tin. Roll the paper tightly around the log, twisting the ends. Refrigerate for at least an hour before eating. Serve in the paper, opened up and cut into 2cm rounds.

2. GINGER, LIME AND COCONUT TAPIOCA PUDDING
(SERVES 4)

Tapioca is a resistant starch (RS) made from the root of the cassava plant, originating in Brazil. It's available as flour, flakes or the little balls (pearls) you use to make pudding. Once cooked and chilled, tapioca will firm up and set, or serve it warm like rice pudding. Or, as the Taiwanese have made famous, Bubble tea. It is fairly high in carbohydrates, the majority coming in the form of sucrose, while a smaller amount comes from amylose. Cassava has the ability to reduce inflammation, thanks to the saponins it contains. It can also break down natural body waste like uric acid, and help bring back balance to your gut flora. Tick, tick, tick.

1 tbsp	fresh ginger, grated
¼ cup	tapioca pearls, white (uncoloured)
500ml	coconut milk
1	egg, beaten
1 tsp	lime zest, grated
Pinch	cinnamon
	Stevia liquid or powder to taste, or ½ tbsp coconut palm sugar
1 tbsp	hemp seeds or chopped toasted almonds to garnish

Method Squeeze the juice from the ginger into a medium-sized pot, then add in the remaining ingredients. Whisk to combine. Let it sit for a few minutes before gently simmering over a medium heat, stirring the whole time, until the tapioca is soft and translucent, about 10 minutes. Serve your pudding warm and a bit runny, or spoon into mason jars and keep it for breakfast. Either way, add a sprinkling of hemp seeds or chopped toasted almonds to cover your protein and crunch needs.

3. SMASHED MIXED BERRIES AND MACADAMIA
(SERVES 2)

Most of us know berries are loaded with antioxidants that fight premature ageing, inflammation and disease. Now we know how important their abundant fibre is for gut health. The recommended daily intake for fibre is about 25g for men and 38g for women, so these ruby beauties just got a lot more important at 4g a cup. If you're feeling like a creamier dessert, you can swirl 2 tablespoons of yoghurt, mascarpone or creme fraiche through the smashed berries before serving.

2 cups	frozen berries
½ cup	raw macadamias, soaked in clean water for a few hours
2 tbsp	cacao nibs
¼ tsp	vanilla extract or powder
1 tsp	lime zest, grated or 2 drops lime essential oil
1 tbsp	maple syrup or 2–3 drops liquid stevia (optional)
1 tbsp	hemp seeds to garnish (optional)
2 tbsp	yoghurt, mascarpone or creme fraiche, optional

Method Place all the ingredients (apart from the hemp seeds) in a food processor and pulse slowly. You don't want this pureed, merely broken down a little. You could also use a mortar and pestle for this step, or put the ingredients in a bowl and squash with a potato masher, keeping the mixture chunky. Serve with hemp seeds, if you have some on hand.

4. LABNEH
(SERVES 2)

I grew up with my Lebanese mother's labneh. She made the yogurt in a big plastic drum, as she was so used to cooking for many people. It is a great food to help achieve a healthy gut microbiome and to boost immunity. It's also a delightful way to add creaminess to meals like sautéed mushrooms, soup, or as a dessert like sorbet. Instead of leaving it to drain in the colander, you can hang the muslin parcel from a kitchen sink faucet to drain for 24 hours. Leaving it out for closer to 48 hours will give you a harder cheese, one you can slice and fry in olive oil, like we do with haloumi.

4 cups (around 1kg) organic whole milk yoghurt (preferably goat or sheep's)

1 tsp unrefined salt

Extra virgin olive oil and za'atar, chopped fresh basil or fennel seeds, or honey and a dusting of raw cacao powder to serve.

Method Tip your yogurt into a large bowl, then stir in the salt. Line a colander with (bleach-free) muslin or a linen tea towel, and place over a large bowl. Pour the yogurt mixture into the towel, then pick up the edges of the muslin and tie them together. Set aside on the counter, or in the fridge to drain for at least 24 hours. Reserve the whey that drains out of the yoghurt and use it as the base for a smoothie, or dilute and use it to feed your plants. To serve, spread your labneh into a shallow bowl, then drizzle with oil, za'atar or basil. For a sweet version, drizzle with honey and fennel seeds, or honey and a dusting of raw cacao powder.

5. TAHINI, SESAME AND HONEY BISCUITS
(MAKES ABOUT 12)

These little beauties will take you about 5 minutes to prep, plus only 15 minutes in the oven. They'll keep for about a week in a stored container in the pantry, and are perfect for dessert or for a mid-afternoon slump or sugar cravings. Stick to one per serve for a nice hit of calcium, protein and gut-loving fibre and essential fatty acids.

½ cup sesame seeds

1½ cups almond meal

½ tsp bicarbonate soda

¼ tsp salt

⅓ cup tahini, hulled

⅓ cup	sweetener (honey, raw agave, maple syrup or coconut nectar)
1 tsp	vanilla essence, paste or powder
½ tsp	ground cinnamon
½ tsp	ground cardamom

Method Preheat oven to 180°C. In a bowl, mix the dry ingredients together, except for the sesame seeds. Set aside. In a separate bowl, mix together the wet ingredients, then mix the wet into the dry. Roll into walnut-sized balls then roll in sesame seeds. Place on a greased baking tray and bake for about 15 mins or until golden brown.

chapter sixty-four
TEAS

Tea began as a medicine and grew into a beverage.

OKAKURA KAKUZŌ, *THE BOOK OF TEA*

Use the following method for all nine tea recipes, unless otherwise specified. They all make one cup.

Method   Bring 1 cup of water to boil. Crush herb leaves and/or flowers or fresh or dried spices then put in your teapot, or cup with an inbuilt strainer. Pour boiled water in and let the raw ingredient steep for a few minutes. (Average time is 10 minutes for a medicinal effect, but overnight is better.) Drink a cup as needed, or wanted, up to three times a day.

1. CHAI SPICED MATCHA

It's pretty easy to find recipes for chai these days. Here's my 21st century version of this timeless spiced tea, with a hint of Japan. The addition of cardamom takes this tea from healing medicine for your gut to also balancing your hormones and blood sugar.

¾ cup   filtered water

¼ cup   mylk

2   green cardamom pods, squashed with the flat side of a knife

2   black peppercorns

¼ tsp   fennel seeds

1   cinnamon quill

1–2   thin slices of fresh ginger

1 tsp   matcha powder

Method   Place all ingredients (apart from the matcha) in a medium saucepan. Bring to the boil over medium heat, then drop to a simmer for 5 minutes to develop the flavours. Meanwhile, add your matcha to a mug. Strain chai through a fine sieve into a wide-mouth pouring jug, then pour into your mug with the matcha. Discard the spices, to your compost bin. Whisk your tea and let it steep for 2 minutes, covered. Sweeten as you like.

2. IMMUNITY TEA

This is a lovely tea with many healing properties: anti-inflammatory, antibacterial, antiparasitic and improves circulation. Cayenne stimulates the circulatory system by opening up capillaries; it also helps regulate blood sugar, ease a sluggish digestion, and is a great way to kickstart your metabolism. It also contains antiviral and antifungal properties, to help avoid colds during the flu season. Add some manuka honey, if you like.

1 tsp   fresh ginger, grated

1 tsp   fresh turmeric, grated

¼ tsp   cayenne, ground

1   garlic clove, grated or crushed

1 tbsp   lemon juice

3. HEAVY METAL DETOX

All four spices here are helpful when dealing with fluid retention and also improving digestion, so they will be effective at eliminating heavy metals. Coriander contains dodecenal, which is twice as strong as most antibiotics at fighting infections and removing dangerous microbes from the body. It won't be your favourite tea of all time, due to the taste, so add some mint or honey. Grind the spices first for a fuller flavour.

> ½ tsp   cumin seeds
> ½ tsp   coriander seeds
> ½ tsp   fennel seeds
> ½   garlic clove crushed (optional)

4. TUMMY TIME

If you suffer from less than perfect digestion or bloating, you will love this tea. Fenugreek and licorice are powerful laxatives, great at removing excess waste and toxins through the bowels, so avoid drinking too many cups before leaving the house! Chicory helps reduce sinus congestion and is also excellent at eliminating toxins through our kidneys and bowel, so it will help to remove even more waste from the body. Some people think chicory tastes like coffee, so if you are a coffee lover, you're going to like this one.

> ½ tsp   fenugreek, ground
> ½ tsp   licorice powder
> 1 tsp   chicory root, powder

5. POST-MEAL BLISS

This is my go-to tea after dinner. If you grow your own herbs and spices, it's easy to enjoy fresh herbal tea daily. Picking them fresh is satisfying and ensures the healing properties of the teas are still intact.

6	leaves of both lemon balm and mint
1	stalk lemongrass, bruised and roughly chopped
2	thin slices of fresh ginger

6. MENOPAUSE TEA

Rooibos is made using leaves from a shrub called Aspalathus linearis, native to the Western Cape province of South Africa. It's valued for its exceptionally high levels of antioxidants. Rooibos is a caffeine-free herbal tea, lower in tannins and oxalic acid than regular black or green tea. It is created by fermenting the leaves, which turns them a red-brown colour. Drink rooibos in a similar way to black tea, so add mylk and a sweetener if you like. Sage is an antihydrotic herb (meaning anti-water), so is recommended for hot flushes and excess sweating, and Red Clover is a phyto-estrogen, meaning a healthy plant source of estrogen. If you don't have all three herbs on hand, then using just one or two of them in this tea will be helpful also.

1 tsp	rooibos
3	sage leaves
1 tsp	red clover flowers or tea bag

7. LOVELY LAXATIVE

Burdock has antibacterial and antifungal properties. Traditionally used by herbalists to treat acne and abscesses, it increases circulation to the skin and helps detoxify via the liver. Burdock root strengthens immunity, while purifying the blood. It also improves liver and gut function, which helps your body become more effective at ridding itself of toxins. You'll need to decoct these herbs, as you'll be using the root (not the stems or flowers), so they take longer to work their magic. Make lots of this tea and have it on hand to have a few times a day when things just aren't moving. Add a slice of ginger root too, if available.

> 1 tsp   burdock root
>
> 1 tsp   dandelion root
>
> 1 tsp   yellow dock root
>
> 1 tsp   licorice root

Method   To make a decoction, place the ingredients in a pot with 1½ cups of clean water and bring to the boil. Drop to a simmer for 10–15 minutes, then strain and drink.

8. TULSI, ROSE AND CALENDULA

This is another of my favourite home brews from my garden. Tulsi, otherwise known as holy basil, is a pretty incredible herb. It's great for nourishing the adrenal glands, as well as healing the heart, boosting immunity, and lifting a bad mood. Plus it's so easy to grow. Calendula is wonderful for improving the condition of your skin. Rose, besides being beautiful, is an aphrodisiac and antidepressant, and helps bring our energy down from our head to our heart. The measurements are for dried herbs, so add 1 tbsp of each if you're lucky enough to have them fresh.

> 1   tsp tulsi
>
> 1 tsp   rose petals
>
> 1 tsp   calendula flower

9. YERBA MATÉ

Yerba maté tea is a South American beverage, made by steeping the ground leaves and stems of the yerba maté plant. You'll find it at most health food stores and well-stocked supermarkets. It contains some caffeine, and has about 90% more antioxidants than green tea. It can slow signs of ageing, increase mental clarity and focus, and is used to keep healthy cholesterol levels by maintaining clean arteries. Yerba maté helps our body use carbohydrates more efficiently, aids digestion by stimulating increased production of bile and other gastric acids, and helps reduce the gut bacteria that can contribute to bad breath and gut issues. (You can use yerba maté in an espresso machine as well.)

> 1 tbsp   yerba maté
> 1 tsp   peppermint, dried
> 1 cup   hot water (never boiling)

Method   Place the leaves in a small teapot. Cover with a little cool water first, then stir. Pour in the boiling water over the top and allow it to steep for a few minutes before straining and sipping.

chapter sixty-five
STOCKS AND BROTHS

In my Lebanese grandmother Veronica's day, it was more about not wasting anything, and also a way of getting flavour into otherwise bland food, rather than making bone broth to heal a leaky gut. I never saw chicken frames, bones or veggie scraps go in the bin growing up. I grew up watching Veronica and her sisters making stocks all the time. She lived to 96, as did Aunty Ruth, and Aunty Dot was 103 years old when she passed away last year. So I guess they were doing something right, besides being wonderful role models and matriarchs.

This is what I do. Each time I cook, I put my veggie scraps in the designated stock bag in the freezer. I also do this with the chicken carcass, after I make a roast chook or chicken soup. I also keep fish frames and prawn shells in a separate bag. When a bag full is full, I put the contents in a large soup pot and make a stock. After I strain it, the stuff in the colander goes into the compost bin. I don't put whole veggies in my stock, I find that a bit of a waste, unless of course they're past their best and at risk of going straight to the compost bin.

Making stock is a satisfying and humbling experience, knowing you're leaving a light footprint, and that your food is going full circle. I can make a lot in one go, as my father gave me an enormous stainless steel pot and colander a few years back. He used it to cook the ridiculous number of mud crabs he caught in pots in the seventies off Moreton Bay. I usually freeze six to ten 1 litre containers with each batch.

Vegetable broth or bone broth?

Collagen is known to help reduce inflammation and support healthy hair, skin, nails, gut lining and joints. This is why bone broth is all the rage right now. But what about animal products being highly acidic? And what about the problems associated with the glutamine in long-cooked bone broth? *See Bone Broth below*

On the other hand, vegetable broth is alkaline, so can help restore balance to an overly acidic system that's been created by too much work, anger, jealousy, medication, stress, coffee, alcohol, meat, environmental toxins and sugar. And veggie broth will also absorb collagen-enhancing nutrients from plants more easily than those made from animal frames. Plant-based foods that will enhance collagen production are seaweed, celery, organic soybeans, kale, beetroot, spinach and olive oil.

OLD FASHIONED STOCK

To make chicken or fish broth/stock, start with a whole chicken or fish (or just the head) when you can. It saves money and waste and will provide you with tonight's dinner, tomorrow's lunch, stock for tomorrow night's dinner, and the carcass to make a future stock/broth. Use about 2 cups veggie scraps like the ones I've listed.

> 1.8 kg   organic chicken
>   Garlic and onion shells
>   Carrot tops and tails
>   Celery leaves and ends

Method Place a whole chicken or fish frame in a large pot and cover well with clean water. Then add in whatever veggie scraps you're using. Bring to the boil and simmer gently for an hour (30 minutes for fish), until the chicken easily falls apart when pulled away from the leg. Using tongs, pull the chicken or fish out and put on a platter that has sides, to prevent spillage/waste. Strain the liquid through a colander and set aside. When cool enough, use your fingers to pull all the flesh off the frame. Now go ahead and use this stock in your recipes, or freeze for later use. You can also freeze the flaked flesh, for up to three months.

BONE BROTH

Bone broth is really just stock that's been cooked for a long time. We now know that slow-cooked bones are a great source of collagen (as is slippery elm) for beautiful skin, hair, nails and teeth; it also guards against a leaky gut, by sealing up the holes causing the 'leak'. People also report that bone broth helps reduce allergic symptoms, improves a struggling immune system and brain health, and helps reduce cellulite by improving connective tissue.

Too much of a good thing? Have you been diagnosed with an autoimmune disease, or suffer from migraines, brain fog, severe mood swings or nervous tics? If so, then bone broth may not be for you. Also, children with nervous system disorders (such as ADD, ADHD and ASD) should not drink long-cooked bone broth. Seizures have been reported after drinking bone broth, even just a small amount. Cooking bones for a long time creates very high levels of glutamine, so if you have leaky brain—as those with Leaky Gut often do—high amounts of glutamic acid/glutamine can trigger seizures if you're prone to them. Autoimmune issues usually means Leaky Gut, and Leaky Gut means leaky brain, and leaky brain means glutamic acid sensitivity.

>   1kg   organic beef or lamb bones; or chicken or turkey
>   carcass; or fish frames
>   1   onion
>   2   celery stalks, roughly chopped

1   large carrot, roughly chopped

1 tbsp   apple cider vinegar

Method Pop the chicken carcass, fish frame or beef bones on a baking tray at a high temperature of around 230°C. Roast until the bones are brown, almost too brown. This takes around 30 minutes. Now you're ready to boil the bones. Place them in the heaviest, biggest stockpot you have, along with your veggies. Don't leave behind the crisped brown or stuck bits on the bottom of the baking tray; loosen them with a little water and a metal spatula and add them to the stockpot also. These are some of the most flavoursome bits. At this stage, add whatever aromatics you like, but keep it simple. Things like black pepper, bay leaves and celery leaves work well, or just use the veggies. Add enough filtered water to just cover the bones, then add the vinegar. Let the pot sit on the stove without heat for about 20 minutes. This lets the acid from the vinegar go to work on the bones, making their nutrients more available to us. Bring to a rapid boil, then drop to a simmer and cover. How long you simmer it can vary, depending on how deep a flavour you want, and how much time you've got. Fish broth really only needs 30 minutes, as after that it starts to develop a bitter taste; chicken broth about 2 hours; beef stock can be simmered anywhere from 1–2 hours. Cool slightly in the pot, remove all the scum and impurities floating on top, then use a fine colander to strain. Use in the next day or two, or freeze in 1 litre containers for up to 3 months.

chapter sixty-six
MYLKS

These days we're drinking all sorts of different milks, and thankfully not just from animals. And we're spelling it with a 'y'! We're now making mylk from nuts, seeds and grains too.

It really is so easy and quick to make your own mylk at home, and they're so much nicer than the store bought ones. All you need is a good blender, and a fine sieve, muslin cloth or a nut bag. These types of mylks don't last long, typically up to four days, so make small amounts often. Try not to stick to the one type of base ingredient, as our guts really do prefer diversity. Soak your base ingredient overnight for an easier blend and smoother end product. Use the leftover pulp in my *Breakfast Bread* instead of the almond meal or add it to the *Acai Breakfast Bowl* or *Chia Puddings*.

MYLK RECIPE
(MAKES ABOUT 750 ML)

3 cups   clean water
1 cup   of the base ingredient. Seeds like pepitas, sesame, sunflower; hemp or raw quinoa; any type of nut like almond, cashew, macadamia, Brazil, hazelnuts; grains like oats or brown rice; coconut (use the flesh from the young fruit or organic dried coconut).

OPTIONS:

1 tsp   each of natural vanilla extract and ground cinnamon
1 tsp   each lemon juice and 1 tbsp sweetener, or to taste
   1   organic date and 1 tsp vanilla extract
1 tbsp   maple syrup

Method Cover your base ingredient in filtered water and soak overnight. Drain the next day (I use this water on my plants). Pop the base ingredient into the blender with 3 cups of clean water. Blend until smooth. You can use the mylk just like this, with the pulp, or strain it through a fine sieve, a piece of muslin, or a nut bag.

Don't discard the pulp; you can use it up to three times to make less creamy batches of the mylk. To do this, cover the pulp with filtered water—I do this in my blender—let it sit for about an hour, blitz it again, then strain. This is called 'second mylk', and so on.

Mylk will last up to four days in an airtight container in the fridge. So will the pulp, which you can use to make biscuits, cakes, pancakes and curries. Or freeze it for up to 3 months.

chapter sixty-seven
WEEKLY PLANNERS

Feel free to have the same meal for lunch and dinner on your IF days, to make things easier on you.

WEEK 1

Monday
Breakfast: Cinnamon Loaf with Cashew Butter
Herbal Tea: Chai Spiced Matcha
Lunch: Roast Veggie, Nuts and Quinoa Salad, with Avocado Mayonnaise
Dinner: Chicken with Eggplant, Saffron and Capers
Dessert: Pistachio, Peppermint and Matcha Halva
Mylk: Golden Milk

Tuesday—IF Day
Breakfast: Gut Sweeper Smoothie
Herbal Tea: Tummy Time
Lunch: Oriental Chicken Soup
Dinner: Kohlrabi and Coconut Soup
Dessert: Coconut and Lime Sorbet
Mylk: LSD—Latte Spiced Dandelion

Wednesday
Breakfast: Golden Mushrooms
Herbal Tea: Yerba Maté
Lunch: Almond and Chia Fritters with Green Tahini Sauce
Dinner: Steamed Veg with Basil and Hemp Hummus
Dessert: Smashed Mixed Berries and Macadamia
Mylk: Carrot Cake Milkshake

Thursday—IF Day
Breakfast: Curb the Cravings Smoothie
Herbal Tea: Menopause Tea
Lunch: Spiced Indian Soup
Dinner: Jerusalem Artichoke and Garlic Soup
Dessert: Chocolate Puddings
Mylk: Sleepy Time

Friday
Breakfast: Buckwheat Porridge
Herbal Tea: Tulsi, Rose and Calendula
Lunch: Potato Salad with Salsa Verdi
Dinner: Thai Tofu and Vegetable Curry
Dessert: Tahini, Sesame and Honey Biscuits
Mylk: Mock Mocha

Saturday
Breakfast: Breakfast Bread
Herbal Tea: Lovely Laxative
Lunch: Steamed Kingfish with Mushroom Pâté and Oven-Baked
  Root Chips
Dinner: Steamed Veg with Basil and Hemp Hummus
Dessert: Lime and Coconut Tapioca Pudding
Mylk: Creamy Green Calmness

Sunday
Breakfast: Acai Healing Bowl
Herbal Tea: Post-Meal Bliss
Lunch: Gado Gado
Dinner: Pumpkin Miso Soup
Dessert: Lubneh with Fresh or Stewed Fruit
Mylk: Pumpkin Pie

WEEK 2

Monday
Breakfast: Buckwheat Porridge
Herbal Tea: Tummy Time
Lunch: Buckwheat Risotto with Fennel, Mint and Peas
Dinner: Hazelnut Crumbed Flathead with Broccolini Salad and
   Black Tahini Sauce
Dessert: Pistachio, Peppermint and Matcha Halva
Mylk: Sleepy Time

Tuesday—IF Day
Breakfast: Protein Power Smoothie
Herbal Tea: Immunity Tea
Lunch: My Favourite Fish Soup
Dinner: Cream of Mushroom
Dessert: Walnut Brownie Pud
Mylk: Creamy Green Calmness

Wednesday
Breakfast: Breakfast Bread
Herbal Tea: Chai Spiced Matcha
Lunch: Millet Patties with Kale and Hemp Pesto
Dinner: Roast Chicken with Crusted Pumpkin Wedges and
   Cauliflower Mash

Dessert: Smashed Mixed Berries and Macadamia
Mylk: Mock Mocha

Thursday—IF Day
Breakfast: Liver Loving Smoothie
Herbal Tea: Immunity Tea
Lunch: Roasted Rainbow Soup
Dinner: Seafood Chowder Soup
Dessert: Strawberry, Macadamia and Orange Sorbet
Mylk: Carrot Cake Milkshake

Friday
Breakfast: Breakfast Bread
Herbal Tea: Tummy Time
Lunch: Millet Patties with Kale and Hemp Pesto
Dinner: Pumpkin Miso Soup
Dessert: Tahini, Sesame and Honey Biscuits
Mylk: LSD—Latte Spiced Dandelion

Saturday
Breakfast: Golden Mushrooms
Herbal Tea: Yerba Maté
Lunch: Roast Veggie, Nuts and Quinoa Salad, with Avocado
Mayonnaise
Dinner: Poached Chicken with Eggplant Mash
Dessert: Chocolate Puddings
Mylk: Pumpkin Pie

Sunday
Breakfast: Cinnamon Loaf with Vanilla Cashew Butter
Herbal Tea: Chai Spiced Latte
Lunch: Potato Salad with Salsa Verde
Dinner: Almond and Chia Fritters with Green Tahini Sauce

Dessert: Ginger, Lime and Coconut Tapioca Pudding
Mylk: Carrot Cake Milkshake

WEEK 3

Monday
Breakfast: Blueberry, Brazil and Quinoa Breakfast Bowl
Herbal Tea: Menopause Tea
Lunch: Potato Salad with Salsa Verdi
Dinner: Pumpkin Miso Soup
Dessert: Pistachio, Peppermint and Matcha Halva
Mylk: Sleepy Time

Tuesday—IF Day
Breakfast: Hormone Happiness Smoothie
Herbal Tea: Yerba Maté
Lunch: Creamy Thai Soup
Dinner: Jerusalem Artichoke and Garlic Soup
Dessert: Labneh with Honey and Raw Cacao Powder
Mylk: Creamy Green Calmness

Wednesday
Breakfast: Breakfast Bread
Herbal Tea: Post Meal Bliss
Lunch: Steamed Veg with Basil and Hemp Hummus
Dinner: Millet Patties with Kale and Hemp Pesto
Dessert: Lime and Coconut Tapioca Pudding
Mylk: Mock Mocha

Thursday—IF Day
Breakfast: Ignite Immunity Smoothie
Herbal Tea: Tummy Time
Lunch: Spiced Indian Soup

Dinner: Oriental Chicken Soup
Dessert: Jaffa Mousse
Mylk: Carrot Cake Milkshake

Friday
Breakfast: Cinnamon Loaf with Cashew Butter
Herbal Tea: Tulsi, Rose and Calendula
Lunch: Gado Gado
Dinner: Kingfish with Mushroom Pâté and Oven-Baked Root Chips
Dessert: Tahini, Sesame and Honey Biscuits
Mylk: Sleepy Time

Saturday
Breakfast: Golden Mushrooms
Herbal Tea: Chai Spiced Latte
Lunch: Millet Patties with Kale and Hemp Pesto
Dinner: Thai Tofu and Vegetable Curry
Dessert: Ginger, Lime and Coconut Tapioca Pudding
Mylk: LSD—Latte Spiced Dandelion

Sunday
Breakfast: Breakfast Bread
Herbal Tea: Yerba Maté
Lunch: Hazelnut Crumbed Flathead with Broccolini Salad and Black Tahini Sauce
Dinner: Flax Crackers with Cashew Cheese
Dessert: Matcha and Avocado Ice Cream
Mylk: Golden Mylk

WEEK 4

Monday
Breakfast: Breakfast Chia Bowl
Herbal Tea: Tummy Time
Lunch: Roast Veggie, Nuts and Quinoa Salad with Avocado
  Mayonnaise
Dinner: Chicken with Eggplant, Saffron and Capers
Dessert: Labneh with Honey and Fennel Seeds
Mylk: Pumpkin Pie

Tuesday—IF Day
Breakfast: Heavy Metal Detox Smoothie
Herbal Tea: Tulsi, Rose and Calendula
Lunch: Kohlrabi and Coconut Soup
Dinner: Cream Of Mushroom Soup
Dessert: Lime and Coconut Tapioca Pudding
Mylk: Creamy Green Calmness

Wednesday
Breakfast: Blueberry, Brazil and Quinoa Breakfast Bowl
Herbal Tea: Menopause Tea
Lunch: Gado Gado
Dinner: Kingfish with Mushroom Pâté and Oven-Baked Root
  Chips
Dessert: Smashed Mixed Berries and Macadamia
Mylk: Golden Mylk

Thursday—IF Day
Breakfast: Mojo Rising Smoothie
Herbal Tea: Post Meal Bliss
Lunch: Roasted Rainbow Soup
Dinner: Seafood Chowder Soup

YOUR 40-DAY TRANSFORMATION

Dessert: Chocolate Puddings
Mylk: Mock Mocha

Friday
Breakfast: Breakfast Bread
Herbal Tea: Chai Spiced Latte
Lunch: Millet Patties with Kale and Hemp Pesto
Dinner: Thai Tofu and Vegetable Curry
Dessert: Tahini, Sesame and Honey Biscuits
Mylk: Carrot Cake Milkshake

Saturday
Breakfast: Cinnamon Loaf with Cashew Butter
Herbal Tea: Lovely Laxative
Lunch: Buckwheat Risotto with Fennel, Mint and Peas
Dinner: Steamed Veg with Basil and Hemp Hummus
Dessert: Tahini, Sesame and Honey Biscuits
Mylk: Sleepy Time

Sunday
Breakfast: Breakfast Bread
Herbal Tea: Tummy Time
Lunch: Hazelnut Crumbed Flathead with Broccolini Salad and
    Black Tahini Sauce
Dinner: Pumpkin Miso Soup
Dessert: Matcha and Avocado Ice Cream
Mylk: Pumpkin Pie

Free e-newsletters
from Hay House, the Ultimate
Resource for Inspiration

Be the first to know about Hay House's free downloads, special offers, giveaways, contests, and more!

 Get exclusive excerpts from our latest releases and videos from *Hay House IN the LOOP*

 Our *Digital Products Newsletter* is the perfect way to stay up-to-date on our latest discounted eBooks, featured mobile apps, and Live Online and On Demand events.

 Learn with real benefits! *HayHouseU.com* is your source for the most innovative online courses from the world's leading personal growth experts. Be the first to know about new online courses and to receive exclusive discounts.

 Enjoy uplifting personal stories, how-to articles, and healing advice, along with videos and empowering quotes, within *Heal Your Life*.

 Have an inspirational story to tell and a passion for writing? Sharpen your writing skills with insider tips from *Your Writing Life*.

Sign Up Now!

Get inspired, educate yourself, get a complimentary gift, and share the wisdom!

Visit www.hayhouse.com.au to sign up today!

We hope you enjoyed this Hay House book. If you'd like to receive our online catalogue featuring additional information on Hay House books and products, or if you'd like to find out more about the Hay Foundation, please contact:

Hay House Australia Pty. Ltd.,
P.O. Box 7201, Alexandria, NSW 2015
Phone: +61 2 9669 4299
www.hayhouse.com.au

Published in the USA by:
Hay House, Inc., P.O. Box 5100, Carlsbad, CA 92018-5100
Phone: (760) 431-7695 • *Fax:* (760) 431-6948
www.hayhouse.com®

Published in the United Kingdom by:
Hay House UK, Ltd., The Sixth Floor, Watson House,
54 Baker Street, London, W1U 7BU
Phone: 020 3927 7290
www.hayhouse.co.uk

Published in India by:
Hay House Publishers India, Muskaan Complex, Plot No. 3, B-2,
Vasant Kunj, New Delhi, 110 070
Phone: 91-11-4176-1620 • *Fax:* 91-11-4176-1630
www.hayhouse.co.in

Access New Knowledge.

Anytime. Anywhere.

**Learn and evolve at your own pace
with the world's leading experts.**

www.hayhouseU.com